DIVERCITIES

Understanding super-diversity in deprived and mixed neighbourhoods

Edited by Stijn Oosterlynck, Gert Verschraegen and
Ronald van Kempen

Paperback first published in Great Britain in 2020 by

Policy Press
University of Bristol
1-9 Old Park Hill
Bristol
BS2 8BB
UK
t: +44 (0)117 954 5940
pp-info@bristol.ac.uk
www.policypress.co.uk

North America office:
Policy Press
c/o The University of Chicago Press
1427 East 60th Street
Chicago, IL 60637, USA
t: +1 773 702 7700
f: +1 773-702-9756
sales@press.uchicago.edu
www.press.uchicago.edu

British Library Cataloguing in Publication Data
A catalogue record for this book is available from the British Library

Library of Congress Cataloging-in-Publication Data
A catalog record for this book has been requested

ISBN 978-1-4473-3818-5 paperback
ISBN 978-1-4473-3817-8 hardcover
ISBN 978-1-4473-3820-8 ePub
ISBN 978-1-4473-3821-5 Mobi
ISBN 978-1-4473-3819-2 ePdf

Cover design by Hayes Design
Front cover image: istock
Printed and bound in Great Britain by CMP, Poole
Policy Press uses environmentally responsible print partners

This book is dedicated to the memory of Professor Dr Ronald van Kempen. Ronald coordinated the large-scale collaborative European research project DIVERCITIES (see www.urbandivercities.eu) until the very last days of his life. DIVERCITIES focused on the question of how to create social cohesion, social mobility and economic performance in today's hyper-diverse cities. The DIVERCITIES project provided the framework for the organisation of three conference sessions titled 'The challenge of diversity: Does urban diversity contribute to the ideal city?' at the annual RC21 conference in August 2015 in Urbino, Italy. This book is based on a selection of papers that were presented in these conference sessions. Ronald was involved in organising the conference sessions and co-authored the book proposal, but sadly passed away before work on the book started.

We will remember Ronald as a highly committed and prolific scholar, who made a lasting impact on social sciences research on diversity and social inequality in cities, housing and urban policy.

Contents

Contents

List of table and figures

Tables

Figures

Notes on contributors

Ympkje Albeda is an urban sociologist. She obtained a Master's degree in Urban Sociology and Constitutional and Administrative Law. Her PhD research at the University of Antwerp focuses on community dynamics in diverse urban neighbourhoods. She is currently working at the University of Applied Sciences in Leiden, the Netherlands.

Georgia Alexandri is a post-doctoral researcher at the Autonomous University of Madrid (UAM), Spain. Her research interests are urban processes of dispossession such as gentrification and the financialisation of housing and land. After completing her PhD on gentrification in the city of Athens at Harokopio University (Athens), she worked as a research associate for the European Union (EU) Seventh Framework Programme DIVERCITIES project at the National Centre of Social Research (EKKE, Athens). She was recently awarded a Marie Curie Fellowship to join the School of Geography at the University of Leeds and explore the way debt is changing social and spatial dynamics in post-crisis Southern European cities.

Dimitris Balampanidis holds a PhD in Urban Social Geography from Harokopio University (Athens) (2016) and an MSc in Urban and Regional Planning from the National Technical University of Athens (2011), Greece. He is currently a Research Assistant at the National Centre for Social Research in Athens, Greece. His research and publications focus on immigrants' housing pathways and entrepreneurial activities, ethnic residential segregation and intercultural coexistence, as well as on housing policies, urban and regional planning. He has conducted several research projects at the Urban Environment Laboratory (National Technical University of Athens), the research department UMR Géographies-Cités (Université Paris 1 Panthéon-Sorbonne, CNRS) and the École Française d'Athènes (EfA).

Eduardo Barberis is a sociologist and tenure track researcher at the University of Urbino Carlo Bo, Italy, where he lectures on urban sociology and immigration policy, and coordinates the Centre for Applied Transcultural Research. His research interests include the study of the local dimension of social policy and migration processes. Among his recent publications are 'Chinese immigration to Italy and economic relations with the homeland' (with A. Violante) in S. Guercini et al's book *Native and immigrant entrepreneurship* and a paper on school segregation in Italian metropolitan areas with A. Violante Belgeo (2016).

Panagiotis Bourlessas is a PhD candidate in Urban Studies at the Gran Sasso Science Institute in the Social Sciences Unit at L'Aquila, Italy. His doctoral research focuses on the geographies of homelessness in Athens city centre and uses ethnographic methods. His further research interests include mobility, materiality and visuality.

Maria Budnik holds a Master's degree in Urban Geography. After her studies at the University of Leipzig in Germany she was involved in the European Union Seventh Framework Programme research project DIVERCITIES on governing urban diversity at the Erfurt University of Applied Sciences, Germany. She developed a research interest in social justice and social cohesion.

Anika Depraetere is a Research Fellow at the Centre for Research on Environmental and Social Change (CRESC) of the University of Antwerp, Belgium and the Laboratory for Education and Society (LeS) of the Catholic University of Leuven, Belgium. Her research focuses on the political implications of social work practices. She recently published a paper on the citizenship practices of undocumented migrants in *Citizenship Studies* (with S. Oosterlynck, 2017).

Ayda Eraydin is Professor in the Department of Urban and Regional Planning at Middle East Technical University, Turkey. Her research interests are planning theory and practice, resilience in planning and development, local economic development, and the sociospatial dynamics of cities and regions. Her recent publications include articles on regional resilience in Turkish regions in *Regional Studies* (2016), the role of regional policies in the *Cambridge Journal of Regions, Economy and Society* (2016) and on the state response to contemporary urban movements in Turkey (with T. Taşan-Kok) in *Antipode*.

Maxime Felder is a doctoral student at the Department of Sociology of the University of Geneva, Switzerland. His research focuses on social relations in urban contexts, dynamics of co-existence and co-presence and on social networks. He investigates how urbanites relate to their environment and to the 'strangers' living around them. He has also written on citizenship, through the analysis of citizenship ceremonies and of coming-of-age rituals organised by Swiss municipalities. His latest publications include a chapter with L. Pignolo on place identity in shopping streets (2017) and an article with L. Pignolo on the co-existence and processes of familiarisation in urban environments in *Sociologie* (2017).

Katrin Großmann is Professor in Urban Sociology at the University of Applied Sciences Erfurt, Germany. From 2007 to 2014 she worked at the Helmholtz Centre for Environmental Research where she was involved in a number of international and national research projects, such as Shrink Smart, ConDENSE and DIVERCITIES. Governance for sustainability in urban spaces is a cross-cutting theme throughout her research. This includes energy vulnerability in relation to housing markets and residential mobility, shrinking cities and neighbourhood change with a special interest in large housing estates, social inequality and residential segregation, sustainability trade-offs and conflicts in urban development.

Annegret Haase is a post-doctoral researcher at the Helmholtz Centre for Environmental Research at the Department of Urban and Environmental Sociology at UFZ in Leipzig, Germany. Her main research interests include sustainable urban transformation, shrinkage and re-urbanisation, land use change and urban green areas, sociospatial processes in cities, inequalities and urban diversity, urban governance and post-Socialist cities. She has recently published articles on greening cities and social inclusion in *Habitat International* (2017), complexity and assemblage thinking and neighbourhood change in *Urban Geography* (with Grossmann, 2015) and re-urbanisation and gentrification in Leipzig in *Geografie* (2015).

Christian Haid is an architect and urban sociologist working in Berlin, Germany. He has worked as an Assistant Professor and Lecturer in Architecture, Urban Planning and Urban Studies at the University of Hanover, Humboldt University Berlin and Technical University (TU) Berlin. He further worked as a researcher in the European Union Seventh Framework Programme research project DIVERCITIES on governing urban diversity at the Helmholtz Centre for Environmental Research Leipzig and the University of Applied Science Erfurt. As a DFG Fellow in the interdisciplinary graduate programme 'The World in the City' at the Centre for Metropolitan Studies, TU Berlin, he developed his doctoral thesis on informal practices in the city of Berlin. His research interests are in critical urban studies, urban informality and stateness, postcolonial studies, urban theory from the south, diversity and governance.

Christoph Hedtke holds a Bachelor's degree in Geography and is currently finishing his Master's degree in Urban Geography at the University of Leipzig, Germany. As a student assistant he was involved in the European Union Seventh Framework Programme research project DIVERCITIES on governing urban diversity. In his research he focuses on urban development, public participation and international migration.

Jamie Kesten worked on the DIVERCITIES project as a Research Associate at the Bartlett School of Planning, University College London, UK. His recent publications include *Multiculture and community in new city spaces* with Allan Cochrane, Giles Mohan and Sarah Neal and *The politicisation of diversity planning in a global city: Lessons from London* with Mike Raco. He is currently working as a community organiser for the Thames Ward Community Project in the London Borough of Barking and Dagenham.

Katharina Kullmann is a sociologist and worked in the European Union Seventh Framework Programme research project DIVERCITIES on governing urban diversity at the Helmholtz Centre for Environmental Research in Leipzig, Germany. She is currently planning a PhD thesis. Her research interests are urban governance, the interplay between different political levels and questions about how to improve decision-making and local democracy.

Tatiana Moreira de Souza is a Postdoctoral Fellow at the Bartlett School of Planning, University College London, UK. She holds a first degree in Architecture and Urbanism from the University of Sao Paulo, Brazil and an MSc in Urban Regeneration and a PhD in Planning Studies from University College London. Her research interests cover urban planning, regeneration and housing policy in European cities, social mix policies, diversity and social relations in urban contexts, residential mobility and neighbourhood change.

Stijn Oosterlynck is Associate Professor in Urban Sociology at the University of Antwerp, Belgium. He is the chair of the Centre for Research on Environmental and Social Change (CRESC) and of the Antwerp Urban Studies Institute. His research is concerned with place-based forms of solidarity in diversity, urban governance, social innovation and welfare state restructuring, civil society politics and the political sociology of urban development. He recently co-edited the book *Place, solidarity, diversity* (Routledge, 2017) and has had published, among others, articles on innovative forms of solidarity in diversity in *Ethnic and Racial Studies* (2016) and citizenship practices of undocumented migrants in *Citizenship Studies* (with A. Depraetere, 2017).

Javier Ruiz-Tagle is a PhD candidate in Urban Planning and Policy from the University of Illinois at Chicago, USA and Assistant Professor at the Institute of Urban and Territorial Studies at the Pontifical Catholic University of Chile. He specialises in topics regarding residential segregation, housing policies, neighbourhood effects, urban sociology and comparative studies. He has published, presented and won honours and awards with his work in Chile, the US and Europe. His current lines of research revolve around urban political economy and sociospatial neighbourhood change. He is working as Section Editor for the Wiley-Blackwell *Encyclopaedia of urban and regional studies* and as Co-Editor for *A companion to urban and regional studies* (also Wiley-Blackwell).

Galia Shokry is a doctoral fellow of the ERC-funded GreenLULUs project of the Barcelona Laboratory for Urban Environmental Justice and Sustainability affiliated with the Institute of Environmental Science and Technology of the Autonomous University of Barcelona, as well as the Healthy Cities and Environmental Justice Programme of the Mar Institute (IMIM-PRBB). Her current research examines how urban greening for environmental protection and social resilience creates new insecurities and social and racial inequities in distressed neighbourhoods. She is also interested in how greening strategies are contested or the benefits extended, and how new senses of place and belonging are constructed. Galia previously worked with the DIVERCITIES team at the Université Paris-Est.

Anouk K. Tersteeg is an urban geographer. She obtained an MSc(Res) in Urban Studies at the University of Amsterdam and conducted her PhD research in the Faculty of Geosciences at Utrecht University. Her work focused on resident experiences with living in hyper-diverse contexts. Besides urban diversity, her main interests lie in the fields of housing and urban policy. She currently works as a policy adviser at the housing corporation GroenWest in Woerden.

Joke Vandenabeele is an Associate Professor at the Laboratory for Education and Society in the Faculty of Psychology and Educational Sciences, University of Leuven, Belgium. In her research she deals with educational matters at the crossroads of education and society, thereby articulating new societal challenges as richly and diversely as possible through the development of theory. In doing so, she contributes to the development of new practices, for example, on sustainable development, solidarity, community development and participatory practices. Recent publications include a joint article with Peter Reyskens, 'Parading urban togetherness: A video record of the Brussels's Zinneke Parade' in the journal *Social & Cultural Geography*.

Bart van Bouchaute is Lecturer in Politics and Policy at the social work programme of Artevelde University College Ghent, Belgium. His research is concerned with the politicising role of social work practices and civil society organisations.

Ronald van Kempen was a Full Professor in Urban Geography at the University of Utrecht, the Netherlands. His research focused on urban spatial segregation, urban diversity, housing for low-income groups, urban governance and its effects on neighbourhoods and residents, social exclusion and minority ethnic groups. He coordinated the European Union Seventh Framework Programme DIVERCITIES on governing urban diversity. He has published more than 200 reports and articles, most of them in social and urban geography journals.

Gert Verschraegen is Associate Professor of Sociology at the University of Antwerp, Belgium. His research interests are in the areas of social theory, cultural sociology and the sociology of governance. Recent publications are *Making human rights intelligible: Towards a sociology of human rights* (co-edited with Mikael Rask Madsen, 2013) and *Imagined futures in science, technology and society* (co-edited with Frédéric Vandermoere, Luc Braeckmans en Barbara Segaert, 2017).

Acknowledgements

We would like to acknowledge the generous funding we received from the European Union's Seventh Framework Programme for research, technological development and demonstration under grant agreement no 319970.SSH.2012.2.2.2-1, 'DIVERCITIES: Governance of cohesion and diversity in urban contexts'.

Introduction: Understanding super-diversity in deprived and mixed neighbourhoods

Stijn Oosterlynck, Gert Verschraegen
and Ronald van Kempen

For a long time, cities have worked as a magnet for very different types of people. As centres of trade and commerce, economic production and consumption, education and other forms of human activity, most cities have an extended history as sites of cultural exchange and human diversity. In the past decades, however, cities have become even more diverse, a fact that is adequately captured by the growing literature on 'super-diversity'. According to Steven Vertovec (2007), who famously coined this term, contemporary cities have seen an increasing diversity of migration in terms of countries of origin, ethnic groups, languages and religions, gender, age profiles and labour market experiences. Complex migration and asylum regimes have further contributed to the process of diversification through the multiplication of immigration legal statuses (civic stratification) (Zetter, 2007; Nash, 2009). Super-diversity has become especially apparent in cities that are designated as 'global cities' (Sassen, 1991), on the basis of their ability to draw heterogeneous people from all parts of the world. However, medium-sized and provincial cities and towns in North America and across Europe are also increasingly characterised by a 'diversification of diversity' (Erel, 2011), although the scale of diversification can vary drastically between neighbourhoods.

As we can expect continuing migration flows, a high degree of ethnic, religious and socioeconomic diversity will undoubtedly be the norm in 21st-century cities, or at least in some of its neighbourhoods. In this book we are concerned with the question of how urbanites from different ethnic and cultural backgrounds, occupying different socioeconomic positions, speaking different languages and often with different legal statuses, can make a common life together in their city or neighbourhood. This question is paramount because living with diversity can translate into very different forms of interaction. While increasing urban diversity can lead people to communicate and relate to each other across cultural, socioeconomic and other divides, it can also create tensions between groups that were formerly isolated from each other. Some of the longstanding residents complain that they are being overwhelmed by the number of newcomers, experiencing a sense of loss and perceiving increased competition for housing, employment and use of public space. Although super-diverse cities rarely display continuous manifestations of conflicts, counter-reactions in the form of identity politics and an increased demand for cultural assimilation can be observed. The other side of the coin may well be the withdrawal and retrenchment among some members of minority groups who no longer feel welcome.

Although a certain amount of conflict is unavoidable, neighbourhoods and cities with a high degree of diversity are mostly characterised by cohabitation (see, for example, Cohen and Sheringham, 2016). In many cities, cultural contact in particular spaces like streets, parks, markets, cafes or sometimes in people's homes occurs peacefully. Attentive observers have highlighted how an ethos of mixing is normal in urban public life and has created an extraordinary varied cultural mélange in which old axes of identification on the basis of singular and neatly delineated cultures have almost disappeared (see, for example, Gidley, 2013; Wessendorf, 2014). Studies of social life in super-diverse cities also show how diversity both creates problems and provides opportunities. While in public debates policy-makers have mostly emphasised the negative aspects of diversity with overly dramatic statements on 'the failure of multiculturalism' or 'the loss of community', this volume is much less pessimistic and highlights the active and creative ways in which people regulate, live and deal with diversity on a micro scale. All contributors to this volume foreground in their chapters the various strategies to live with diversity, covering interactions from the stigmatisation of disliked minorities over a reluctant acceptance of newcomers to warm relations of solidarity and friendship. Although tensions are present, most contributions show that living in diversity is possible and can take place in many different ways. Such variation is also visible in urbanites' everyday living practices and in their valuations of living in super-diverse urban neighbourhoods. The contributions to this volume hence zoom in on how people can live very different lives, even when living close together: for some, their diverse neighbourhood is extremely important; for others, their activities all take place elsewhere in the city.

In exploring how social and cultural differences, in their various dimensions, are experienced locally, and what new forms of interaction emerge in contexts of super-diversity, this volume also pays particular attention to how the specific urban or neighbourhood context matters. It is clear that cities differ substantially and that within cities, quite a number of neighbourhoods show a large diversity, often accompanied by large differences in lifestyles and socioeconomic inequality. This is why the authors to this volume argue for fine-grained attention to be paid to the neighbourhood and even housing context, and how this shapes different forms of interaction. While some neighbourhoods have a large diversity of poor households, others are characterised by processes of gentrification and displacement, leading to new socioeconomic differentiations. Within some neighbourhoods residents may live spatially mixed or more separated. While some buildings are socially and ethnically mixed, others have a rather homogeneous set of inhabitants.

In this introductory chapter we set the scene for the other contributions by giving a short overview of the current discussion on diversity in deprived and mixed neighbourhoods. We first discuss how the idea of urban diversity has become an important topic in the public and political discourse. We then present how the topic of diversity at the urban and neighbourhood level is being empirically studied in Urban Sociology and Urban Studies, paying attention to both classical and more contemporary approaches. To conclude we shortly introduce the different contributions to this book and lay out the different thematic connections between them.

From multicultural to super-diverse cities

Although many cities have had longstanding forms of ethnic, linguistic and religious pluralism, contemporary international migration has significantly increased the demographic diversity in European cities since at least the latter half of the 20th century. This trend is not merely a demographical given, but also spills over into public and political debates about how to respond to challenges posed by increased population diversity. An important change of reference occurred with the term 'multiculturalism' which was coined in the 1970s. It emerged as an umbrella term referring to a set of institutional arrangements for the recognition of cultural minorities and the accommodation of group-differentiated rights (Young, 1990; Kymlicka, 1995). After first being launched in 1971 in Canada as an explicit political programme, the notion quickly diffused throughout North America, Australia and Western Europe. Inspired by the multicultural idea, various Western European countries tried, or at least discussed, different approaches to the challenges posed by population heterogeneity, including setting up minority councils, affirmative action measures in education and employment, or quota representation of migrants in political parties, administration or the police. Although multiculturalism never developed into a coherent ideology or policy model, it led to an increasing recognition of cultural minorities and of ethnic identity as an important issue. While older notions of assimilation, which dominated policy thinking until the 1970s, emphasised the way in which migrants orient themselves to the expectations, norms and values of the majority society, multiculturalism at least introduced the idea that the institutions of the majority society must also adapt and accommodate for migrant experiences. This was particularly the case in urban settings, which were at the forefront of demographic and immigration changes.

Over time, however, the notion of multiculturalism became increasingly criticised in Europe and beyond (Vasta, 2007; Alexander, 2013). It was met with resistance, by conservative thinkers who defended the primacy of national traditions and cultural homogeneity, as well as by progressive commentators, who argued that actually existing multicultural policies ignored socioeconomic inequalities and prioritised cultural traditions over individual freedom (see, for example, Brubaker, 2001; Joppke, 2004; Vertovec and Wessendorf, 2010). At the same time, the term 'multiculturalism' lost some of its lustre as a scholarly and analytical concept. Since the 1990s, philosophers, sociologists and anthropologists have problematised the idea of clearly defined ethnic groups and highlighted the constructed nature of ethnic communities as units of analysis (Glick Schiller et al, 2006; Wimmer, 2013). In this critique multiculturalism was seen as a form of cultural essentialism that tended to reify differences between cultural or ethnic groups, while obscuring the variety within them.

In the last decade, the critique of multiculturalism has given way to a broader expression and recognition of different kinds of differences, such as gender, education, age cohorts and generations, and for the dynamic interplay between them. Steven Vertovec (2007) has described the emerging 'super-diversity' of immigrant backgrounds, socioeconomic positions, legal statuses and trajectories of adaptation that makes a neat distinction between separate ethnic communities impossible. Tasan-Kok and colleagues (2018) have coined the term 'hyper-diversity' to indicate that cities are not only diverse in socioeconomic, social and ethnic terms, but also display differences with respect to lifestyles, attitudes and activities. It is important to emphasise that this shift from an 'ethnic lens' to a 'diversity lens' was not only a matter of changes in the academic agenda, but also resulted from the waves of new migration that have transformed the demographic profile of urban areas. While 40 years ago big cities in Europe and North America were mostly dominated by a small number of immigrant groups, they now boast an enormous diversity of ethnic groups. As Maurice Crul has pointed out, many cities in North America and, more recently Europe, have become 'majority-minority cities', cities that no longer have a dominant ethnic or racial majority group and consist of only minorities (Crul, 2016).

This so-called 'diversity turn' or 'the transition to diversity' has enabled scholars to acknowledge this continuing demographic transformation and to take into account a wider range of differences and similarities between and within groups than conceptual predecessors such as ethnicity or multiculturalism did. It has also transformed scholars' view on the political dimensions of urban diversity, notably with respect to multiculturalist and assimiliationist viewpoints and policies. The idea of assimilation or integration, for instance, has become more complex in cities where there is no longer a clear majority group into which one is to assimilate or integrate (Crul, 2016). Furthermore, when ethnic characteristics alone become less important, and people's attitudes, lifestyles and activities are seen to be shaped by a whole range of other factors, multicultural and assimilationist policies have to be reconsidered, and new alternatives to create liveable neighbourhoods and to improve the position of groups have to be found. The analysis of the daily lives of residents in diversified and disadvantaged urban neighbourhoods is expected to give clues for such new policies.

In sum, the 'diversity turn' has provided a useful new lens to grapple with ongoing ethno-cultural diversification. Although references to super-diversity have by now become pervasive in urban and migration studies, the emphasis on '(super-)diversity' has also received a fair share of criticism. A first critique concerns the conceptual fuzziness of the term. Diversity and its superlative are often assumed to be self-evident notions, but are notoriously slippery and context-dependent terms (Boccagni, 2015). Usage of the term 'super-diversity' can be analytically vacuous, because groups or populations with huge diversity can vary enormously in all dimensions of diversity (socioeconomic, age, lifestyle, ethno-national, cultural, religious, etc). Rather than having a clear analytical added value, the success of the super-diversity concept can precisely be attributed to its 'catch-all' quality: the concept ties together different societal patterns regarding migration-driven diversification and facilitates theorising and research into migration across disciplinary boundaries (Vertovec, 2018).

Second, it has been pointed out that the current success of (super-) diversity also has to do with its evocative and normative power. Diversity often works as a value that can be incorporated into political slogans such as 'united in diversity' (Boccagni, 2015, p 26). This widespread use of super-diversity implies that the demarcation lines between the normative and the analytical, between the political and the merely descriptive, are not always clear. On a political level, the term allows to string together a set of – not necessarily coherent – policies and programmes, appealing to those who emphasise the individual self-reliance of migrants ('neoliberals'), as well as to those who push for more policy recognition of ethno-cultural diversification and its interlocking with other axes of societal differentiation (Faist, 2014). Some have pointed out that super-diversity hardly exists apart from politics, but has been constructed precisely as a 'governance problematic', a problem 'that needs to be understood, managed, acted upon, celebrated, considered, rethought' (Matejskova and Antonsich, 2015, p 2).

Another influential line of critique concerns the question of how super-diversity relates to existing societal divisions, statuses or stratification. Much literature has underlined how the lexicon of diversity resonates with the consumerist and neoliberal logic of contemporary societies, which devalues the struggle against economic inequalities (Michaels, 2006; Lentin and Titley, 2008). Others have emphasised the lack of knowledge about how ethno-cultural differences matter for social inequality and about how new migration patterns produce new hierarchical social positions or stratifications (Faist, 2014).

We think that this lack of a systematic focus on the intersection of diversity and social inequalities makes it useful to cast an empirical light on diversity-related perceptions and practices in cities, and how they relate to other axes of social differentiation. In what follows we discuss in more detail how this book will take up this challenge. First, we briefly describe how diversity *in cities* has been empirically studied and conceptualised in the formative decades of early 20th-century Western urban sociology. We then distil three topics from this classical legacy, namely, segregation, ethnic relations and sociation, which are still very present in contemporary scholarly debates on urban diversity. This allows us to situate the two specific contributions that we aim to make through this collection: (1) a focus on the active and creative ways in which people regulate, live and deal with diversity on a micro-scale; and (2) the relationship between ethno-cultural diversity and social inequality. Finally, we position the chapters in this book within the state of affairs around these topics in the field of Urban Studies and briefly introduce their content.

Diversity at the urban and neighbourhood level

Diversity has always been at the core of our understanding of the urban. In his classic text *Urbanism as a way of life*, Chicago School scholar Louis Wirth formulates a sociological definition of the city that puts 'social heterogeneity' central: 'the city is a relatively large, dense and permanent settlement of heterogeneous individuals' (Wirth, [1938], 1996, p 1). Social heterogeneity is an important feature of urban life, according to Wirth, because it 'tends to break down rigid social structures and to produce increased mobility, instability, and insecurity, and the affiliation of the individuals with a variety of intersecting and tangential social groups with a high rate of membership turnover' ([1938] 1996, p 1). To be sure, Wirth was not only referring to ethnic and cultural diversity here, as he aimed to capture the rich variety of 'personality types' in the city that were the result of increased physical and social mobility in society. But ethnic and cultural differences were inevitably part of the social heterogeneity of US cities in the early 20th century. It led Chicago School scholars to reflect on and analyse spatial specialisation and segregation in cities as an 'ecological' response to urban growth (MacKenzie, 1925), ethnic relations in the city (Plummer, 1997) and forms of social interaction in the city (Simmel, [1905] 2002). Many of these reflections prefigured current research topics around ethnic and cultural diversity in cities.

First, there is the Chicago School conception of the metropolis as organised in a number of what they called 'natural areas' (a term that has since, for good reasons, gone out of use). Ernest Burgess claims that: 'In the expansion of the city a process of distribution takes place which sifts and sorts and relocates individuals and groups by residence and occupation' (1925, p 54). This spatial process of sifting and sorting is intimately connected to the growth of ethnic and cultural minorities in the city, as Burgess refers to the 'homeless migratory men of the Middle West' and the 'immigrant colonies' such as the Black Belt, Chinatown and Little Sicily in the zone in transition. Indeed, the ghetto and the zone in transition are two of the most widely analysed of these urban areas (far beyond Chicago School sociologists) as they aim to capture how ethnic and cultural minorities settle and organise themselves in growing cities (Burgess, 1928; Rex, [1967], 1974; Portes and Manning, [1986], 2008; Wilson, 1987; Downey and Smith, 2011). For Chicago School sociologists, so-called 'natural areas' and spatial segregation were a normal feature of growing metropolises and even a source of urban integration. Robert Park appreciated that assimilationists believed that 'natural areas' – particularly as they were inhabited by ethnic and cultural minorities – promoted 'moral isolation from mainstream society', but nevertheless provided a more positive view when claiming that:

> ... the process of segregation establishes moral distances which make the city a mosaic of little worlds which touch but do not interpenetrate. This makes it possible for individuals to pass quickly and easily from one moral milieu to another, and encourages the fascinating but dangerous experiment of living together in several different continuous, but otherwise widely separated worlds. (Park, quoted in Park and Burgess, 1925, pp 40-1)

Despite this, over the course of the past century and perhaps even more in the past decades of heated public debate around multiculturalism in Western cities, policy-makers have voiced strong concerns over the perceived social and moral implications of spatial segregation of ethno-cultural minorities, and have consequently argued for social mix policies as a prerequisite for urban social integration (Ostendorf et al, 2001; Uitermark, 2003). Also, as the ecological paradigm gave way to political-economic explanations of urban segregation, spatial segregation was problematised by scholars as a source of social inequality (Massey and Denton, 1988, 1993).

Second, the interest of classical urban sociologists in the mosaic of social worlds, described in Park's above quote, triggered a range of urban ethnographic studies, which, among other topics, also focused on ethnic relations in the early 20th-century metropolis. As Ken Plummer (1997) argues, the Chicago School 'legitimated the serious study of ethnic relations'. The rejection of arguments about the biological and genetic inferiority of minority ethnic groups paved the way for studies of 'race as a process', cultural accommodation and assimilation and the experience of minority ethnic groups. These studies certainly had important biases, not the least the relative ignoring of the role of social class and larger economic dynamics in these social worlds and their spatial patterning.

Third, the Chicago School's interest in forms of interaction in the city is rooted in Georg Simmel's work. Simmel's concept of sociation proved particularly apt to understand the forms of social interaction that emerged in cities in which 'strangers' are omnipresent. Simmel contrasts 'sociation' with 'society'. Whereas society is constituted by permanent interactions that are embedded in clear and consistent structures, sociation refers to the more contingent, transient and informal social interactions that make up urban social life (Simmel, 1950, p 10; Savage et al, 2003, p 12). Understanding how processes of sociation changed in the modern, socially and spatially fragmented metropolis, 'where any overriding social customs and values have been swept away' (Savage et al, 2003, p 17), became one of the prime empirical research concerns of the Chicago School. This focus on 'light' forms of interaction in daily urban life and what it means for the social fabric of multicultural neighbourhoods is today a booming field in Urban Studies (Oosterlynck et al, 2016), often referred to under the headings of 'conviviality', 'living in/with difference' and 'civic indifference'.

These three topics, segregation, ethnic relations and sociation, are still very present in contemporary scholarly debates on urban diversity. Today, the topic of diversity is widely studied at the urban level, most notably from the perspective of the notions of segregation and social mix. What is lacking, however, from much of this literature on urban diversity is a dynamic perspective on the active and creative ways in which people regulate, live and deal with diversity on a micro scale. This is what we aim to offer in this volume. It is also emerging from some recent work on super-diversity (see, for example, Wessendorf, 2013), and has some affinity with Simmel's concern with sociation in the metropolis and early 20th-century urban ethnographies of ethnic relations.

What we aim to add here to the recent literature on super-diversity (and the Chicago School concerns) is a stronger focus on socioeconomic differences: social inequality, poverty and social exclusion. While empirical research on super-diversity has largely been focusing on patterns of social interaction between people from diverse cultural, ethnic and religious origins (see, for example, Gidley, 2013; Wessendorf, 2014; Schönwalder et al, 2016), there is less knowledge about how socio-cultural differences interact with socioeconomic differences and 'how cultural differences exactly matter for social upward and downward mobility' (Faist, 2010, p 298). As migrants often arrive in specific neighbourhoods (see, for example, Saunders, 2010) – usually ethnically diverse, rather deprived and often located in the margins of large cities (for instance, the French banlieues) – there is a clear need for more insight into how new forms of cultural and lifestyle diversity interact with inequalities. This is why almost all contributions to this book take into account socioeconomic differences, inequality and poverty, and how they relate to other types of and conceptions of diversity (ethnic-cultural, socioeconomic, gender, etc).

By enlarging the concept of diversity with a socioeconomic dimension, this volume also provides a better optic for thinking about the broader policy consequences of increasing diversity. As super-diversity leads to unequal opportunities for different groups of urban residents and changes existing social patterns and inequalities, it also has profound implications for urban policies. While the super-diversity perspective has broadened the attention of policy-makers to cultural differences and the wide variety of people's attitudes, lifestyles and activities, there is also a danger that 'cultural difference is separated from issues such as social inequality along class and gender lines' (Faist, 2010, p 303). This is why the different contributors also analyse how the daily lives of residents in diversified and disadvantaged urban neighbourhoods can give clues to new area-based policies that are attentive to both cultural and socioeconomic differences.

Introducing the chapters

Given the aims outlined above, the chapters in this volume can be organised around two themes: the active and creative ways in which people regulate, live and deal with diversity on a micro scale, and the relationship between ethno-cultural diversity and social inequality, most often addressed through a focus on segregation and social mix. Below we position the chapters in this book within the state of affairs around these topics in the field of Urban Studies and briefly describe the argument that is made in each of the chapters.

The micro regulation of urban diversity has long been a concern in Urban Studies. However, in the past decades, this concern often led to rather negative perspectives on urban diversity, as can be seen, for example, in the literature on neighbourhood effects (Bolt and van Kempen, 2011; Galster, 2012), racism, racial stereotyping and discrimination and the urban conflicts and riots associated with it (Garbin and Millington, 2012; Slater and Anderson, 2012) and the erosion of social capital (Putnam, 2007). As for the latter, the topic of the relationship between diversity and social cohesion and social capital has generated much research and controversy among scholars. Research that is particularly grounded in a communitarian tradition sees cultural diversity as a factor challenging and undermining social cohesion, social capital or solidarity (Kymlicka, 2015; Oosterlynck et al, 2016, 2017). Robert Putnam's research on social capital and cultural diversity is a case in point (2007). Putnam observed that in neighbourhoods with higher levels of ethnic diversity residents tend to have fewer friends and acquaintances and are less engaged in the neighbourhood or voluntary organisations. His findings are different from those of group conflict or homogeneity theory, which predict less social relationships, trust and solidarity with the out-group, while Putnam observes this also in the in-group. He concludes that 'diversity seems to trigger not in-group/out-group division, but anomie or social isolation. In colloquial language, people living in ethnically diverse settings appear to "hunker down" – that is, to pull in like a turtle' (Putnam, 2007, p 140), and calls this 'constrict theory'.

Putnam's findings have triggered a stream of research, questioning the mechanistic relationship between ethno-cultural diversity and social capital. Attention was drawn to the impact of, among others, other forms of diversity (Letki, 2008) and different dimensions of social cohesion (Gijsberts et al, 2011). A similar negative reading of urban diversity is to be found in the social mix literature, where (ethnic) social mix is often found to lead to lower levels of social cohesion (Bolt and van Kempen, 2011) and lower levels of social interaction (Bretherton and Pleace, 2011; although for a more positive analysis of social mix strategies, which stresses the importance of investments in the social and physical infrastructures of the neighbourhood, see Chaskin and Joseph, 2010).

More recently, with the aforementioned launching and growing popularity of notions such as super-diversity (Vertovec, 2007) and conviviality (Wessendorf, 2014), positive readings of living with cultural differences in urban neighbourhoods have appeared. The super-diversity perspective challenges migration studies, which, according to Vertovec (2007), still owe a lot to the Chicago School of Urban Sociology and look comparatively at the integration trajectories of different ethnic groups. The diversification of diversity undermines the validity of neat comparisons between ethnic groups, as members of ethnic groups increasingly vary in terms of language, religion, migration channels, immigration status, educational qualifications, and so on. This implies that multiculturalism – through its focus on collective (ethno-cultural) identities and community organisations – is an inadequate policy and intervention paradigm to address the individual needs and ambitions, and inclusion and exclusion dynamics, of migrants.

The impossibility of capturing adequately the migrant experience and, more generally, the urban experience of living in diversity through the lens of collective ethno-cultural identities and ethno-cultural community organisations is also reflected in the literature on conviviality. Conviviality is the 'cohabitation and interaction that have made multiculture an ordinary feature of social life' (Gilroy, 2004, p xi). It is about diversity becoming commonplace, which, according to Wessendorf, requires residents of diverse neighbourhoods to strike a balance between positive relationships and keeping distance, or 'dealing with difference by "being open, but sometimes closed"' (Wessendorf, 2014, p 400). Simon Pemberton and Jenny Phillimore, in a study on migrant place-making in super-diverse neighbourhoods in UK cities, highlight how place attachment of migrants is increasingly based not on 'monolithic ethnic identities' but on neighbourhood identities developed around diversity itself (Pemberton and Phillimore, 2016). Conviviality is supported by civility towards diversity, that is, 'the skills necessary to communicate with people of different backgrounds' (Wessendorf, 2014, p 396; see also Jones et al, 2015), or by cosmopolitan habits, that is, 'the habitual ways cultural differences are transacted and reconciled in the daily conduct of people in culturally diverse settings' (Noble, 2013, p 162). Scholars of conviviality analyse the multiple and concrete ways in which people live together in diversity and the conditions under which this works out well (Nowicka and Vertovec, 2014). Important in this regard are what Amanda Wise (2009) calls 'transversal enablers', people who organise gatherings of neighbourhood residents with diverse backgrounds, engage them in everyday rituals of sharing food, music, and so on, and are acutely aware of 'the problems of an uneven distribution of power in a dominant culture guest/host relationship' (Wise, 2009, p 11).

In Chapter 2, Maxime Felder investigates the complex relation between interest and indifference and separation and exposure between neighbours in four socially and ethnically heterogeneous buildings in the Swiss city of Geneva. He looks at the conditions under which urbanites learn about their neighbours and the factors that contribute to maintaining their strangeness (meant as unusual and unfamiliar characteristics). Felder draws an important distinction between not knowing someone personally but being familiar and not knowing of someone's existence. From his empirical analysis, it seems that good neighbours do not need to be 'like us' as long as they are friendly and do not threaten our interests and privacy. Still, the combination of physical proximity and lack of acquaintance makes neighbours into strangers. Urbanites deal with their life among strangers and the incomplete knowledge they have of their neighbours with a back-and-forth movement between normalising and fantasising. In this way, urban residents balance their need for normality with their attraction to strangeness and diversity.

Jamie Kesten and Tatiana Moreira de Souza tackle similar issues in Chapter 3 on the London Borough of Haringey. They seek to understand the extent to which ethno-cultural diversity and perceptions of it have an impact on social relationships between neighbours and their everyday social activities. Since the overwhelming majority of respondents view the diversity of their neighbourhood positively, Kesten and Moreira de Souza focus solely on this group, examining the contrast between those who engage in meaningful and sustained interactions and relationships across difference and those whose social networks are relatively insular. The positive perceptions of neighbourhood diversity of Haringey residents revolve mainly around the opportunities for new experiences and greater levels of tolerance, understanding and comfort and access to more diverse places of consumption. Kesten and Moreira de Souza then assess the extent to which positive perceptions of diversity translate into meaningful and sustained practice across lines of difference. They observe that for the majority of the Haringey residents relations with their neighbours are 'pleasantly minimal', and that they choose to visit spaces run or attended by people with similar characteristics. They conclude that for the vast majority of residents neighbourhood diversity is a natural part of everyday life, but this typically only extends as far as the public sphere. In the private sphere, the networks and activities of most residents are far more insular than perhaps their perceptions of diversity would suggest.

In Chapter 4, Ayda Eraydin discusses how residents in Beyoğlu, the most diverse district in the Turkish city of Istanbul, designate others, and the effects of this designated 'otherness' on social cohesion in this area. She shows how residents in Beyoğlu use a variety of attributes to define others, most notably socioeconomic and occupational attributes, or whether they are established or new residents or come from the same hometown. Ethnic and cultural differences are not so important in defining others in Beyoğlu, although the aforementioned attributes are strongly linked to certain ethnic and cultural categories since most new residents are migrants with a low socioeconomic status and usually of Kurdish ethnicity. Eraydin's findings also underline that lifestyle is a prominent factor in the definition of others. In Beyoğlu, a majority of the respondents regard living with others as something positive because of the possibility of getting to know different people and learning about their cultures and the tolerant atmosphere that exists in the district. Still, the rapidly changing demographic composition and character of the district is seen as a threat to local social cohesion. For most residents of Beyoğlu, relationships with family members and relatives are vital, especially for immigrants and minority ethnic groups. Eraydin finds that low-income residents tend to develop good trust-based relations with their neighbours. The perception of others is rarely an obstacle to networking among neighbours, unless there are considerable differences in socioeconomic levels and lifestyles.

In Chapter 5, Anika Depraetere, Bart van Bouchaute, Stijn Oosterlynck and Joke Vandenabeele prefer to use the stronger term 'solidarity in diversity' over 'conviviality' or 'cosmopolitanism'. They take issue with the pessimism of many sociologists such as Putnam with regard to the possibility of fostering solidarity in ethno-culturally heterogeneous societies. They propose to seek solidarity not in the shared history and presumably homogeneous culture of the nation-state, but in the here-and-now of specific practices in particular places. To assess the value of this perspective, they examine if and how the introduction of a local currency system in an impoverished and super-diverse neighbourhood in the Belgian city of Ghent stimulates interpersonal practices of solidarity in diversity. They observe that the local currency triggered new activities and stimulated a more diverse group of inhabitants to participate, thus strengthening interdependency in the neighbourhood and generating new forms of solidarity, especially between residents in similar economically disadvantaged positions. Some of these new forms of solidarity in diversity have a transformative effect, that is, they question existing and normalised social structures and relationships. The authors focus on how the currency system transforms the symbolical constitution of the labour market, the taken-for-granted ways of appropriating public space, and the allocation of positions within the neighbourhood. Social professionals play a crucial role in all of this.

Besides conviviality, solidarity in diversity and associated concepts, interculturalism is yet another notion that has recently emerged to address the shortcomings of multiculturalism (Meer and Modood, 2012; Anthias, 2013). Interculturalism focuses on the communication and dialogue between diverse groups and the dynamic and interdependent nature of identities, which cannot be limited to closed ethnic and national categories. Interculturalism can have different interpretations in an urban context, but in line with the impersonal social relations, light social interaction and indifferent and blasé attitude identified by Simmel ([1905] 2002) as typical for urban social life, Bart van Leeuwen formulates intercultural urban citizenship as a 'side-by-side' citizenship (van Leeuwen, 2010). This type of citizenship facilitates living in and with urban diversity by nurturing a certain degree of indifference towards others.

In Chapter 6, Eduardo Barberis focuses on interculturalism in the context of emerging national and local models of incorporating international migrants in Italy, and the city of Milan more specifically. Barberis explains that Italy is a latecomer in the debate on immigrant policies, but that it is nevertheless an interesting case because (1) it has no policy legacy in this field and does not have an explicit and consistent immigrant policy; (2) it is at the forefront of localising migration policy in Europe; and (3) it explicitly uses an intercultural approach that is not based on a retreat from multiculturalism. Although interculturalism is often presented as a consistent policy approach, which seeks a middle ground between assimilationist and multiculturalist models, Barberis argues that in Italy interculturalism is a form of assimilationism that works through an implicit subordination of immigrant rights and life chances to the goal of social cohesion. Barberis shows how migrant incorporation policies are affected by the weakness of the Italian welfare state: national measures are implemented inconsistently and common features develop more by chance than by design through the accumulation of (assumedly) successful local practices, European Union (EU) influences and court judgments. After an analysis of national policies, Barberis focuses on two local measures in Milan that target new generations from an immigrant background, and presents them as examples of the piecemeal intercultural incorporation model in Italy: symbolic citizenship and a local dedicated information desk. These examples are aimed at showing how 'second generations' challenge the boundaries of the Italian nation-state and require a rethinking of national and local identity, while at the same time producing local answers that are not particularly consistent. Barberis concludes that inconsistent national discourses on diversity produce short-term measures that are unable to cope systematically with minorities' needs and consider the visibility of diversity as disturbing.

The second way in which this volume aims to make a contribution to the literature on urban diversity is by taking a closer look at the relationship between ethno-cultural diversity and socioeconomic inequality. This relationship can be analysed in several ways. Perhaps the most established way of doing this is through a focus on spatial segregation (and the associated notion of social mix; see Massey and Denton, 1989). Spatial segregation is, of course, not identical to social inequality. However, spatial segregation is, to an important extent, the result of the spatialisation of socioeconomic inequalities through the housing market. In the wide-ranging literature on neighbourhood effects, there is an ongoing concern with the impact of living in a disadvantaged neighbourhood on the life chances of its residents (for example, a spatial mismatch in labour markets, territorial stigma, low-quality infrastructure and public services, etc; see Galster, 2012). Since the 1920s, there has been an abundance of studies measuring spatial patterns of concentration, both of different income groups as well as minority ethnic groups. Much of this literature has focused on refining (operational) definitions and measures of spatial segregation and identifying its causes and effects. The majority of this literature is focused on Western Europe and the US, often highlighting that spatial segregation and neighbourhood effects are in general higher in the US than in Europe (Musterd, 2005). This is explained, among others, by referring to the lower levels of social inequality in Europe and the impact of established welfare states. Segregation research has also focused on specific instances of spatial segregation, such as ghettos (Wilson, 1987; Wacquant, 2007), gated communities, ethnic enclaves (Portes and Manning, [1986] 2008) and suburbs (Schuermans et al, 2014).

Closely associated with segregation is the aforementioned notion of social mix. Policy-makers across the Western world have called for and implemented social mix policies in disadvantaged and multicultural neighbourhoods, claiming that social mix improves social integration and supports the social mobility of impoverished groups (Sarkissian et al, 1990). Still, the majority of academics been sceptical about the proclaimed benefits of social mix, because the mere spatial proximity of different groups does not automatically lead to diverse social networks (Ostendorf et al, 2001; Bolt and van Kempen, 2011; Arthurson, 2012).

In Chapter 7, Javier Ruiz-Tagle confronts the issues of segregation and social mix head on by comparing two socially diverse neighbourhoods in Chicago (Cabrini Green and Near North) and Santiago (La Loma and La Florida area). Ruiz-Tagle aims to understand how social relationships can be modified by a change in spatial configurations. He questions whether intergroup physical proximity triggers other processes of integration, notably functional (access to opportunities and services), relational (non–hierarchical interactions) and symbolic (shared elements of identification) integration. He argues that in the literature on segregation and integration there is an excessive fixation on the spatial causes of social problems and an under-estimation of power relationships in socially mixed neighbourhoods. This shows in his two case studies, where he finds little relevant benefits of social mix for the poor. Social mix leads to more amenities and some institutional change, but not to upward social mobility for the poor. Ruiz-Tagle also describes how intergroup relationships in these socially mixed neighbourhoods are marked by fear, distrust and avoidance and governed by increased material and symbolic competition. He concludes that the physical proximity of social mix conceals the persistence of inequality and the forces that are actively maintaining segregation. He pleads for a critical approach that addresses the three structural factors of residential segregation: social stratification systems, housing allocation systems and welfare systems in space.

In Chapter 8, Dimitris Balampanidis and Panagiotis Bourlessas focus on vertical multi-ethnic coexistence or the socio-spatial dynamics of segregation and social mix in the same building, a residential apartment building in Athens, Greece. Over the last 25 years Athens has become increasingly ethnically diverse. Athens is characterised by low levels of spatial segregation and high levels of ethnic mix both at the neighbourhood level and within residential buildings. However, for Balampanidis and Bourlessas, living together does not mean that inequality disappears. In their analysis they focus explicitly on the link between diversity and inequality, since this link is missing all too often from urban analysis. Indeed, on closer inspection, in Athens vertical social differentiation within buildings seems to offer an alternative to neighbourhood-level segregation, with quite a strong correlation between ethnicity and floor of residence. In the studied building, Balampanidis and Bourlessas observe relations of tolerance, solidarity and friendship, but also, despite the vertical spatial proximity, social distance, lack of contact and racist and xenophobic attitudes between different ethnic groups. The authors therefore characterise vertical coexistence within the building as 'living together but unequally'.

Segregation and social mix are related to neighbourhood choice (or lack of choice, for those families at the bottom of the income distribution). In Chapter 9, Anouk Tersteeg and Ympkje Albeda analyse neighbourhood choice and satisfaction, more specifically what attracts people to diverse and deprived urban areas, and how perceptions of local diversity play a role in this. They argue that the importance of diversity for neighbourhood choice and satisfaction has hardly been studied among non-middle-class residents, and aim to change this through a qualitative study of neighbourhood choice and satisfaction among residents of different social classes in highly diverse and disadvantaged neighbourhoods in Antwerp (Belgium) and Rotterdam (the Netherlands). They find that the primary motive for choosing to live in a diverse neighbourhood is the availability of affordable housing. For poor residents and migrants, the presence of family and friends in the neighbourhood is also an important motive. Only for some interviewees, mostly of minority ethnic backgrounds, neighbourhood ethnic diversity is an important factor for their neighbourhood choice, mainly because they prefer to live in neighbourhoods that are not dominated by a majority group.

Although for most residents ethnic diversity is not an important settlement motive, aspects of diversity contribute to their neighbourhood satisfaction. For example, for members of minority groups, not being the only person who is 'different' increases satisfaction. Despite the rather negative discourses on diverse and disadvantaged neighbourhoods in public and political debates, Tersteeg and Albeda find that residents are in general quite satisfied and that diversity contributes to the decision to remain in the neighbourhood – also among the low-income groups. Finally, Tersteeg and Albeda do not find much evidence for diverse social networks, which confirms the aforementioned social mix literature; still they observe more diverse weak ties with neighbours and acquaintances than expected on the basis of the literature.

Regarding diverse social networks, authors writing on living with difference like Gill Valentine, warn against the 'romanticisation of encounter'. Harking back to earlier research on the contact hypothesis, she claims that contact between members of different groups is not necessarily meaningful in the sense that it changes people's values and produces respect for difference (Valentine, 2008). Existing inequalities are an important reason for this since contact in itself is insufficient to counter individual prejudices. She claims that scholars have to pay closer attention to the 'relationships between individuals' prejudices and the processes through which communities become antagonised and defensive in the competition for scarce resources and in the debate about conflicting rights' (Valentine, 2008, p 333). Urban politics, then, needs to address social inequality at the same time as diversity. The 'complex nature of belonging and social hierarchy' (Anthias 2013, p 323) has been strongly thematised by the intersectionality approach, which analyses the relationships between a multiplicity of identities, ranging from class and gender over sexuality and ability to ethnicity, and how these combine to produce social inequalities. It sees ethnicity as only one social division among others and is therefore well positioned to address the linkages between inequality and diversity in an urban context.

In Chapter 10, Katrin Großmann, Georgia Alexandri, Maria Budnik, Annegret Haase, Christian Haid, Christoph Hedtke, Katharina Kullmann and Galia Shokry adopt an intersectionality approach to analyse which categories are mobilised by residents to describe the social groups in their area and which normative assessments are attached to those descriptions. This intersectionality approach allows them to see social stratification at work in how inhabitants of diverse neighbourhoods in Leipzig, Paris and Athens perceive, describe and judge their social environment. The three cities that are analysed represent different histories of diversification (for example, short- or long-term migration history), and all three of them have experienced societal disruptions and change. They observe that the residents' own positionality shapes how they categorise other residents and judge their social environment. They also find that the construction of social groups in diverse neighbourhoods in these cities draws on a variety of rather classic social categories and is influenced by national discourses. Stigmatisation often occurs at the intersections of these categories. Also, neighbourhood change is an important factor in the construction of social groups.

In the concluding chapter, we reflect on some important insights that we can draw from the chapters in this volume on how citizens actively shape their life in super-diverse urban places and how ethno-cultural differences intersect with social inequality.

References

Alexander, J.C. (2013) 'Struggling over the mode of incorporation: Backlash against multiculturalism in Europe', *Ethnic and Racial Studies*, 36(4), 531-56.

Anthias, F. (2013) 'Moving beyond the Janus face of integration and diversity discourses: Towards an intersectional framing', *The Sociological Review*, 61(2), 323-43.

Arthurson, K. (2012) *Social mix and the city. Challenging the mixed communities consensus in housing and urban planning policies*, Collingwood, VIC: Csiro Publishing.

Boccagni, P. (2015) 'The difference diversity makes: A principle, a lens, an empirical attribute for majority–minority relations', in T. Matejskova and M. Antonsich (eds) *Governing through diversity: Migration societies in post-multiculturalist times*, Basingstoke: Macmillan, 21-38.

Bolt, G. and van Kempen, R. (2011) 'Successful mixing? Effects of urban restructuring policies in Dutch urban neighbourhoods', *Tijdschrift voor economische en sociale geografie*, 102(3), 361-8.

Bretherton, J. and Pleace, N. (2011) 'A difficult mix', *Urban Studies*, 48(16), 3433-47.

Brubaker, R. (2001) The return of assimilation? Changing perspectives on immigration and its sequels in France, Germany, and the United States', *Ethnic and Racial Studies*, 24(4), 531-48.

Burgess, E.W. (1925) 'The growth of the city: An introduction to a research project', in E.W. Burgess and R.E. Park (eds) *The city*, Chicago, IL: University of Chicago Press, 47-62.

Burgess, E.W. (1928) 'Residential segregation in American cities', *The Annals of the American Academy*, CXXXX, 105-15.

Chaskin, R.J. and Joseph, M.L. (2010) 'Building "community" in mixed-income developments', *Urban Affairs Review*, 45(3), 299-335.

Cohen, R. and Sheringham, O. (2016) *Encountering difference: Diasporic traces, creolizing spaces*, Cambridge and Malden, MA: Polity Press.

Crul, M. (2016) 'Super-diversity vs assimilation: How complex diversity in majority-minority cities challenges the assumptions of assimiliation', *Journal of Ethnic and Migration Studies*, 42(1), 54-68.

Downey, D.J. and Smith, D.A. (2011) 'Metropolitan reconfiguration and contemporary zones of transition: Conceptualizing border communitices in postsuburban California', *Journal of Urban Affairs*, 33(1), 21-44.

Erel, U. (2011) 'Complex belongings: Racialization and migration in a small English city', *Ethnic and Racial Studies*, 34(12), 2048-68.

Faist, T. (2010) 'Cultural diversity and social inequalities', *Social Research*, 77(1), 297-324.

Faist, T. (2014) 'Diversity unpacked: From heterogenities to inequalities', in S. Vertovec (ed) *Routledge international handbook of diversity studies*, London: Routledge, 265-73.

Galster, G.C. (2012) 'The mechanism(s) of neighbourhood effects: Theory, evidence and policy implications', in M. van Ham (ed) *Neighbourhood effects research: New perspectives*, New York: Springer, 23-56.

Garbin, D. and Millington, G. (2012) 'Territorial stigma and the politics of resistance in a Parisian banlieue: La Courneuve and beyond', *Urban Studies*, 49(10), 2067-83.

Gidley, B. (2013) 'Landscapes of belonging, portraits of life: Researching everyday multiculture in an inner city estate', *Identities: Global Studies in Culture and Power*, 20(4), 361-76.

Gijsberts, M., van der Meer, T. and Dagevos, J. (2011) '"Hunkering down" in multi-ethnic neighbourhoods? The effects of ethnic diversity on dimensions of social cohesion', *European Sociological Review*, 28(4), 527-37.

Gilroy, P. (2004) *After Empire. Melancholia or convivial culture*, London: Routledge.

Glick Schiller, N., Caglar, A. and Guldbransen, T.A. (2006) 'Beyond the ethnic lens: Locality, globality, and born-again incorporation', *American Ethnologist*, 33(4), 612-33.

Jones, H., Neal, S., Mohan, G., Connell, K., Cochrane, A. and Bennett, K. (2015) 'Urban multiculture and everyday encounters in semi-public, franchised cafe spaces', *The Sociological Review*, 63(3), 644-61.

Joppke, C. (2004) 'The retreat of multiculturalism in the liberal state: Theory and policy', *The British Journal of Sociology* (https://doi. org/10.1111/j.1468-4446.2004.00017.x).

Kymlicka, W. (1995) *Multicultural citizenship: A liberal theory of minority rights*, Oxford: Clarendon Press.

Kymlicka, W. (2015) 'Solidarity in diverse societies: Beyond neoliberal multiculturalism and welfare chauvinism', *Comparative Migration Studies*, 3(1), 1-19.

Lentin, A. and Titley, G. (2008) 'More Benetton than barricades? The politics of diversity in Europe', in Council of Europe, *The politics of diversity*, 9-30.

Letki, N. (2008) 'Does diversity erode social cohesion? Social capital and race in British neighbourhoods', *Political Studies*, 56(1), 99-126.

MacKenzie, R. (1925) 'The ecological apprach to the study of the human community', in R.E. Park and E.W. Burgess (eds) *The city. Suggestions for investigation of human behavior in the urban environment*, Chicago, IL: University of Chicago Press, 63-79.

Massey, D.S. and Denton, N.A. (1988) 'The dimensions of residential segregation', *Social Forces*, 67(2), 281-315.

Massey, D.S. and Denton, N.A. (1989) 'Hypersegregation in US metropolitan areas: Black and Hispanic segregation along five dimensions', *Demography*, 26(3), 373-91.

Massey, D.S. and Denton, N.A. (1993) *American apartheid. Segregation and the making of the underclass*, Cambridge, MA: Harvard University Press.

Matejskova, T. and Antonsich, M. (eds) (2015) *Governing through diversity: Migration societies in post-multiculturalist times*, London: Palgrave Macmillan.

Meer, N. and Modood, T. (2012) 'How does interculturalism contrast with multiculturalism?', *Journal of Intercultural Studies*, 33(2), 175-96.

Michaels, W.B. (2006) *The trouble with diversity: How we learned to love identity and ignore inequality*, New York: Metropolitan Books.

Musterd, S. (2005) 'Social and ethnic segregation in Europe: Levels, causes, and effects', *Journal of Urban Affairs*, 27(3), 331-48.

Nash, K. (2009) 'Between citizenship and human rights', *Sociology*, 43(6), 1067-83.

Noble, G. (2013) 'Cosmopolitan habits: The capacities and habitats of intercultural conviviality', *Body & Society*, 19(2-3), 162-85.

Nowicka, M. and Vertovec, S. (2014) 'Comparing convivialities: Dreams and realities of living-with-difference', *European Journal of Cultural Studies*, 17(4), 341-56.

Oosterlynck, S., Schuermans, N. and Loopmans, M. (eds) (2017) *Place, diversity and solidarity*, London: Routledge.

Oosterlynck, S., Loopmans, M., Schuermans, N., van den Abeele, J. and Zemni, S. (2016) 'Putting flesh to the bone: Looking for solidarity in diversity, here and now', *Ethnic and Racial Studies*, 39(5), 764-82.

Ostendorf, W., Musterd, S. and de Vos, S. (2001) 'Social mix and the neighbourhood effect. Policy ambitions and empirical evidence', *Housing Studies*, 16(3), 371-80.

Park, R.E. and Burgess, E.W. (1925) *The city*, Chicago, IL: University of Chicago Press.

Pemberton, S. and Phillimore, J. (2016) 'Migrant place-making in super-diverse neighbourhoods: Moving beyond ethno-national approaches', *Urban Studies*, 1-18.

Plummer, K. (1997) 'Introduction: Chicago Sociology. The foundations and contributions of a major sociological tradition', in K. Plummer (ed) *The Chicago School: Critical assessments*, London: Routledge.

Portes, A. and Manning, R.D. ([1986] 2008) 'The immigrant enclave. Theory and empirical examples', in D.B. Grusky (ed) *Social stratification. Class, race, and gender in sociologicla perspective*, Philadelphia, PA: Westview Press, 646-57.

Putnam, R.D. (2007) '*E. pluribus unum*: Diversity and community in the twenty-first century, The 2006 Johan Skytte Prize Lecture', *Scandinavian Political Studies*, 30(2), 137-74.

Rex, J.A. ([1967] 1974) 'The sociology of a zone of transition', in R.E. Pahl (ed) *Readings in urban sociology*, Oxford: Pergamon Press, 211-31.

Sarkissian, W., Forsyth, A. and Heine, W. (1990) 'Residential social mix: The debate continues', *Australian Planner*, 28(1), 5-16.

Sassen, S. (1991) *The global city: New York, London, Tokyo*, Princeton, NJ: Princeton University Press.

Saunders, D. (2010) *Arrival city: How the largest migration in history is reshaping our world*, London: William Heinemann.

Savage, M., Warde, A. and Ward, K. (2003) *Urban sociology, capitalism and modernity*, Houndmills: Palgrave Macmillan.

Schönwalder, K., Petermann, S., Hüttermann, J., Vertovec, S., Hewstone, M., Stolle, D. et al (2016) *Diversity and contact: Immigration and social interaction in German cities*, London: Palgrave Macmillan.

Schuermans, N., Meeus, B. and de Decker, P. (2014) 'Geographies of whiteness and wealth: White, middle class discourses on segregation and social mix in Flanders, Belgium', *Journal of Urban Affairs*, 37(4), 478-95.

Simmel, G. ([1905] 2002) 'The metropolis and mental life', in G. Bridge and S. Watson (eds) *The Blackwell city reader*, Oxford: Blackwell, 11-19.

Simmel, G. (1950) *The sociology of Georg Simmel*, Glencoe, IL: The Free Press.

Slater, T. and Anderson, N. (2012) 'The reputational ghetto: Territorial stigmatisation in St Paul's, Bristol', *Transactions of the Institute of British Geographers*, 37(4), 530-46.

Tasan-Kok, T., van Kempen, R., Raco, M. and Bolt, G. (2013) *Towards hyper-diversified European cities: A critical literature review*, Utrecht: Faculty of Geosciences, University of Utrecht.

Uitermark, J. (2003) '"Social mixing" and the management of disadvantaged neighbourhoods: The Dutch policy of urban restructuring revisited', *Urban Studies*, 40(3), 531-49.

Valentine, G. (2008) 'Living with difference: Reflections on geographies of encounter', *Progress in Human Geography*, 32(3), 323-37.

van Leeuwen, B. (2010) 'Dealing with urban diversity: Promises and challenges of city life for intercultural citizenship', *Political Theory*, 38(5), 631-57.

Vasta, E. (2007) 'From ethnic minorities to ethnic majority policy: Multicultualism and the shift to assimilationism in the Netherlands', *Ethnic and Racial Studies*, 30(5), 713-40.

Vertovec, S. (2007) 'Super-diversity and its implications', *Ethnic and Racial Studies*, 30(6), 1024-54.

Vertovec, S. (2018) 'Talking around super-diversity', *Ethnic and Racial Studies*, doi: 10.1080/01419870.2017.1406128.

Vertovec, S. and Wessendorf, S. (2010) *The multiculturalism backlash: European discourses, policies and practices*, Abingdon: Routledge.

Wacquant, L. (2007) 'French working-class banlieue and black American ghetto: From conflation to comparison', *Qui Parle*, 16(2), 1-34.

Wessendorf, S. (2013) 'Commonplace diversity and the "ethos of mixing": Perceptions of difference in a London neighbourhood', *Identities*, 20(4), 407-22.

Wessendorf, S. (2014) '"Being open, but sometimes closed". Conviviality in a super-diverse London neighbourhood', *European Journal of Cultural Studies*, 17(4), 392-405.

Wilson, W.J. (1987) *The truly disadvantaged. The inner city, the underclass and public policy*, Chicago, IL: University of Chicago Press.

Wimmer, A. (2013) *Ethnic boundary making. Institutions, power, networks*, Oxford: Oxford University Press.

Wirth, L. ([1938], 1996) 'Urbanism as a way of life', *American Journal of Sociology*, 44(1), 1-24.

Wise, A. (2009) 'Everyday multiculturalism: Transversal crossings and working class cosmopolitans', in S. Velayutham and A. Wise (eds) *Everyday multiculturalism*, New York: Springer, 21-47.

Young, I.M. (1990) *Justice and the politics of difference*, Princeton, NJ: Princeton University Press.

Zetter, R. (2007) 'More labels, fewer refugees: Remaking the refugee label in an era of globalization', *Journal of Refugee Studies*, 20(2), 172-92.

2

Who are the strangers? Neighbour relations in socially and ethnically heterogeneous residential buildings in Geneva

Maxime Felder

Introduction

In the first sentence of her book, *The lonely city*, British writer Olivia Laing (2016, p 3) asks the reader to imagine him- or herself standing at the window at night, when dark and illuminated windows compose the urban landscape. 'Inside', she writes, 'strangers swim to and fro, attending to the business of their private hours. You can see them, but you can't reach them, and so this commonplace urban phenomenon, available in any city of the world on any night, conveys to even the most social a tremor of loneliness, its uneasy combination of separation and exposure.'

As Laing suggests, urban anonymity might not mean that neighbours are totally indifferent towards and ignorant of each other. The lonely urbanite, standing at the window, is observing others living their lives. The particular loneliness he or she feels comes from the paradoxical situation of being alone yet surrounded by thousands of people. But were urbanites 'blasé', as Georg Simmel argues (1903), would they be affected by the sight of other lives? In this chapter I seek to investigate the complex relation between interest and indifference between neighbours.

We might know people living alongside us as intimate friends or we might ignore their existence. Yet, as Olivia Laing suggests, neighbour relations often consist of both 'separation and exposure'. What people learn from the exposure, and what remains hidden by the separation, is the focus of the first part of this chapter. More specifically, I look at the conditions under which urbanites learn about their neighbours, and the factors that contribute to maintaining their 'strangeness'.[1] Do urbanites categorise their neighbours according to how different or similar they are? Since cities' populations are heterogeneous in many respects, probably more than ever before (Tasan-Kok et al, 2013), this raises the question of the extent to which categorical differences like ethnicity, race and socioeconomic position contribute to the 'strangeness' between neighbours.

The second part of the chapter focuses on the consequences of overhearing and witnessing parts of neighbours' private lives, while often not knowing them personally. Do people tend to find a plausible explanation for the 'strange' behaviour of their neighbours in order to maintain a sense of normality and of intelligibility, as Harold Garfinkel ([1967] 1999), Erving Goffman (1971), Barbara Misztal (2001) and Talja Blokland (2017) argue? Or is it part of what makes city life 'stimulating'? I argue that the need for normality is balanced by an attraction to strangeness and diversity, seen as essential ingredients of a 'lively' urban neighbourhood. Finally, I address the question of whether this attraction is specific to an urban-seeking (Lockwood, 1995) middle class that plays a central role in gentrification processes.

My arguments are based on a study conducted in Geneva city centre. I draw from interviews with the tenants of four apartment buildings, where I systematically investigated the wide range of relations between tenants, including those that do not involve face-to-face interaction.

Dealing with strangers in the city

Anonymity in big cities inspired the early urban scholars: how do people live among people they do not know? As Simmel suggests, people adapt to urban settings by being indifferent to their environment. It would be impossible, he wrote, 'to behave like in the small town, in which one knows almost every person he meets and to each of whom he has a positive relationship' (Simmel, 1903, p 15). As a consequence, city dwellers sometimes 'do not know by sight neighbours of years standing' (Simmel, 1903, p 15). Simmel's argument is that mutual reserve and indifference allow the urbanite to feel free and independent, and that the social differentiation characterising cities is stimulating. In the first quarter of the 20th century, Park elaborates the famous metaphor of the city 'as a mosaic of little worlds which touch but do not interpenetrate' (Park, 1925, pp 40-1). He emphasises the stimulation caused by the possibility of passing from one milieu to another, which provides the 'fascinating but dangerous experiment of living at the same time in several different … worlds' (Park, 1925, pp 40-1). It introduces, he writes, an element of 'adventure, which adds to the stimulus of city life and gives it for young and fresh nerves a peculiar attractiveness' (Park, 1925, pp 40-1). Decades later, scholars like French philosopher Roland Barthes (1967) and Chicago political scientist Iris Marion Young (1990) refer to this aspect of urban life as the 'erotic' dimension of the city. From a social class perspective, this aspect of urban life is particularly valued by 'new', 'urban-centred' middle classes (as opposed to 'urban-fleeing' middle classes; see Lockwood, 1995).

During the second half of the century, sociologists developed a better understanding of how urbanites navigate in a 'world of strangers' (Lofland, 1973). Lofland argues that city dwellers 'did not lose the capacity for the deep, long-lasting, multifaceted relationship' but 'gained the capacity for the surface, fleeting, restricted relationship' (1973, pp 177-8). For instance, they learned to practice 'civil inattention' by acknowledging another person's presence yet at the same time 'express[ing] that he does not constitute the target of special curiosity' (Goffman, 1971, p 84). However, these observations regarding fleeting relationships concerned the public space, and the fate of neighbourhoods' communities was subject to different theories proclaiming their loss or survival (Wellman, 1979). The emerging consensus was that although few neighbourhoods were 'urban villages' (Gans, 1962), most urbanites were not isolated. Their social networks, however, had become more geographically dispersed (Wellman, 1979; Fischer, 1982), and the neighbourhood's relevance as a context for sociability had diminished (Blokland, 2003).

At the end of the 20th century, in France and the UK, studies confirmed the fading relevance of neighbours to urbanites' social networks (Abrams and Bulmer, 1986; Héran, 1987; Guest and Wierzbicki, 1999; Grafmeyer, 2001; Buonfino and Hilder, 2006). Globalisation and individualisation had weakened the relevance of place, and consequently of local ties such as neighbour relations. In Ulrich Beck's words, contemporary urbanites are no longer 'obligated and forced ... into togetherness' (Beck, 1994, p 15). However, we shall reject the 'image of an emerging society of bad neighbours' (Abrams and Bulmer, 1986, p xi). Regarding neighbour relations, British scholars note that 'people lay emphasis on the need for privacy and reserve, alongside the general disposition towards friendliness' (Young and Willmott, 1986, p 55). More recent works confirm that an ideal relation to neighbours is often seen as including a 'respectful distance' (Savage et al, 2005) that has to be skilfully worked out (see also Crow et al, 2002 and for the US, see Rosenblum, 2016).

In the context of increasing attention being placed on the diversification of urban populations, due to new waves of migration and lasting inequality, neighbour relations came to be seen as inter-ethnic relations or as class relations (see, for example, Wise and Velayutham, 2009). More specifically, the impact of diversity on these relations has been debated. The combination of physical proximity and social distance is double-edged, as Talja Blokland has shown. On the one hand, 'some level of acquaintance, however superficial and fluid – creates a comfort zone that allows people to feel they belong, even though they may have no local friends or family, never talk to their direct neighbours, and not even like the place where they live' (Blokland and Nast, 2014, p 1156). On the other hand, the limited knowledge of one another also allows for social distinction and identifications: 'they' are not as clean, tidy, respectable and civilised as 'we' are (Blokland, 2003, pp 99-109; van Eijk, 2011).

The question is then, who are the strangers? Based on Norbert Elias and John Scotson's (1965) case study in a suburb of Leicester, Andreas Wimmer (2004) investigated three neighbourhoods in Basel, Bern and Zürich. His interviewees were divided between a group of long-term residents from diverse origins, and newcomers – Swiss and immigrants – who they accused of being untidy and unruly. Like in Elias and Scotson's study, individual characteristics mattered less than the length of residence and the difference of cohesion between each group. Similarly, regarding the US, Rosenblum argues that Americans typically try to establish whether their neighbours are 'decent folk' or not. This distinction would be based on a 'modest practical assessment that these neighbors intend us no harm, will take our elementary interests into account, and are available for the rudiment of give and take' and implies 'disregard' for other characteristics like origin or social status (Rosenblum, 2016, p 12).

This brief overview on more than a century of urban theory shows that dealing with the proximity of the unknown and the strange is an essential aspect of life in a city, involving indifference, attraction and conflict. Yet the status of neighbours remains unclear. Do they belong to the familiar or parochial realm, or are they also strangers, like those inhabiting the public realm (Lofland, 1998)? Moreover, fleeting neighbour relations have been described as involving indifference or as inducing social distinctions and potential conflicts (van Eijk, 2011). But can they contribute to the urban environment's appeal, whereby many find urban life more attractive than suburban life?

Methods and data

I chose to carry out interviews with inhabitants of four residential buildings in Geneva city centre, across various neighbourhoods. All four buildings are located in central and densely populated areas. They are socially mixed and the median income is lower than the average for the canton (Langel and Rietschin, 2013); 50 to 60 per cent of the population of all four buildings are of foreign nationality, which is a little more than the city mean. I chose morphologically commonplace buildings, with five to six storeys and neither high nor low status. Each building hosts between 14 and 21 apartments, each with between two and five-and-a-half rooms, most of them costing between 2,000 and 3,000 Swiss francs (CHF) (€1,870-2,810) per month. The exceptions were a few subsidised apartments available for around 1,000 CHF (€930), and a loft costing around 4,500 CHF (€4,200).

The aim was to meet with all residents, in order to avoid the over-representation of the individuals most willing to be interviewed. I was not able to meet with every tenant and had to try to convince those who argued they knew neither their neighbours nor their neighbourhood. I conducted 49 interviews of around one hour each with representatives of 44 households. I talked briefly with nine more, but could not interview them formally for different reasons, some of which could be considered as forms of refusal (constant rescheduling). Six people explicitly declined. The remaining seven households were simply never home when I knocked on their door or did not even open the door. Most interviews were one-to-one, although I occasionally met with couples and with families while children were present. On five occasions I interviewed children and their parents, or tenants and subtenants, separately.

Families with children – including single parents – lived next to heterosexuals and same-sex couples, singles and shared apartments. All of them were tenants, some of them subtenants. The youngest were in their late 20s while the eldest were over 80. University professors lived side by side with bank employees, teachers, unemployed people and recipients of disability benefits. My interviewees represented 18 nationalities, and a majority declared an income between 70 and 150 per cent of the national median, while a minority were either considered as low income or high income, following the Swiss Federal Office for Statistics' definitions. The most well-off earned as much as six times more than their most modestly earning neighbour, while some newcomers paid rent up to three times higher than long-term residents.

The interviews took place at the interviewees' homes, across 2015 and 2016. We talked first about their residential history, daily routines and use of the neighbourhood and wider city. In the second part of the interview I used an A4 sheet of paper with a schematic representation of the building. Each apartment was represented by a square, and for each of them I asked, 'Do you know who lives here?' When analysing the transcripts, I paid close attention to the kind of relation interviewees spoke of. I additionally noted how they described their neighbours, the kind of information they knew about each other, and how they first became aware of each other.

Neighbours are strangers

The interviewees' neighbour relations vary from anonymity – when someone doesn't know who lives in a certain apartment – to intimacy: in one particular building two couples regularly go on holiday together, and in two of the buildings tenants had become romantically involved, subsequently moving in together. This confirms that neighbouor relations refer to a context more than to a specific type of relation (Abrams and Bulmer, 1986, p 21). However, by asking systematically what interviewees knew about the neighbours they often claimed not to know, I discovered a range of different relation types varying from actual anonymity to 'public familiarity' (when 'individuals are able to socially place others, to recognise them, and even to expect to see them', as stated by Blokland, 2017, p 126). The term 'anonymity', I believe, is often misused to characterise a situation where neighbours do not know each other personally. The following pages, however, should provide evidence of the important difference between not knowing someone personally but being more or less familiar and not knowing of the neighbour's existence.

A large number of the neighbours were familiar with each other. Through fluid encounters (Blokland, 2017) and occasional chats with some of their fellow tenants, interviewees were able to recognise them. Occasional events were opportunities to learn more about people living in the building. A yearly neighbours' party (*Fête des voisins*) was organised in three of the four buildings, gatherings that are encouraged by the city authorities but are privately organised. People attending the party – more or less the same group every year – know more about each other compared to the ones who never go. At these events I was able to witness tenants asking for and sharing information about other residents, and circulating information and rumours in the process. Tenants also get to know and help each other in the exceptional case of a burglary or a flood. More ordinarily, they learn about their neighbours when facing an irritation or a conflict. They investigate individuals responsible for noise and disturbances, for leaving the front door unlocked, or for abandoning bicycles or bin bags in the hallway. Such tensions do not automatically result in face-to-face encounters with the guilty party: tenants often either resign themselves to the fact of an unwanted situation, or complain to other neighbours or to the building's management. However, these issues lead residents to investigate their neighbours. Apart from face-to-face encounters, familiarity was fostered via rumours, door decorations, names on the doorbell and voices heard through the walls.

Familiarity remains a limited and partial knowledge of the other. When describing their neighbours, interviewees most often used life cycle and household type as denominator ("an elderly woman", "a young couple"). Observable features like visible ethnic characteristics or audible accent led interviewees to speak of "an Asian woman" or "an English-speaking man". Surprisingly, the term 'foreigner' did not appear as a generic term, probably because of the heterogeneity of the foreign-originating population.[2] Some households were identified in reference to children, pets or possessions, for example, "the parents of the young boy", "the owners of the cat" or "the guy riding a scooter". With few exceptions, information known about the neighbours was too limited to help in assessing how 'similar' or 'different' they were (for more details, see Felder, 2016).

Rather than classifying them into groups, or according to an 'us' versus 'them' paradigm, tenants described their neighbours based on how they conform to the ideal of the 'good neighbour', following the triptych of 'friendliness, helpfulness, and respect for privacy' (Abrams and Bulmer, 1986, p 30). The exchange of greetings serves as a test. As Rosenblum puts it, this ritual of civility is how, by 'gesture or word we acknowledge one another as neighbors' (Rosenblum, 2016, p 13). Those who greet too briefly or fleetingly were considered "cold" or "shy", and those not smiling were called "grumpy". Then, anyone performing adequately – in the interviewees' opinions – was considered "nice" or "friendly". Neighbours often know too little to classify each other into the binaries of 'similar' or 'different'. The classifications of 'friendly' and 'unfriendly' are both an alternative, adapted to the case of restricted knowledge, and a sign of limited expectations. 'Good neighbours', it seems, do not need to be like us, as long as they are friendly and do not threaten our interests and our privacy. This category is focused on the requirement of day-to-day coexistence.

Interviewees clearly differentiate between 'good neighbours' and 'friends'. Only a few of them have befriended a neighbour, and they referred to two main differences. First, unlike friendships, neighbour relations are highly determined by proximity, and would most likely not be sustained if one of the parties moved away. When neighbours become friends, proximity loses some of its relevance. Second, friendship involves 'progressively breaking down the barriers of privacy', while those barriers are 'essential to mere friendliness' (Abrams and Bulmer, 1986, p 94). The tenants I met were less interested in developing friendships than in preserving the efficiency of neighbour relations (Cousin, 2014). This would allow them to maintain privacy (as 'the control we have over information about ourselves', Fried, 1984, p 209), while having someone to ask for help if need be.

The main concern, then, is to distinguish among more or less familiar strangers who is 'friendly' and who is not. But because tenants tend to move in and out, this social exploration is never completed. Indeed, interviewees always consider a part of their building as *terra incognita*, not knowing anything about who lives in certain apartments. This contradicts the assumption that proximity alone leads to at least minimal contact. Simmel is right about the fact that urbanites 'do not know by sight neighbours of years standing' (1903, p 15). However, his explanation based on the 'mental attitude ... of reserve' (Simmel, 1903, p 15) should not overshadow the influence of the configuration of the urban setting and how it is used by city dwellers.

For instance, no common space is to be found around the buildings I investigated. They are conjoined, so that the facade goes from one crossroads to the other with no interruption. The high density[3] in Geneva comes from intensive land use rather than from building height. This contributes to the fact that city dwellers do not spend time around their home and are not seen conducting their daily activities by their neighbours. Similarly, the lack of common areas within the buildings reduces chances of encounters as well as the visibility of each other's daily lives. One exception is the laundry room; its use is organised by the estate management in a way that generally prevents conflict but also encounters between tenants.

As I was knocking on doors to meet tenants and ask for an interview, I realised why casual encounters in the stairways are as rare as interviewees had told me. On at least four occasions I was staring at an apartment door, getting no answer, when I heard someone entering the building below me. I went down to 'casually' bump into the potential interviewee. Before I could even reach the ground floor, he or she was already in the elevator, which I could only see moving up, stopping at an upper floor. As I climbed the stairs again, I could hear an apartment door closing, leaving me with no idea about who had just got home. This is one reason why some tenants have not seen some of their neighbours in several years, and it has little to do with an attitude of reserve.

Three buildings from my sample have the classic configuration described above: a main door directly on the street, a staircase and an elevator, and two or three apartments on each of the five or six floors. The fourth building, however, is built differently. It consists of two blocks with a courtyard in between and external walkways. Apartment doors and kitchen windows face each other, making it impossible to enter or leave without getting noticed. Consequently, tenants knew more about who lived opposite them, being able to observe whether they were home or not, and noticing prolonged absences. The more curious observer – or perhaps those spending more time in their apartment – even knew about the coming and going of lovers. In general, the tenants of this building could rely a lot more on observation when compared with the other interviewees, which further underlines the role of architecture in promoting or hindering the creation of familiarity. I should add that some tenants from the fourth building have found it challenging to get used to this exposure. An elderly couple, for instance, have never got used to it, and while they have chosen not to move out, they keep their distance with other neighbours and rarely open their curtains. Public familiarity, in the case of immediate neighbours, is not positive *per se*: it also allows for social distinctions, gossip, and might imply dynamics of exclusion.

Architecture cannot be addressed without considering the practices and the kinds of lifestyles it hosts. Interviewees explained that home is where they seek to be alone, or with their partner or children, considering it a private area. When I explained my research project and asked for an interview, the discussions always took place on the doorstep. I was most often received in the kitchen and only ever by appointment. In my numerous visits to the four buildings, I never saw a door left open, nor witnessed a conversation on a doorstep or in a hallway. These observations reflect the idea of the home as 'the place of peace, the shelter' against the 'anxieties of the outer life', as described by Ruskin in 1865 (cited by Sennett, 1991). This idea, writes Sennett (1991, p 20), symbolises 'the modern fear of exposure'. Some of the interviewees have never even had a neighbour over for a coffee. Others had only been invited to one to three households with whom they have more contact.

Even neighbours who consider themselves good friends regretted the rarity of meetings. Indeed, work, hobbies and social lives kept my interviewees away from home for most of the day. Moreover, from both my attempts to get interviews and from the interviews themselves, I realised that each building had its 'frequent travellers' and its 'multi-locals' (Duchêne-Lacroix, 2013). The former travel for work a few days or weeks every couple of months, or spend their weekends elsewhere, for leisure or to visit friends and relatives. The latter have a second home, sometimes in the mountains, or live part time at their partner's place. Recent research has shown that 28 per cent of Switzerland's residents live in more than one place (Schad and Hilti, 2015).

Based on these observations, I suggest that home is not necessarily surrounded by a parochial realm. First, it varies from one setting to another. In the fourth building, for example, the degree of acquaintanceship is higher than in the three others, and therefore closer to Lofland's definition of the parochial realm. And second, the perspective varies from one individual to another, depending on how familiar their neighbours are. For many interviewees, their doorstep is the only buffer zone between the privacy of their home and the public realm. Consequently, 'stranger' takes on a different meaning. In the context of familiarity, 'stranger' might refer to a person who is 'different' or belonging to an out-group. However, within a context of reduced familiarity, stranger would rather define those 'who [are] personally unknown to the actor of reference, but visually available to him' (Lofland, 1973, p 18; see also Sennett, 1992, p 48).

In other words, it is the combination of physical proximity and lack of acquaintance that turns people into strangers. As Abrams and Bulmer (1986, p 249) noted, 'proximity enables one's neighbours to know things about one which one might much prefer not to have known.' Because of this forced intimacy, 'wanted or not, we may have bits of intimate knowledge without strong attachment, commitment, or trust', writes Rosenblum (2016, p 42). In the next section I analyse how they deal with this incomplete knowledge of those with whom they share an address.

The tension between normalising and fantasising

Throughout my fieldwork I was surprised by how much people could say about their neighbours with the support of the schematic representation of the building, even if they effectively knew little about them. Much of what they said consisted of trying to make sense of the little they knew by fitting it into a coherent story or character. Based on the peculiarities and incongruities they sometimes inadvertently observed or overheard, they 'vigorously sought to make the strange actions intelligible and to restore the situation to normal appearances' (Garfinkel, [1967] 1999, p 47). To do so, people built coherent stories about others, turning them into characters, with the help of suppositions and extrapolations. One resident talked about his neighbour upstairs, a woman he sometimes heard shouting and throwing things across her apartment:

> 'She's an alcoholic. [A neighbour] told me how he often finds her lying in the stairwell between two floors and has to help her get to her apartment. She has a troubled past.... She's also invented a dead son, allegedly, at least.... That's what I heard. We just say hello. If I have to help her I do it of course, but we don't have much more contact.'

Other interviewees told similar stories about her, adding some variations about possible mental illness. Gossip helped them form a coherent story about this woman, including a justification for her behaviour (alcoholism) and a reason for her alcoholism (a troubled past). This form of storytelling made her behaviour appear if not acceptable, at least understandable.

In a famous breaching experiment led by Stanley Milgram and John Sabini (1978) in the New York City subway in the 1970s, an experimenter asked commuters to give up their seats, sometimes without justifying his or her request, and sometimes explaining, "I can't read my book standing up." One of the results was that people were more likely to give up their seat when no explanation was given. Without explanation, people figured a good one out by themselves. By attributing meaning to the social norm violation – for example, by supposing that the enquirer is sick and therefore needs to sit – the violation is normalised. In our case, labelling the neighbour alcoholic and attributing to her a 'troubled past' is a way of normalising her behaviour.

Normalising does not mean endorsing, however. Barbara Misztal reminds us that the idea of 'normality' has two distinct meanings. What she calls 'situational normality' is based 'on our perception of the regularity of events and people's behaviour (its factual dimension)', while 'normative normality' is based on our 'classification of action as rule/norm following (its normative dimension)' (Misztal, 2001, p 314). Her analysis is much inspired by Goffman's framing theory. She considers trust to be an outcome of situational normality, since trust stems from the predictability and reliability of social order, which helps reduce the complexity of a situation (for more details, see Blokland, 2017, pp 103-5). The example provided above shows that an otherwise deviant, disturbing or worrying situation can become a situational normality when it appears predictable and legitimate. Interviewees never endorsed the woman's behaviour, but neither did they fear it.

This tendency to normalise peculiarities and incongruities points to an 'existential need for normalcy', coming from a 'desire to experience continuity and from defense against the pressure to make sense of everyday situations over and over again' (Blokland, 2017, p 104, based on Goffman and Garfinkel). Anthony Giddens, for instance, underlined the necessity of 'basic trust', without which one would live in 'a state of mind which could best be summed up as existential angst or dread' (Giddens, 1991, p 100). And yet, it seems that unpredictability, to a certain extent, is part of the urban environment's attractiveness.

Living among strangers, both in the sense of 'unknown' and 'different', appears in my interviews as a desirable feature of an urban environment. A young woman from France explains that:

> 'The atmosphere in the streets in Geneva is different from our small town in the north of France, where most people speak in French. It is something I like here, when you're on the bus and you hear different languages. We do not interact, but it is nice hearing it, and you feel like you are not the only foreigner.'

Because she is highly educated and belongs to a desirable category of foreigners, she might belong to the 'new middle class' that is 'more inclined to find a diverse neighbourhood attractive' (Blokland and van Eijk, 2010, p 315). As stated in the literature review, in the context of gentrification, scholars have argued that middle-class groups value a diverse neighbourhood more than other social groups, but have rather homogeneous networks. Judith Butler, for example, condemns the category of the gentrifier that 'values the presence of others ... but chooses not to interact with them', treating them as 'a kind of social wallpaper, but no more' (Butler, 2003, p 2484). This argument raises the question of whether the attraction for the 'unknown' and the 'different' is a form of 'cultural voyeurism', and whether it contributes to the reproduction of inequalities.

First, as has been argued by many scholars, there is a general trend to preserve some distance from neighbours – no matter how 'similar' or 'different' they are – as a reaction to a relatively forced physical proximity. Moreover, research on working-class (Gans, 1962, p 20; Devine, 1992, p 75) *and* on upper-middle-class groups (Andreotti et al, 2015, pp 165-8) has highlighted this preference for friendliness over friendships with respect to neighbours. Instead of focusing on neighbour relations, scholars have suggested investigating neighbourhood institutions like schools (Nast and Blokland, 2013) and childcare centres (Small, 2009) as settings where resources are shared and social capital is built.

Second, individuals with more resources are indeed more likely to be 'diversity seekers' (that is to mention 'diversity' as a positive feature of their neighbourhood, as in Blokland and van Eijk, 2010). At the same time, low-income groups undoubtedly have less control over the kind of diversity they live in compared to those whose resources allow them a greater freedom in the choice of their place of residence (like the managers studied by Andreotti et al, 2015). Yet taste is probably not as determined by class, as Pierre Bourdieu argues (on Frankfurt School theorists' argument about class-obscuring mass culture, see Gartman, 1991), and it cannot be assumed that low-income groups have a general preference for socially or ethnically homogeneous environments, and are less able to enjoy 'the novel, strange and surprising' elements that a city has to offer (Young, 1990, p 239).

Less educated interviewees also value diversity as a cosmopolitan experience. Far from being 'middle class', an unemployed woman with no degree declares that residing in her neighbourhood "feels like travelling around the world, without leaving Geneva." As a counter-example, she points out the homogeneity of some wealthy residential neighbourhoods in Geneva, just outside of the city centre. Repeatedly, interviewees contrast their 'vibrant' and 'lively' neighbourhoods with the same residential areas, which symbolise boredom and the toxic homogeneity of a self-segregating upper middle class.

Third, the debate on the preference for diversity and whether or not people's practices reflect their discourses[4] mostly focuses on a conception of diversity as a mix of ethnicities and social classes. I believe, however, that the appeal of 'diverse' urban environments has to do with a more comprehensive form of otherness. Following my first argument, I argue that much of 'the novel, [the] strange and [the] surprising' which provides 'pleasure and excitement' (Young, 1990, p 239) to urbanites stems from the typically urban combination of physical proximity and social distance, and not only from categorical differences.[5] Living alongside people whom one does not know personally, but with whom one shares the same space, provides us with a glimpse of other lives, exposing and potentially amplifying their peculiarities.

Lyn Lofland considers the fact that 'one takes pleasure in the very incompleteness of the information one is able to gather exactly because incompleteness gives reign to imagination' (1998, p 81) as a source of interactional pleasure in urban life. She adds, 'we overhear or oversee just enough to catch a glimpse of enticing real-life dramas; the filling out of the drama is a work of the imagination.' She explains that she likes watching people and found herself 'amused to elaborate stories that explained the behavior [she] had witnessed' (Lofland, 1998, p 91).

Columbia sociologist Peter Bearman explains what happens when a CCTV system replaces the costly doormen in New York City. During his ethnographic work, he discovered that some tenants spent 'much of their time monitoring the traffic in the lobby' on their TV. Bearman notes that,

> ... the absence of sound recording makes lobby videos more exciting to watch, since the triviality of most interactions one can observe makes it difficult to generate more interesting theories about what might be going on. The monitors then provide a shell for the fantasy life of tenants, which is almost always more stimulating than the real life they are observing. This may be one of the reasons that it is so much fun to watch essentially nothing. (Bearman, 2009, pp 107-8)

This argument could be supported by more accounts of 'window watchers', like Gans' working-class *West Enders*, for whom 'watching [the] social life from the window – elbows on a pillow – was a popular spare time activity' (Gans, 1962, p 21), or like Mrs Jones and her husband, who 'soon after moving in [in Brooklyn] discovered what she has come to think of as the apartment's best feature: its view into the neighbors' private lives' (Scelfo, 2009, D1).

My interviewees provided more examples. One of them asked me if we could do the interview in her office. She had an executive position in administration. Meeting her had not been easy, since she did not participate in the neighbours' party where I introduced myself. As we were reviewing each square of the schematic representation of her building, she pointed at the apartment next to hers and explained:

> 'It used to be very mysterious.... We could hear someone in there, but never saw him. In many years, we saw him

once, a young man. It really fed fantasies. The same goes for the couple living next to him. I find them very strange, very strange. [Me: 'What do you mean?'] I don't know, but I would not be surprised to learn that they.... [Silence. Me, joking: 'do drug trafficking?'] 'Even worse.' [Me: 'Could they be murderers?'] Yes. They are extremely polite, and nice, but always stay in the background, just like you would do if you had something to hide.'

I did not have the chance to interview the 'mysterious couple', but I met them briefly. To me, they are an unremarkable couple in their 50s and I would guess that they are Swiss, like her, and with a similar social background. Paradoxically, similarity could be the very reason why a little oddity is incomprehensible to her. If they had been of different ethnic or social background, she might have explained their behaviour by these differences. Their strangeness stems from neither clashing values nor practices – like she said, she finds them very polite – nor from categorical differences.

Moreover, their strangeness partly comes from her turning a trivial situation into an interesting story. In this case, too, the incompleteness of the information is key and purposeful. If she had been seriously suspicious, she could have asked one of the few neighbours she knows quite well, "the one who knows everything", as she calls him. She never asked, admitting that she enjoys the thrill of uncertainty. "It's funny, she said, all the things we can imagine about neighbours." This concluding remark also signals that she is not entirely serious when she says her next-door neighbours might be murderers.

The stories about the 'alcoholic woman' and about the 'mysterious couple' illustrate the tension that arises in the void created by lack of acquaintance. Through suppositions and imagined stories, interviewees tried, on the one hand, to make sense of behaviours and actions they did not fully understand, and on the other, they managed to keep the story interesting, maintaining the illusion that they are part of an interesting and diverse urban milieu. The 'fascinating' experiment of living in a 'mosaic of little worlds' – as Park (1925, pp 40-1) characterises the appeal of urban life – results probably as much from lack of acquaintance creating space for imagination as from urbanites developing very distinct lifestyles.

Not all interviewees valued this definition of the urban setting as a place where 'things happen' and where one encounters 'the strange' and 'the different'. However, it seems that stories about neighbours' peculiarities can be entertainment for everyone, be it in the form of complaints or as an object of curiosity and interest. More importantly, it shows that the interpenetration of people's private lives due to physical proximity is not simply a downside to city living. As long as this interpenetration does not diminish our sense of privacy, and as long as 'home' still feels like a safe space, it may contribute to 'the stimulus of city life', by adding an element of 'adventure' (Park, 1925, pp 40-1).

Conclusion

In this chapter I hope to have contributed to the 'effort to move away from the emphasis on face-to-face interaction' (Wilson, 2016, p 9) and show the relevance of other forms of relations[6] with the more or less familiar strangers with whom we coexist on an everyday basis. In the Geneva city centre apartment buildings where I conducted this study tenants were prompt in declaring that they did not know their neighbours; therefore, it is tempting to refer to anonymity. During interviews, however, it became clear that tenants gathered, willingly or not, some knowledge of the people living alongside them. The combination of exposure due to the proximity, and distance maintained in reaction to this forced proximity, results in neighbours becoming 'strangers'.

My argument challenges the notion of this 'strangeness' being the result of a regrettable decline in neighbourliness and a threat to social cohesion (see Dunkelman, 2014). The analysis of my interviews confirms that which other scholars have argued for decades: tenants have limited expectations regarding their neighbours. 'Good neighbours' are at best friendly and at least do not threaten our interests and our privacy. Except when it comes to the norms governing the brief and occasional encounters, being 'similar' or 'different' is of lesser importance regarding day-to-day coexistence.

Central to neighbours' coexistence is the norm of civil inattention that involves not showing interest in the affairs of each other, so that no one feels judged or observed. However, it does not mean that neighbours ignore each other (Lofland, 1998, p 31). Therefore, civil inattention should not be mistaken for an absence of relations; quite the opposite. As this chapter has aimed at showing, relations made of both long-term proximity and lack of acquaintance can be meaningful. The lack of acquaintance leaves a grey area where imagination is used to fill a gap.

I have shown that tenants deal with the incompleteness of information about their neighbours in two ways. On the one hand, they manage to frame what they learn or observe in a way that makes sense to them. In doing so, they rarely express a moral judgement but rather try to establish whether they should worry and what they should expect in the future. Labelling a woman as alcoholic and telling a dramatic story about her past is a way of attributing meaning to past and future incidents involving her. On the other hand, interviewed tenants *enjoyed* generating stories that explain what might be occurring. The incompleteness of the information opens up room for fantasy and stimulation. In this way, people moved back and forth between normalising deviance and making triviality interesting.

I recognise that neither civility – be it in the form of 'civil inattention' (Goffman, 1971) or of 'civility toward diversity' (Lofland, 1998, p 32) – nor attraction to diversity guarantee mutual respect and address inequalities in power and resources. However, the close proximity of tenants is not only insufficient to create this mutual respect and to overcome inequalities, but it probably even prevents it to some extent. Because 'good neighbours' leave each other alone, apartment buildings are not likely to work as 'micropublics' (2002), as Amin defines spaces where stereotypes and boundaries are overcome and perceptions are reshaped. Yet anyone that has been involved in neighbour conflicts – which might range from mere inconveniences to sexist and racist violence – knows that civil coexistence should not be taken for granted. The question is then whether individuals' privately held attitudes and opinions are of more relevance than the collective achievement of peaceful coexistence. As far as neighbour relations are concerned, I think the answer is no.

Acknowledgements

The Swiss National Science Foundation financed this project (no 155747). I would like to thank Stijn Oosterlynck and Gert Verschraegen as well as the anonymous reviewer for their helpful comments. Earlier versions have benefited from comments by the organisers and the participants in the session 'The challenge of diversity: Does diversity contribute to the ideal city?' at the RC21 2015 Conference, and by Talja Blokland and her PhD Colloquium's participants. My thanks also go to Eamon Ali for his copyediting and proofreading assistance.

Notes

[1] As used here, 'strangeness' conveys the qualities of being unusual and unexpected, as well as the quality of being unfamiliar. It refers to the figure of the 'stranger as an unknown' rather than to the figure of the stranger as an 'outsider' (Sennett, 1992, p 48).

[2] Indeed, half of Geneva's residents do not have Swiss nationality, and a third of the Swiss living in Geneva have an additional nationality or have had another nationality in the past.

[3] The investigated buildings are located in areas with a density of between 17,000 and 35,900 inhabitants per square kilometre.

[4] Blokland and van Eijk (2010), among others, suggest that they do *not*.

[5] I use the notion of social distance in reference to how intimate two individuals are, and not to how socially similar they are, like in the Bogardus social distance scale. Typically, neighbours can feel similar and yet keep a 'friendly distance' that I refer to as a social distance as opposed to physical distance.

[6] In his seminal definition of a 'social relationship', Max Weber suggests avoiding the reification of the concept, positing that a 'social relationship' exists as soon as 'the action of each [actor] takes account of that of the others and is oriented in these terms' (Weber, 1978, pp 26-7). Weber also considers as a 'mutual orientation' a situation where 'even though partly or wholly erroneously, one party presumes a particular attitude toward him on the part of the other and orients his action to this expectation' (Weber, 1978, pp 26-7). This definition would encourage one not to under-estimate the importance of non face-to-face interactions and even of imagined relations.

References

Abrams, P. and Bulmer, M. (1986) *Neighbours: The work of Philip Abrams*, Cambridge: Cambridge University Press.

Amin, A. (2002) 'Ethnicity and the multicultural city: Living with diversity', *Environment and Planning A*, 34(6), 959-80.

Andreotti, A., Le Galès, P. and Moreno Fuentes, J.F. (2015) *Globalized minds, roots in the city. Urban upper middle-classes in Europe*, Oxford: Blackwell.

Barthes, R. (1967) 'Sémiologie et urbanisme', in *L'aventure sémiologique*, Paris: Seuil, 261-71.

Bearman, P. (2005) *Doormen*, Chicago, IL: University of Chicago Press.

Beck, U. (1994) 'Preface', in U. Beck, A. Giddens and S. Lash (eds) *Reflexive modernization: Politics, tradition and aesthetics in the modern social order*, Stanford, CA: Stanford University Press.

Blokland, T. (2003) *Urban bonds*, Cambridge: Polity Press.

Blokland, T. (2017) *Community as urban practice*, Cambridge: Polity Press.

Blokland, T. and van Eijk, G. (2010) 'Do people who like diversity practice diversity in neighbourhood life? Neighbourhood use and the social networks of "diversity-seekers" in a mixed neighbourhood in the Netherlands', *Journal of Ethnic and Migration Studies*, 36(2), 313-32.

Blokland, T. and Nast, J. (2014) 'From public familiarity to comfort zone: The relevance of absent ties for belonging in Berlin's mixed neighbourhoods', *International Journal of Urban and Regional Research*, 38(4), 1143-60.

Buonfino, A. and Hilder, P. (2006) *Neighbouring in contemporary Britain*, London: The Young Foundation.

Butler, T. (2003) 'Living in the bubble: Gentrification and its "others" in North London', *Urban Studies*, 40(12), 2469-86.

Cousin, B. (2014) 'Entre-soi mais chacun chez soi', *Actes de la recherche en sciences sociales*, 204(4), 88-101.

Crow, G., Allan, G. and Summers, M. (2002) 'Neither busybodies nor nobodies: Managing proximity and distance in neighbourly relations', *Sociology*, 36(1), 127-45.

Devine, F. (1992) *Affluent workers revisited: Privatism and the working class*, Edinburgh: Edinburgh University Press.

Duchêne-Lacroix, C. (2013) 'Éléments pour une typologie des pratiques plurirésidentielles et d'un habiter multilocal', *E-Migrinter*, 11, 151-67.

Dunkelman, M.J. (2014) *The vanishing neighbor. The transformation of American community culture*, New York: Norton.

Elias, N. and Scotson, J.L. (1965) *The established and the outsiders: A sociological enquiry into community problems*, London: Frank Cass.

Felder, M. (2016) 'La diversité sur le palier. Catégorisations ordinaires d'un voisinage hétérogène à Genève', *Lien social et politiques*, 77, 220-39.

Fischer, C. (1982) *To dwell among friends: Personal networks in town and city*, Chicago, IL: University of Chicago Press.

Fried, C. (1984) 'Privacy', in F.D. Schoeman (ed) *Philosophical dimensions of privacy*, New York: Cambridge University Press, 203-22.

Gans, H. (1962) *The urban villagers: Group and class in the life of Italian-Americans*, New York: Free Press.

Garfinkel, H. ([1967] 1999) *Studies in ethnomethodology*, Cambridge: Polity Press.

Gartman, D. (1991) 'Culture as class symbolization or mass reification? A critique of Bourdieu's distinction', *American Journal of Sociology*, 97(2), 421-47.

Giddens, A. (1991) *The consequences of modernity*, Stanford, CA: Stanford University Press.

Goffman, E. (1971) *Relations in public: Microstudies of the public order*, New York: Basic Books.

Grafmeyer, Y. (2001) 'Les sociabilités liées au logement', in J.-Y. Authier (ed) *Du domicile à la ville*, Paris: Anthropos, 103-31.

Guest, A.M. and Wierzbicki, S.K. (1999) 'Social ties at the neighbourhood level: Two decades of GSS evidence', *Urban Affairs Review*, 35(1), 92-111.

Héran, F. (1987) 'Comment les Français Voisinent', *Economie et statistique*, 195(1), 43-59.

Laing, O. (2016) *The lonely city*, Edinburgh: Canongate.

Langel, M. and Rietschin, R. (2013) *Mixité sociale et niveau de revenus dans le canton de Genève*, Genève: Office cantonal de la statistique.

Lockwood, D. (1995) 'Introduction: Making out the middle class(es)', in T. Butler and M. Savage (eds), *Social change and the middle classes*, London: University College of London Press, 1-14.

Lofland, L.H. (1973) *A world of strangers. Order and action in urban public space*, New York: Basic Books.

Lofland, L.H. (1998) *The public realm: Exploring the city's quintessential social territory*, New York: Aldine de Gruyter.

Milgram, S. and Sabini, J. (1978) 'On maintaining urban norms: A field experiment in the subway', in A. Baum (ed) *Advances in environmental psychology*, Hillsdale, NJ: Lawrence Erlbaum, 31-40.

Misztal, B.A. (2001) 'Normality and trust in Goffman's theory of interaction order', *Sociological Theory*, 19(3), 312-24.

Nast, J. and Blokland, T. (2014) 'Social mix revisited: Neighbourhood institutions as a setting for boundary work and social capital', *Sociology*, 48(3), 482-99.

Park, R.E. (1925) 'The city: Suggestions for the investigation of human behavior in the urban environment', in R.E. Park, E.W. Burgess and R.D. McKenzie (eds) *The city*, Chicago, IL: University of Chicago Press, 1-46.

Rosenblum, N. (2016) *Good neighbors: The democracy of everyday life in America*, Princeton, NJ: Princeton University Press.

Ruskin ([1865] 2002) *Sesame and lilies*, New Haven, CT and London: Yale University Press.

Savage, M., Bagnall, G. and Longhurst, B. (2005) *Globalization and belonging*, London and Thousand Oaks, CA: Sage.

Scelfo, J. (2009) 'Window watchers in a city of strangers', *The New York Times*, 11 November.

Schad H. and Hilti, N. (2015) 'Die Mobilität multilokal Wohnender', *Verkehrszeichen*, 2, 4-7.

Sennett, R. (1991) *The conscience of the eye: The design and social life of cities*, New York: Alfred A. Knopf.

Sennett, R. (1992) *The fall of the public man*, New York: W.W. Norton & Company.

Simmel, G. (1903) 'The metropolis and mental life' in G. Bridge and S. Watson (eds) (2002) *The Blackwell city reader*, Oxford and Malden, MA: Wiley-Blackwell.

Small, M.L. (2009) *Unanticipated gains: Origins of network inequality in everyday life*, New York: Oxford University Press.

Tasan-Kok, T., van Kempen, R., Raco, M. and Bolt, G. (2013) *Towards hyper-diversified European cities. A critical literature review*, Utrecht: Utrecht University.

van Eijk, G. (2011) '"They eat potatoes, I eat rice": Symbolic boundary making and space in neighbour relations', *Sociological Research Online*, 16(4).

Weber, M. (1978) *Economy and society. An outline of interpretative sociology*, Berkeley, CA: University of California Press.

Wellman, B. (1979) 'The community question: The intimate networks of East Yorkers', *American Journal of Sociology*, 84(5), 1201-31.

Wilson, H.F. (2016) 'On geography and encounter: Bodies, borders, and difference', *Progress in Human Geography*, 1-21.

Wimmer, A. (2004) 'Does ethnicity matter? Everyday group formation in three Swiss immigrant neighbourhoods', *Ethnic and Racial Studies*, 27(1), 1-36.

Wise, A. and Velayutham, S. (eds) (2009) *Everyday multiculturalism*, Basingstoke: Palgrave Macmillan.

Young, I.M. (1990) *City life and difference*, Princeton, NJ: Princeton University Press.

Young, M.D. and Willmott, P. (1974) *Family and kinship in East London*, Harmondsworth: Penguin.

3

Experiencing diversity in London: Social relations in a rapidly changing neighbourhood

Jamie Kesten and Tatiana Moreira de Souza

Introduction

This chapter investigates how residents of the London Borough of Haringey perceive the ethnic and socioeconomic diversity of their local neighbourhood. It demonstrates the extent to which this diversity, and perceptions of it, has an impact on relationships between neighbours and residents' everyday practices and social activities. Diversity has been a recurrent theme in discussions over living in cities as residents have become increasingly diverse in socioeconomic and ethnic terms, as well as with regards to lifestyles, attitudes and activities. Since the 1990s, migration patterns to the UK have become increasingly varied and now include more and more countries and an array of other variables, such as 'differential immigration statuses and their concomitant entitlements and restrictions of rights, divergent labour market experiences, discrete gender and age profiles, patterns of spatial distribution, and mixed local area responses by service providers and residents' (Vertovec, 2007, p 1025). This context, which Steven Vertovec (2007) described as one of 'super-diversity', coexists with growing social inequality. Many studies have focused on the impact that diversity has on the sense of community within urban areas and neighbourhoods in the UK. While some have reported on residents living 'parallel lives' (Cantle, 2001), many others have focused on the possibilities of convivial everyday encounter and interaction (Amin, 2002; Sennett, 1999; Neal et al, 2013, 2015).

This chapter makes three main contributions to wider literature on super-diverse urban neighbourhoods and the experiences of their residents – first, in the sampling approach the research adopted. Studies such as Pemberton and Phillimore (2016, p 1) have sought to understand 'how place-making proceeds in super-diverse urban neighbourhoods where no single ethnic group predominates' by interviewing European

Union (EU) and non-EU migrants. This chapter demonstrates that the experiences of recent migrants are only part of the story. To truly understand the dynamics of super-diverse areas like Haringey, where no single ethnic group predominates, it is important to acknowledge that a significant proportion of the population is long established – and often British-born – black and minority ethnic (BME) groups for whom the label of migrant is ill-fitting and inaccurate. It is also necessary to acknowledge the experiences and perceptions of the equally long-established White British working-class residents and that in many cases the most recently arrived are the new middle class – often White British – gentrifiers. This chapter is based on research that spoke to residents from all of these groups. It recognises the distinction between the experiences of, and perceptions towards, neighbourhood diversity of the long-established and recently arrived as well as between those who may still reasonably be perceived (or perceive themselves) as migrants and those for whom this terminology is unsuitable. Second, as a result of this broader engagement with residents of super-diverse neighbourhoods, the chapter is able to demonstrate the role that socioeconomic position plays in determining cross-cultural exchanges. And third, it offers a valuable insight into the impact of gentrification on super-diverse neighbourhoods as the influx of middle-class residents brings rapid changes to the physical and social fabric of the area that threaten pre-existing cohesion within the community.

Haringey is the fifth most ethnically diverse and thirteenth most deprived borough in England, where over 100 languages are spoken (Haringey Council Services, 2015). It is an example of a London borough with sizable numbers of a wide range of different BME groups and migrant communities where historically, unlike many other boroughs, no single ethnic group has dominated statistically. Since almost all respondents viewed the diversity of their neighbourhood positively, the focus here is solely on examining the contrast between those who noted that they engage in meaningful and sustained interactions and relationships across difference and those whose social networks were relatively insular. This was done to understand (1) the factors that affect cross-cultural interaction; and (2) the disconnection between perceptions and practices in relation to neighbourhood diversity.

The chapter draws on findings from 41 semi-structured interviews with residents living in the eastern wards of the borough, which are the focus of Haringey Council's regeneration plans (see Figure 3.1). Interviews were conducted in cafes, coffee shops, libraries and community centres between October 2014 and March 2015.

Respondents were identified via four methods: resident groups and pre-existing contacts from local organisations; online via locally oriented forums; users of a local food bank; and via snowball sampling and personal contacts. This range of sampling methods enabled access to residents from a variety of different backgrounds and experiences including those who were very well established, engaged in their community, and participating in local civic organisations; those less socially active but still civically minded and concerned with local issues; as well as those who were far less engaged in neighbourhood life and, in many cases, experiencing degrees of financial and emotional hardship.

Figure 3.1: Map of the London Borough of Haringey

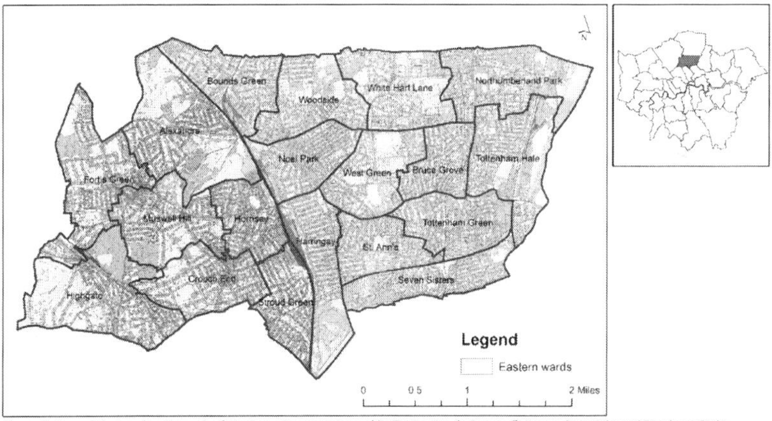

Figure 1: Map of the London Borough of Haringey. Source: Mapped by T. Moreira de Souza, © Crown Copyright and Database Right [2017]. Ordnance Survey (Digimap Licence) , <http://digimap.edina.ac.uk>.

Source: Moreira de Souza (2017)

The sample was developed with the importance of reflecting the demographics of the case study area in mind in terms of age, gender, country of birth, ethnic background, religious belief, sexual orientation, disability, level of education, occupation, household income, household composition, household type, household tenure, area of residence, length of time in current residence and length of time in area, and sampling approaches were adjusted accordingly at various stages of the fieldwork. Most participants were aged 25-44 (42%) or 45-64 (29%), 30 out of 41 were female and 56 per cent of the sample defined themselves as either 'White British' or 'White Other' while others identified as being from a range of 'Black' (23%), 'Asian' (7%), 'Mixed' (7%) and 'Other' (7%) ethnic backgrounds. Those born in the UK accounted for 54 per cent, while the remaining respondents were born overseas across 14 different countries from Europe, Africa, North and South America, South Asia and the Caribbean.

This chapter begins with a review of the literature around issues of encounters in diverse environments. It then moves on to present examples of the types of positive perceptions of neighbourhood diversity expressed by Haringey residents, centred around the opportunity for new experiences and greater levels of tolerance, understanding and comfort on the one hand, and access to more diverse places of consumption on the other. Next, it uses both the 'meaningful' and 'minimal' relations and interactions between neighbours to outline some of the common characteristics of those with more open and more closed local social networks and practices of neighbouring. Finally, it concludes by outlining the factors affecting the likelihood of these interactions taking place, and reflects on the significance of the disconnection highlighted between the positive perceptions of neighbourhood diversity and the minimal nature of interactions across lines of difference.

Resident encounters in ethnically diverse urban environments

Policy discourses and the daily experiences of those living in diverse cities and neighbourhoods with regards to their perceptions and practices of diversity have been widely discussed by academics. Since the 2001 riots in Oldham, Bradford and Burnley, concerns about social cohesion in British cities have increased among policy-makers, with strong criticism of multiculturalist policies that were perceived to exacerbate divisions between groups. Much of the concern was based on the idea that residents were living parallel lives, or, in other words, not interacting with and being ignorant of the culture and customs of other local residents who were different to them. Since then, more attention has been put on fostering a concept of citizenship based on common principles and shared solidarity (Cantle, 2001, p 21) – exemplified by the creation of the 'Life in the UK' citizenship test, which is largely based on an 'imagined, unified and essentially white British identity' (Clayton, 2009, p 482). According to Fortier (2007, p 106), the 'strategies for fostering social cohesion' in Britain, and Europe more broadly, represent 'one example where the state seeks to engineer modes of living together and affective relations that draw on injunctions of intimacy through which the limits of the civil nation are drawn.' However, as Amin (2002, p 959) notes, aside from the existence of national policies with regards to ethnic relations and diversity, it is important to focus on the 'micropolitics of everyday social contact and encounter' to understand the ways in which interaction with difference develops. For Amin the terms of engagement within, and the constitution of, micropublics are 'crucial for reconciling and overcoming ethnic cultural differences' (2002, p 959). Similarly, Clayton (2009, p 494) argues that it is through people's everyday lived experiences at the local level that ethnic and social differences are interplayed and through which 'identities and solidarities are constructed, contested and negotiated.'

Residents of mixed urban neighbourhoods, such as the ones studied in this chapter, experience encounters with difference whenever they leave their homes. This was extensively discussed by Lyn Lofland (1973) who noted that urbanites are constantly experiencing both anonymity and interactions with unknown others in public space, and as such they use tools such as what she termed 'appearential ordering', which relies on visual information (clothing, hair, markings), and 'spatial ordering', which associates certain locations with certain groups or certain types of people, in order to cope with difference and make sense of their environment (Lofland, 1973, p 27). In her investigations of social interaction across difference in the 'super-diversified' London Borough of Hackney, Susanne Wessendorf (2013, 2014) developed the notion of 'commonplace diversity', referring to the fact that diversity has become normal in people's daily lives. This normalcy has resulted in people using civility as a pragmatic tool that allows them to either engage further or avoid deeper contact with people different to them (Wessendorf, 2014). Wessendorf also developed the idea of an 'ethos of mixing' referring to residents' expectation that 'people "should mix" and interact with their fellow residents of other backgrounds' in public and associational spaces by conducting themselves in ways that show openness towards diversity (2013, pp 407-8). She noted that respondents were happy with the coexistence of separation (in the private sphere) and mixing (in public and associational spaces), but they were not comfortable with groups that removed themselves from 'local life, ranging from economic activities to participation in civil society or institutions such as schools' (2013, p 419). Such separation seems more acceptable and preferred by middle-class households, who use differentiation as a way to safeguard their status, be it through the careful selection of schools for their children (Butler, 2003; Boterman, 2013) or of spaces in which to socialise (Savage et al, 2005; Watt, 2009).

Policy expectations lie in the premise that mixed neighbourhoods and the shared use of public spaces in them will expose residents to diversity, and that social interaction among different groups will contribute to social integration and an increased sense of belonging (Cattell et al, 2008; Curley, 2010). Yet some studies have shown that it cannot be implied that people's everyday lived experiences in diverse environments will result in respect or positive views of difference. Gill Valentine (2008) has shown that racism and prejudice can coexist with positive encounters, warning that the discourses of conviviality and the celebration of multiculturalism fail to adequately acknowledge the fact that interactions can be courteous despite privately held negative feelings towards difference. Caroline Holland et al (2007) found that coexistence in public spaces in Aylesbury, UK, did not culminate into different groups interacting. In fact, different groups carved out their own spots in a local park and individuals or groups who were considered 'undesirable' or 'out of place' were moved on or dispersed in certain public spaces (Holland et al, 2007, p 65). Nonetheless, the literature highlights that awareness of difference is increased when people encounter diversity in public spaces (Peters and de Haan, 2011), and that there are more opportunities for meaningful encounters (which can challenge prejudices and negative perceptions of difference) in spaces that facilitate repeated visits and through activities that require mutual assistance.

Another dimension of living in diverse neighbourhoods is that of neighbouring, a relationship that is bounded by physical proximity. Since physical proximity alone is not enough to guarantee whether neighbours will share similar lifestyles or social characteristics or will have the volition to interact, it can be assumed that relationships between neighbours, be it in relatively homogeneous or mixed neighbourhoods, are based on unpredictability (Mann, 1954; Abrams and Bulmer, 1986; van Eijk, 2011). Indeed, as Painter (2012, p 524) notes, '[a]t the outset we do not know if our neighbours are like or unlike us, whether we will be inclined to love or hate them, how they will feel about us, or how far they will be knowable at all.' The literature on neighbouring also discusses the existence of expectations with regard to a certain code of conduct because physical proximity facilitates the involuntary transference of personal information (such as the noise and smells that transcend walls and information obtained through the observation of routine activities; see van Eijk, 2011). Fortier (2007, p 116) highlights the multifaceted nature of relations between ethnically and culturally diverse neighbours by emphasising how 'the management of multicultural intimacy is both about physical relations in geographically bounded areas, as well as about the conception of nonphysical relationships in terms of a spatial social imaginary.' This is evidenced using the examples of community cohesion policy discourse in Britain that 'presupposes that interethnic mixing cannot occur without spatial and physical (non-erotic) proximity' and relations between British Asian and White residents of Bradford, which were to be found characterised by segregation and division (Fortier, 2007, p 107).

Perceptions of neighbourhood diversity

This section explores the positive perceptions of diversity among Haringey residents with a view to understanding how they experience it in their neighbourhood. It is particularly interested in the relationship between residents' perceptions of neighbourhood diversity and their lived practices and experiences manifested in how they describe their relations with their neighbours and other people locally. As noted previously, existing literature highlights an ambiguous and, at times, seemingly paradoxical relationship between perceptions and practices in relation to diversity (see, for example, Clayton, 2009; van Eijk, 2012; Wessendorf, 2013, 2014). This normalcy of diversity is argued to often be typified by a positive – but arguably somewhat superficial – appreciation of difference (Wessendorf, 2014). It is with this in mind that this chapter seeks to understand the perceptions of respondents towards their diverse neighbours and neighbourhoods and the extent to which these positive perceptions correlated with meaningful relations across difference.

Our findings indicate that in the context of London, the most ethnically diverse city in Europe and the 'most cosmopolitan place on earth' (Benedictus and Godwin, 2005), the diversity of the neighbourhood, and the experience of living with difference (Valentine, 2008) was something that many took for granted. For example, Victor (resident names have been anonymised), a longstanding Black British resident of Wood Green in his early 30s who was born and raised in Tottenham, summed up the feeling expressed (both explicitly and implicitly) by many towards the diversity of their neighbourhood, remarking: "The thing is, it's normal, I grew up around loads of different cultures, a lot of my friends were from all over the world, it's not something I even thought about before you asked me that question". While Donna, originally from the USA and in a long-term same-sex relationship and with a son in primary school, commented on her neighbourhood of Bruce Grove in Tottenham that: "You expect it to be diverse, you expect people to be fairly open-minded ... you expect it to be just very, very diverse and kind of accepting and open." This expectation of open-mindedness informed their choice of neighbourhood. Overall, perceptions of neighbours can loosely be characterised as adhering to the notion of 'commonplace diversity' in that ethnic, religious and linguistic diversity was 'experienced as a normal part of social life and not as something particularly special' (Wessendorf, 2013, p 407).

The most common and significant positive aspects of neighbourhood diversity described by respondents can be split into two categories: *fostering new experiences and greater levels of tolerance, understanding and comfort* and *access to diverse places of consumption locally* (including shops, cafes and restaurants).

Fostering new experiences and greater levels of tolerance, understanding and comfort

A number of residents placed immense value on the opportunity to meet and interact with others different to themselves in their neighbourhoods as this enabled them to gain an enhanced understanding of a variety of cultures, histories and perspectives. For example, Dorota, who was in her early 20s living in student accommodation in Tottenham Hale and originally from Poland, remarked: "When you talk to people like that, who are completely different to you, it really helps you to understand many things better." This sentiment was shared by Darren, also in his early 20s and living with his parents in Wood Green but born and raised in Dominica, who described how "[…] one of the best things to me, personally, living in Haringey is the fact that it's multicultural … the opportunities to meet and experience a different culture, a different lifestyle." Some residents, like Geoff, a White British Noel Park resident in his late 30s, were even able to give specific examples of how living in Haringey had made them more open-minded and more aware of the world, stating:

> '… the Turkish guy that lives here told me a lot about his story, it's a real eye opener…. I wasn't too clever on all my views on immigration before but, speaking to people … it's made me realise … it's important to help these people – I didn't really think that before – I used to think "oh, close the border", n'all that, I don't think like that no more.'

For Geoff, and others moving to Haringey having previously lived in 'predominantly White' places, his ethnically and culturally diverse neighbourhood offered the opportunity to break down barriers and develop a greater level of intercultural understanding, appreciation and acceptance of the various backgrounds of his neighbours. He, like many others, saw the diversity of his neighbourhood as an indisputable improvement and was extremely positive about the impact that his experiences of living there had given him, recounting various examples of sustained and meaningful interactions and relationships across lines of difference. This sense of diversity offering residents new experiences and levels of understanding was noted as particularly significant for children and young people. For example, John, a White British single father in his mid-60s living in North Tottenham, reflected that it "teaches tolerance and understanding that there are different ways of living, different religions, different cuisines, different ways of thinking … and the schools, certainly celebrate that by teaching and observing all the major religious festivals … and having meals, y'know, from the Caribbean cooking and roast beef and Yorkshire pudding." However, while numerous other residents shared these positive perceptions of neighbourhood diversity, many struggled to articulate why they felt this way and struggled to give concrete examples of how the diversity of their local area impacted their day-to-day lives, such as Steve, a White British resident of St Ann's in his mid-50s:

> 'Why does it matter to me? I mean, instinctively, I would say "that's great", but thinking about why does it, actually, matter to me, apart from it fitting in with my subscribed view of the world of tolerance and inclusivity [pause] … it's so easy to say "oh yeah, this is what I prefer, this is what I like" – but is it, actually … a superficial pay-off for me, that it's great 'cos I get to see lots of different things and hear lots of different things, rather than anything deeper than that … is it enough?'

There was also evidence indicating that the area's sociocultural diversity acted as a magnet for certain incomers, particularly those who imagined or stated that they would feel out of place in an ethnically homogenous environment, and those who sought a sense of familiarity with those of a similar nationality, ethnicity or sexual orientation. Several migrant and BME residents lauded the diversity of their neighbourhood as providing them with a sense of comfort and security. This feeling was often attributed to the specific nature of diversity in Haringey where, as mentioned earlier, unlike some other London boroughs, no single ethnic group is dominant. This dynamic enabled interviewees from a range of backgrounds and lifestyles to avoid feeling like 'an outsider' or the embodiment of difference for being the only same-sex couple or the only non-White British person in a predominantly heterosexual or White British environment. Jade, a South Tottenham resident in her late-20s from a 'Mixed: White and Asian' background, explained the difference in comfort she feels living in South Tottenham compared to her former university in Derby in the north of England as: "… definitely something that attracts me and makes me feel more comfortable.… If I was living in an area that was less diverse, I think – because I'm mixed race – I would feel not as comfortable, or I'd be more aware of it, where this is more neutral for me, I'm kind of used to the diversity, so I don't necessarily see it, but if I was somewhere less diverse, I would notice." Valencia, a Tottenham resident in her mid-40s and originally from Mexico, notes that the fact that the residents of Wood Green are from a variety of ethnic backgrounds and cultures provided not just comfort but a sense of security as a migrant, which she did not feel in her previous home:

> 'I didn't feel safe in Newcastle, there were people from other places, but most people are like people from Newcastle … here, it's like "oh, okay"… it's just another one of those countries, y'know, all the many people that live here.'

It was clear from the research, as evidenced by Jade, Valencia and others, that the diversity of the city and the neighbourhood performed two clear functions. First, it provided an opportunity to learn about different cultures and ways of life and to interact across difference in ways that were shown to increase levels of tolerance and understanding. This was noted as particularly enlightening for those with little prior experience of living in a diverse urban environment. Second, it made it possible for residents who did not fit a 'mainstream' profile in terms of ethnicity, religion, cultural background or sexual orientation to feel at home and reduced their sense of alienation and isolation as 'others' defined in relation to a so-called 'host' population.

Access to diverse places of consumption

The positive perceptions of neighbourhood diversity and the experiences it offers residents often became a reflection on the diverse nature of local places of consumption. This perception of engagement with diversity through consumption concurs with Hage's (1997, p 17) finding that residents of Sydney's inner-city suburbs tended to conceive of and express multiculturalism in terms of the 'quantity and quality of available "ethnic" food, and primarily "ethnic" restaurants' in their streets or neighbourhoods. It was common for some residents to praise the opportunity to purchase foods and other products from around the world due to the various specialised grocery stores, bakeries, cafes and restaurants within the neighbourhood. Margaret, a White British resident of Tottenham in her late 50s, among many others, reflected positively on the fact that "in Tottenham, you've got so many places to eat ... you've got fabulous Turkish food shops, which is wonderful, and you're not that far from Green Lanes [an area of Haringey well known for its Turkish restaurants]." It was a recurring theme among many interviewees to note the diversity of small shops and 'ethnic' businesses available as one of their neighbourhood's best features. Debbie, a White British resident of South Tottenham in her late 20s, spoke at length about the benefits of her local Turkish shop which included an in-house greengrocer and bakery in contrast to what she saw as the alternative: "I don't wanna have to walk down streets that are like homogenous and full of Tesco's ... and Costa's and other places.... I want to have local shops and local things and things that people eat from my local community and things that I can try which are different and different people that I can meet." Steve, a White British resident of St Ann's in his mid-50s, beamed about his local Greek-Cypriot grocery store as a form of "community hub" and praised the fact that it afforded him the opportunity to be able to "buy fresh coriander late at night" or go "shopping on Christmas Day". Other residents like Layla, a White British resident of Bruce Grove in her early 50s, reflected fondly on how the representation of her neighbourhood's diversity in its local places of consumption meant she could, "...walk down the end of [her] road and ... [she doesn't] need to go on holiday to half the places in Europe...."

These examples are indicative of the overwhelming majority of respondents who perceived the diversity of their neighbourhood in a highly positive way. In many cases, the wide mix of residents and variety of local places of consumption were referred to as the area's best features due to the opportunity for new experiences, cross-cultural understanding and appreciation for various forms of difference, particularly among children. This positive perception of diversity was often evident even without a specific question being asked.

It was possible to identify different reasons for valuing diversity among various 'types' of residents. While residents from a range of backgrounds praised the opportunity to gain new experiences through meeting and interacting with people different to themselves, there was a clear split between residents from BME and migrant backgrounds for whom diversity often offered a sense of comfort and security, and residents of 'White British' and 'White Other' backgrounds who were far more likely to highlight the presence of diverse places of consumption when explaining why they valued neighbourhood diversity. However, this emphasis on the consumption of diversity does not necessarily result in meaningful interaction with ethnic subjects.

Interactions across difference

This section assesses the extent to which these positive perceptions of diversity translated into meaningful and sustained practice (such as interactions, bonds and relationships across lines of difference). It pays particular attention to how residents' identities and experiences affected the likelihood of interactions across difference taking place, as well as the issues that were found to hamper diverse interactions. Reported relationships between neighbours of different backgrounds varied significantly, in line with previous research on 'neighbouring' as a process, and, therefore, showing various degrees of 'neighbourliness' (Abrams and Bulmer, 1986). The analysis of the interviews allowed for the identification of two groups: those who gave examples of sustained and meaningful relationships and interactions with their diverse neighbours, and those whose cross-cultural interactions were more superficial or 'pleasantly minimal' in nature. It is to these two distinct groups that the analysis now turns.

Meaningful forms of neighbouring, strong bonds and patterns of interactions

Evidencing the everyday or 'commonplace' nature of neighbourhood diversity in Haringey, and without specifically mentioning (or being asked about) any aspect of the diversity of the neighbourhood, many residents praised the presence of strong social bonds, community spirit and patterns of interaction among diverse neighbours. A good example of these meaningful interactions across difference taking place comes from Eudine, a Black Caribbean single mother from Tottenham in her late 40s, who noted that her neighbours were: "[White] English, Black English, Jamaican, Turkish…" and that "everybody gets on well with each other, especially if they know each other and know that you're a neighbour." Eudine demonstrates how bonds of neighbourliness can outweigh other perceived differences given the right circumstances and if forged through regular, sustained and enjoyable interactions. She describes a quite involved level of interaction among her immediate neighbours, who take turns once a month cooking for, and eating with, each other, and reflects on the positive impact this has had on neighbourly relations:

> 'Where I live, in my block, on my floor, … [no matter] what country you come from, or what background you've come from, we have one Sunday a month where one person on that floor cooks for everybody on that floor, for Sunday dinner, so you get different cultures that way and you taste different food and that's just once a month and it's just making our floor acceptable.'

The sharing of food between neighbours from different ethnic backgrounds was also mentioned by several other residents as an enjoyable engagement with diversity. For example, Abyan, in her early 20s and who had moved to Tottenham from Somalia when she was a toddler, notes: "My neighbourhood's wicked, my street, White Hart Lane, is cool because if we cook something for ourselves, we have people over, we just share it out to each other – they do the same thing as well – so it's really nice, it's a bit friendly." While according to Shane, a White British resident of Tottenham in his late 20s, living in Haringey offers him the opportunity to gain a window into other parts of the world through food:

> 'From my point of view, it's very positive.… I go to my friend's house, I can taste some food from Africa, [and] I can go to my friend's house, taste some food from Portugal, we bring different things to the table.… They show you parts of their world.'

The sharing of food between neighbours was perceived as an enjoyable engagement with diversity by interviewees. Such practices constituted what Hage (1997, p 13) defined as 'a homely and an interactive culinary multiculturalism', as they allowed for the sharing of knowledge, experiences and biographies. Such experiences stimulate feelings of reciprocity and trust considerably, and 'produce capacities for the recognition or acknowledgement of otherness' (Wise, 2009, p 35).

Other residents also praised the strong bonds between neighbours. Rupinder, a Portuguese national and resident of Bruce Grove in her mid-50s, commented: "the best thing, I would say, is that kind of human connection with people who live in the area … there is a high level of solidarity." She was particularly fond of the older, mostly Black Caribbean, residents of her neighbourhood, describing how their approach to neighbourliness added to her sense of security and social bonding in her neighbourhood:

> '[…] these older members of the street, they make sure they know everybody who lives there. Even if you come exhausted from work, they'll greet you and ask you how was your day n'all, that old-fashioned way, and many people are retired, and they just monitor the street to see if anybody tries to break into your home, they're on the phone immediately, calling the authorities, they won't tolerate that at all, so there is a mutual concern for wellbeing and also like a vigilante force you could call it.'

While respondents were generally aware of much of the demographic profile of their neighbourhood and able to describe the ethnicity, age, socioeconomic status and occupation of many of their neighbours to some extent, these markers were often less significant to them than individual volition to interact with others in the neighbourhood or participate in activities. As demonstrated by Eudine, Shane and Rupinder, in many cases it was possible to disassociate notions of neighbourliness and community from perceptions of similarity, allowing for a more inclusive form of neighbourly relations. The overall feeling was that there were more issues in common between people living in the research neighbourhoods than divisions, many of them related to their sense of attachment to the area. One response that was indicative of many others on the connection between diversity and relations with neighbours comes from Donna who remarked that the fact that she did not "match" with her neighbours was not a problem. For Donna, the "beauty of London" is that "nobody's the same and nobody would expect to be the same" but that "what we might be the same on are some of the things that we care about". She continued to explain:

> 'The match is about community here and I think where this neighbourhood – and Tottenham overall – does really well, manages really well, is to bring people together around community, around where we are, and around our place and our community, rather than being the same, or thinking the same, necessarily. Obviously, you've gotta have a certain amount of similarity in terms of, umm, y'know, what you think is acceptable, but that's fairly broad.... I think the matching is about concepts of community ... it's not about what we look like, or who we are … it's not at

all about being the same, it's about coming together with our difference and caring about our community.'

In addition to the practices, common bonds and civic values described there were also many examples of helpfulness and neighbourly support. These provided fairly basic but important forms of cooperative action and reciprocity. Alice (an 80-year-old South Tottenham resident of mixed heritage originally from South Africa), for instance, noted that neighbours would watch out for each other's properties during holidays. Others noted that neighbours would frequently: take in a parcel; hold extra sets of keys for neighbours; assist the elderly or less mobile with shopping; water plants during a neighbour's absence; or share knowledge of planning and neighbourhood issues. Other manifestations included multiple accounts of banal and everyday friendliness with many examples of residents inviting each other to their homes, of children playing and befriending each other, and of mutual kindness and practical and emotional support in times of family crisis. Such activities quickly established levels of trust and local social norms that gave individuals a sense of community and place.

These examples demonstrate that a degree of neighbourliness is indeed possible in super-diverse neighbourhoods; the presence of mixed groups of individuals does not necessarily lead to mutual disconnection. Relationships are forged through day-to-day interactions in place and lead to the formation of positive, collective forms of support. These relationships were most evident among younger residents, those with young children and those on lower incomes from a broad range of ethnic backgrounds. Ultimately, as demonstrated by Donna, connections between neighbours were most often made around common interests and concerns, with individual identities seen as less important.

Pleasantly minimal relations and interactions

Having noted that a sizable proportion of residents praised strong community bonds, our research nevertheless indicated that for the majority, relations with their neighbours could be characterised as "pleasantly minimal" or "hi/bye" relationships where they would often greet each other in the street but little more. Many residents also reported that they most often chose to frequent spaces run or attended by people who shared similar characteristics.

While the focus of the research this chapter draws on was on social interactions and relationships between residents from different ethnic and cultural backgrounds, it became clear that in fact divisions in social class were often the hardest to overcome, a finding that mirrors Wessendorf's (2014) study of Hackney. The previous section highlighted numerous examples of positive interactions and meaningful relationships between residents from a variety of different ethnic and cultural backgrounds. The vast majority of these examples involved residents of a similar, and most often lower, socioeconomic status. There were some examples of skilled and higher-earning BME residents reporting regular interactions and meaningful relationships with those of a different ethnic background and social status. However, most White British middle-class residents reported that their social networks and activities took place primarily among others like themselves. A number of these respondents explicitly mentioned doing "middle-class activities", and pursuing specifically "middle-class" practices of cultural consumption despite living in relatively deprived areas. For example, having praised the diversity of her neighbourhood for the new experiences and diverse spaces of consumption it offered her, Debbie reluctantly noted when it came to where and how she chose to spend her leisure time: "I don't think I really live, particularly, in this space, like I don't think I live in the environment socially." She also reflected on how the activities she did partake in did not bring her into contact with a wide range of people: "I do yoga, festivals about clouds and cheese ... like [laughter] come on, this is middle-class stuff, but I know exactly what it is, and I also berate myself at the same time because I'm so aware of what I'm doing." Debbie describes her yoga class as full of "middle-class hippies, or lefties like me" and, while noting a sense of regret at the insular nature of her activities, explains:

'The thing is though ... they talk about community cohesion and community integration and about communities coming in with one another, interacting, and that's fine, but you can't force it ... naturally, people end up staying with people that they can identify with and can relate to and have some form of common bonds with, and I have a common bond with people in Haringey, in that I live there and that I share this space with them and, in doing so, I do feel part of a community with them, which is why I'm not bashing them over the head and they're not bashing me over the head because we do feel part of a community, but y'know [pause] I do wince that what I'm doing is rather middle-class.'

Despite Debbie's reluctance or even embarrassment when discussing her activities and the composition of her social network, she explains that she believes that people feel most comfortable socialising among those with whom they are similar, implying a distinction between an un-defined 'us' and 'them' on more than one occasion. As such, for Debbie and others who viewed diversity positively but had minimal interactions across lines of difference, there was an expectation that diversity could be valued but would not necessarily permeate every aspect of their lives in both the public and private spheres. There was a sense that it could be appreciated more for the potential opportunities it presents than actual relationships sustained, a finding that was indicative of many other White British middle-class respondents. So, while for some, cross-cultural interactions served as an essential function of neighbourhood life, for others they were viewed as something they were pleased with but did not necessarily participate in regularly.

There were, however, some White British respondents who expressed a desire to interact more and form stronger bonds across difference, but expressed frustration at what they described as a lack of opportunity. Steve, the primary care-giver for his two young sons, compared the experiences of his children, "I love the fact that, for my children, it's just normal for them to be among so many children of different backgrounds, different languages", with his own and those of other adults in the neighbourhood, "[…] there's no way that any adult I know has that daily contact and quite reasonably intimate contact, sustained contact, with such a broad range of backgrounds, ethnicities and languages." At times he was almost envious of the opportunities for meaningful cross-cultural interaction and relationships that they were experiencing, making clear that his networks and those of his friends were nowhere near as linguistically and ethnically diverse.

Despite perfectly civil relationships with their diverse neighbours, residents from some other cultural, religious and/or ethnic groups reported feeling more 'at ease' with those they felt a shared sense of affinity. As a result, these residents displayed stronger patterns of in-group socialisation and bonding and weaker evidence of cross-group bonding. This was true for Abdi, in his mid-40s and Anwar, in his mid-30s, both Tottenham residents of Somali origin. They noted that the size of the Somali community locally and the strength of the bonding capital within it meant that they did not feel the need to interact much with non-Somalis. Religion also played an important binding role. Abdi was aware that while many of his interests were common outside of his Somali community (for example, watching football matches on television), the ways in which he sought to practice these hobbies and pastimes as a Muslim were at odds with others (an alcohol-free environment), and this was one reason for his tendency to do so exclusively with other Somali Muslims in local Somali-run cafes. Religion played an important binding role for other residents with migrant backgrounds, particularly those from communities with sizable and growing numbers and strong religious identities. Combinations of religious and ethnic-national identity created some powerful forms of bonding capital which, at times, appeared to be a contributing factor to patterns of minimal cross-cultural bonds being formed.

The examples provided demonstrate that social networks and interactions across difference in Haringey do not necessarily become stronger over time, even for individuals who are long-term residents. They can be very difficult to establish and equally difficult to maintain, being often fleeting in nature and gradually evaporating as individuals' life courses evolve. In most cases they are combined with strong social networks based on shared cultural, ethnic, religious, class or occupational characteristics. Our research indicated that these more insular networks and relationships were common among residents of a higher social status who, due to the nature of the deprived urban area they lived in and their tendency to socialise primarily with those of a similar social status, interacted least frequently with those from a different ethnic or cultural background to themselves. These types of networks were also evident among those with strict religious beliefs and practices which, in many cases, inhibited the desire and opportunity for cross-cultural interactions.

Interactions across difference varied significantly in our case study. While some residents reported deeper bonds with their neighbours, much of it materialised through the sharing of food or the realisation that fellow residents shared common interests – many of them related to place – others reported a stronger preference for interactions and participation in activities with similar others. This preference, however, did not stop this group from conducting civil interactions with their neighbours and from perceiving diversity as a neighbourhood asset.

Conclusion

Our research has demonstrated that positive perceptions of neighbourhood diversity do not necessarily lead to meaningful relationships and interactions across lines of difference. It was true that for the vast majority of residents the diversity of their neighbourhood was a natural part of everyday life and not something particularly noteworthy. However, this typically only extended as far as the public sphere. When looking in more detail at the private sphere, the networks and activities of most residents were far more insular than perhaps their perceptions of diversity would suggest. Such a finding bears similarity to Wessendorf's notion of the 'ethos of mixing' as interactions across difference did not 'go beyond simple expectations of interaction' and could also be described as 'an implicit grammar of living in a super-diverse area' (Wessendorf, 2013, p 408).

There were, nevertheless, a sizable number of residents who participated in more meaningful interactions and several factors that had an impact on the likelihood that they would do so. Patterns of interaction were often influenced significantly by the ethnic identity, religious and cultural practices, and socioeconomic status of residents. White British middle-class residents were the least likely to interact in a sustained and meaningful manner with those different to themselves. For many of these residents, neighbourhood diversity was often perceived as a positive and exciting opportunity but not necessarily something that had a significant impact on their networks or activities. Their interaction with diversity was mainly based on the experience of consumption, not on the experience of social interactions with different others, supporting Hage's (1997) criticism of celebratory forms of multiculturalism that are based on the appreciation of the cultural experience despite the absence of interaction with ethnic subjects. The nature of their middle-class status means that they are mobile enough to 'opt in' and 'opt out' of diverse activities and places of consumption locally. Conversely, residents more likely to interact with those different to themselves frequently offered an 'active' explanation for their positive definition of diversity based on the activities they do. They typically held a 'minority identity' (for example, non-British, non-White, non-heterosexual), were often from a lower socioeconomic status and more likely to value and depend on local neighbourhood support. Being a parent of young children was also shown to have an impact on attitudes towards interaction across difference. Although many did not describe particularly ethnically or socioeconomically diverse social networks, they were far more likely to mention a desire to interact more with their diverse neighbours having seen and praised their children's opportunity and ability to do so. Younger people who had been raised around — and attended school with — peers from a wide range of backgrounds also described having friendships with those from different ethnic, cultural and religious backgrounds the most. Their experience of diversity as 'commonplace' meant that common interests, many of them attached to place, often took precedence over common identities in shaping social networks.

Following the 2011 riots, regeneration and other broader processes of gentrification are leading to an increasing number of residents from middle-class (and disproportionately White) backgrounds moving into areas of Haringey that have historically been among the most deprived in the country and home to the highest percentage of its BME residents. These demographic changes pose new potential challenges. The local authority might achieve their vision of making Haringey 'a place for diverse communities that people are proud to belong to' (Haringey Strategic Partnership, 2007), as demonstrated by the overwhelming majority of our respondents reporting positive views of the diversity of their area. However, the strong cross-cultural community bonds evidenced in this chapter – which appear to have more profound positive impacts on people's perceptions of difference – could diminish over time as the population changes.

References

Abrams, P. and Bulmer, M. (1986) *Neighbours: The work of Philip Abrams*, Cambridge: Cambridge University Press.

Amin, A. (2002) 'Ethnicity and the multicultural city: Living with diversity', *Environment and Planning A*, 34(6), 959-80.

Boterman, W.R. (2013) 'Dealing with diversity: Middle-class family households and the issue of "black" and "white" schools in Amsterdam', *Urban Studies*, 50(6), 1130-47.

Benedictus, L. and Godwin, M. (2005) 'Every race, colour, nation and religion on earth', *The Guardian*, 21 January (www.theguardian.com/uk/2005/jan/21/britishidentity1).

Butler, T. (2003) 'Living in the bubble: Gentrification and its "others" in North London', *Urban Studies*, 40(12), 2469-86.

Cantle, T. (2001) *Community cohesion. A report of the Independent Review Team chaired by Ted Cantle*, London: Home Office.

Cattell, V., Dines, N., Gesler, W. and Curtis, S. (2008) 'Mingling, observing, and lingering: Everyday public spaces and their implications for well-being and social relations', *Health & Place*, 14(3), 544-61.

Clayton, J. (2009) 'Thinking spatially: Towards an everyday understanding of inter-ethnic relations', *Social & Cultural Geography*, 10(4), 481-98.

Curley, A.M. (2010) 'Neighborhood institutions, facilities, and public space: A missing link for HOPE VI residents' development of social capital?', *Cityscape*, 12(1), 33-63.

Fortier, A. (2007) 'Too close for comfort: Loving thy neighbour and the management of multicultural intimacies', *Environment and Planning D*, 25, 104-19.

Hage, G. (1997) 'At home in the entrails of the West: Multiculturalism, "ethnic food" and migrant home-building', in H. Grace, G. Hage, L. Johnson, J. Langsworth and M. Symonds (eds) *Home/world: Communality, identity and marginality in Sydney's West, Sydney*, Sydney, NSW: Pluto Press, 1-47.

Haringey Council Services (2015) 'Figures about Haringey' (www. haringey.gov.uk/social-care-and-health/health/joint-strategic-needs-assessment/figures-about-haringey).

Haringey Strategic Partnership (2007) *Haringey's Sustainable Community Strategy – A sustainable way forward 2007-2016* (www.ibyd.co.uk/bhf/documents/Haringey_PCT/LocalStrategicPartnership.pdf).

Holland, C., Clark, A., Katz, J. and Peace, S. (eds.) (2007) *Social interactions in urban public places*, Public Spaces Series, York: Joseph Rowntree Foundation by the Policy Press.

Lofland, L. (1973) *A world of strangers: Order and action in urban public space*, New York: Basic Books.

Mann, P.H. (1954) 'The concept of neighborliness', *American Journal of Sociology*, 60(2), 163-8.

Neal, S., Bennett, K., Cochrane, A. and Mohan, G. (2013) 'Living multiculture: Understanding the new spatial and social relations of ethnicity and multiculture in England', *Environment and Planning C: Government and Policy*, 31(2), 308-23.

Neal, S., Bennett, K., Jones, H., Cochrane, A. and Mohan, G. (2015) 'Multiculture and public parks: Researching super-diversity and attachment in public green space', *Population, Space and Place*, 21(5), 463-75.

Painter, J. (2012) 'The politics of the neighbour', *Environment and Planning D: Society and Space*, 30(3), 515-33.

Pemberton, S. and Phillimore, J. (2016) 'Migrant place-making in super-diverse neighbourhoods: Moving beyond ethno-national approaches', *Urban Studies*, 1-18.

Peters, K. and de Haan, H. (2011) 'Everyday spaces of inter-ethnic interaction: The meaning of urban public spaces in the Netherlands', *Leisure/Loisir*, 35(2), 169-90.

Savage, M., Bagnall, G. and Longhurst, B. (2005) *Globalization and belonging*, London: Sage.

Sennett, R. (1999) 'The spaces of democracy', in R.A. Beauregard and S. Body-Gendrot (eds) *The urban moment: Cosmopolitan essays on the late-20th-century city*, Urban Affairs Annual Reviews, Thousand Oaks, CA: Sage Publications, 273-85.

Valentine, G. (2008) 'Living with difference: Reflections on geographies of encounter', *Progress in Human Geography*, 32(3), 323-37.

van Eijk, G. (2011) '"They eat potatoes, I eat rice": Symbolic boundary making and space in neighbour relations', *Sociological Research Online*, 16(4), 1-12.

Vertovec, S. (2007) 'Super-diversity and its implications', *Ethnic and Racial Studies*, 30(6), 1024-54.

Watt, P. (2009) 'Living in an oasis: Middle-class disaffiliation and selective belonging in an English suburb', *Environment and Planning A*, 41(12), 2874-92.

Wessendorf, S. (2013) 'Commonplace diversity and the "ethos of mixing": Perceptions of difference in a London neighbourhood', *Identities*, 20(4), 407-22.

Wessendorf, S. (2014) '"Being open, but sometimes closed". Conviviality in a super-diverse London neighbourhood', *European Journal of Cultural Studies*, 17(4), 392-405.

Wise, A. (2009) 'Everyday multiculturalism: Transversal crossings and working class cosmopolitans', in A. Wise and S. Velayutham (eds) *Everyday multiculturalism*, New York: Palgrave Macmillan, 21-45.

4

'Others' in diversified neighbourhoods: What does social cohesion mean in diversified neighbourhoods? A case study in Istanbul

Ayda Eraydin

Introduction

In the past decades, major cities increased their global functions and became the core of global movements of goods, finance and human capital. As a result, they attracted people from different origins, ethnic backgrounds, religions and culture. The newcomers tended to settle in a few neighbourhoods where they mixed with people belonging to different socioeconomic statuses, occupations and lifestyles. These diversifying cities and neighbourhoods have received increasing interest in the literature. This is mainly concerned with whether this diverse set of people are able to create a cohesive society that can work towards the wellbeing of all its members, create a sense of belonging, promote trust and offer its members the opportunity of upward mobility (Forrest and Kearns, 2001). In other words, it is focused on social cohesion and conviviality towards others in super-diversified neighbourhoods (Vertovec, 2007).

However, studies of neighbourhood diversity and social cohesion have been inconclusive. A number of studies to date have found that despite differences among residents, communities are able to live together in harmony if they accept and respect the identities of *others*. Martin Albrow (1997) claims that individuals with very different lifestyles and social networks can live in proximity without improper interference with each other, while Jan Vranken (2004), sharing a similar view, asserts that relationships that are non-conflictual and mutually supportive between diverse groups can be structured at a neighbourhood level. Putnam (2007), however, takes a different view, claiming that the greater the ethnic diversity in a neighbourhood, the less trust exists, leading to even lower confidence in the so-called out-group, but also to distrust within the in-group. Similarly, Amin (2002) argues that finding a balance between diversity, harmonious living and solidarity can be quite difficult. Although there are different views on the role of diversity in social cohesion, almost all of them agree that relations among existing groups with different identities are important in defining connections between diversity and social cohesion.

The existing studies, however, pay little attention to differences in the way *others* are perceived and defined within diverse neighbourhoods and to the implications of such differences on building relations, solidarity among different groups and mutual trust. The aim of this chapter is to contribute to existing debates on neighbourhood diversity and social cohesion by building on fieldwork in Beyoğlu, Turkey, which is the most diversified district in Istanbul. To do so the chapter explores three main questions: What are the key factors in defining *others?* Is defining *others* an obstacle in networking and building relations among the groups that differentiate themselves from others? How and under what conditions do these networks help to create trust and mutual help among distinct groups?

Compared to existing literature on super-diverse urban neighbourhoods, this chapter highlights lifestyle as an important factor in the perception of diversity and otherness. It also shows that existing group identities are relatively less important in building relations with diverse others. More precisely, the chapter argues that categories of others are relatively blurred at a local level, leading to networking among people with distinct socioeconomic characteristics, cultural backgrounds and ethnicities.

Living with 'others': Networking patterns between people of different groups

As indicated earlier, conviviality and social cohesion are closely connected to how *us* and *others* are defined in a certain society. Unfortunately, to date there has only been a handful of studies (Forrest and Kearns, 2001; Kearns and Parkinson, 2001; Hipp and Perrin, 2006) explaining how others are defined at a neighbourhood level. Therefore, diversified neighbourhoods comprising people with different ethnic, cultural and personal characteristics merit particular attention when attempting to explain how others are defined and the attitude towards people with ethnic and cultural differences that are different from the majority. In distinguishing between *us* and *other*, ethnic, cultural, language and religious differences are used extensively (Riano and Wastl-Walter, 2006), although a number of other characteristics of both people and groups that are assumed to belong to different socioeconomic categories can be quite significant (Wimmer, 2004). That said, the dominance of discourses that define immigrants or minority ethnic groups as *other* is clearly apparent, and these discourses are important in the construction of identity among both the native-born and immigrants and in defining their respective *others*. At this point, language, religious and cultural practices and other symbolic markers are used as indicators of difference, and serve as principal reasons for exclusion and the building of *otherness*, since perceived differences are evident in language and religious practices (Erkamp, 2006). Recently, socioeconomic differences related to lifestyles have also become important in defining *others* (Berzano and Genova, 2015).

Do these differences act as barriers to the building of relations between people of different ethnic, cultural or religious groups, as well as with those with different lifestyles? According to Havekes et al (2014), identifying *others* in terms of their ethnic origin, language, religion, customs and civic values, and their beliefs, preferences and expectations in everyday neighbourhood life can have a negative effect on social inclusion and building social capital. Differences in lifestyles can be the reason for the limited relations among residents of the same neighbourhood. However, the level of social cohesion in diverse neighbourhoods can be adjusted through the building of relationships among the different groups that live together in the same area. Notions of *trust* and *willingness to help* – in other words, *mutual support* – are critical in encouraging interactions between people of different backgrounds and in increasing social cohesion. Nanetti (2006) and Leonardi et al (2011) define social trust as the dimension of social cohesion that encourages widespread confidence in *others*, while another study by Forrest and Kearns (2001) emphasises the positive effect of networks, mutual help, support and interaction in the public sphere on social cohesion. A vital role is played by networks in the construction of social cohesion in different societies, where they act as compensation mechanisms against existing prejudices. Developing social contacts between neighbours, and sharing mutual knowledge, familiarity and interpersonal trust in everyday neighbourhood interactions may also contribute to conviviality and social cohesion and a sense of belonging. For example, Hudson et al (2007), in their study of social cohesion in different British neighbourhoods, underline the feelings of community that come with everyday neighbourhood interactions.

The types of networking patterns that exist in a neighbourhood are crucial in this respect. Social networks between individuals, family members, close friends and members of the same ethnic group can help to create bonding capital (Sabatini, 2008), and can be a primary source of emotional and material support in poor and excluded communities (Labini, 2008). That said, traditional networks can also have a negative effect on the level of socialisation and independence of individuals in society, since people who maintain strong relationships with family members and relatives may have less interest in forming relationships with those whom they are unfamiliar with and those with whom they bear little similarities (Eraydin et al, 2012). This can enhance feelings of *otherness*, as highlighted by Turok and Bailey (2004). There have been several studies documenting the increasing desire among members of ethnic majorities to move out of neighbourhoods with a strong minority ethnic presence and networks (Musterd and de Vos, 2007; Bolt et al, 2008; van Ham and Clark, 2009; Havekes et al, 2014). These studies underline that strong networks among ethnic communities result in low social cohesion in such neighbourhoods when there is limited interaction with *others*. In contrast, weak and cross-cutting social ties between friends and neighbours allow people to get ahead when given access to opportunities and resources in social circles other than their own (Forrest and Kearns, 2001; Stone, 2001; Sabatini, 2008), and such networks can act against people's prejudices and can encourage social cohesion. Moreover, networks built between individuals or social groups with professional and administrative connections and local communities are also vital in aiding households to adapt to changing circumstances and engaging in social relationships with those in authority.

In line with this brief summary of the literature, this chapter focuses on the social networks, trust and mutual support among the various social groups living in Beyoğlu, one of the most distinctive residential and recreational areas in the historical centre of Istanbul.[1]

Case study research in Beyoğlu

Beyoğlu has always been a diversified district, and its social and cultural atmosphere has encouraged the development of civilised relations among people of distinct ethnicities, religions and cultural backgrounds. These relations, which are more evident in public spaces, have reshaped people's behaviours and encouraged them to take into consideration the interests of *others* (Batur, 2001). Throughout the 19th century, Beyoğlu was home to people of European origin (French, Germans,

Italians, British, etc) and non-Muslim Ottomans (Greeks, Armenians and Jews), but lost many of these former residents at the beginning of the Republican period in the 1920s. The population exchange between the Balkan countries and Turkey and the outward migration of people of Greek descent to different cities in Greece after the events of 6-7 September 1955[2] had a negative effect on the cosmopolitan character of the area.

The departure of those of Greek descent led other minorities, as well as some of the families in the higher middle-income groups, to leave Beyoğlu, after which the district became home to many immigrants from different parts of Turkey. During the 1960s and 1970s, Beyoğlu attracted poor immigrant families and other disadvantaged groups, besides minority groups such as Romani and members of the LGBT communities – in short, those who were not welcome in the middle-income neighbourhoods in other parts of Istanbul. In the 1980s, Beyoğlu began to experience an inflow of immigrants from the Middle East and North Africa, including people from Iran, Iraq, Afghanistan, Nigeria and Palestine, among others, while in the last two decades there has been a growing interest in the area among those involved in the arts, and an increasing number of foreigners settling in neighbourhoods like Cihangir. The rising popularity of certain neighbourhoods has coincided with a growing nostalgia for old Beyoğlu, as the core of cosmopolitan Istanbul and the former home of the city's more distinguished residents.

At present, Beyoğlu has a very mixed demographic structure, including poor communities and immigrants from Turkey's less-developed regions,[3] but also people from the creative-professional middle- and high-income classes, artists and people with diverse identities and sexual orientations. The district is also home to a host of Romani and Kurdish people, Syrian refugees and foreign immigrants, along with such minority ethnic groups as Jews, Armenians and Greeks. According to the 2013 census, the population of Beyoğlu was 245,219, of which only 14.9 per cent were born in Istanbul, the others having migrated both from the different regions of Turkey and from abroad. Among the immigrants, 8.3 per cent are foreign, and some of them have no legal status.[4] The Beyoğlu district also hosts residents of different socioeconomic status. While the south-eastern parts of the district are home to more upscale residents in terms of income and education, in the zones to the west and north west, the socioeconomic condition of the residents is remarkably low, leading to physical and socioeconomic deprivation. Recently, the district has been witnessing a gradual change as a result of urban renewal projects in the more deprived areas and the gentrification of certain neighbourhoods (Galata, Cihangir, Tarlabaşı, etc) (Enlil, 2011). Interestingly, the image of the district bears little resemblance to its real population composition; for instance, not so long ago, a journalist with a conservative Muslim profile defined Beyoğlu as a place for minorities, as a place of *others* (Arasyumul, 2007).

The fieldwork in Beyoğlu that aimed to define connections between the perception of others, conviviality and social cohesion was organised in two stages. In the first phase, information on the composition of the population in the district was collected from interviews with two local officials from the municipal government, two central government officials working in the local departments of ministries, representatives of two non-governmental organisations (NGOs) working in Beyoğlu, two academicians carrying out their own research projects in Beyoğlu, and representatives of the Chambers of Planners and Architects. This pilot work was deemed essential, given the lack of any detailed statistical data on the inhabitants of Beyoğlu. The findings of the in-depth interviews were used to define target groups who represented the diversity of the district. In the second stage, 54 semi-structured in-depth interviews were carried out by three researchers with residents of Beyoğlu throughout November 2014. To reach the desired target groups, associations related to the target groups were contacted, several of which[5] were able to put us in touch with someone who would be willing to speak on behalf of their respective group. If the person agreed to take part in the interview, we asked for his/her help in contacting other people who may be willing to speak as representatives of the diverse groups in the district. The semi-structured interviews consisted of open-ended questions on the perception of diversity and socioeconomic and cultural characteristics of the respondents and their social networks. Each interview took about two hours and utilised note-taking and audio recordings that were later transcribed. The primary characteristics of the interviewees were as follows:

- Among the 54 respondents, 32 were male and 22 were female.
- The largest group of interviewees belonged to the 20-29 age group (21), followed by the 30-39 age group (17), the 40-49 age group (7), the 50-59 age group (5) and the over-60s (4). This age composition reflects the dominance of young and active age groups in this district.
- The ethnic distribution of the respondents was as follows: one Nigerian, three Greeks, two Armenians, one of Turkish-Greek origin, two Americans and one Azerbaijani, none of whom were Turkish citizens. In addition, eight respondents were Syrian-Kurdish who had not yet acquired Turkish citizenship. The remaining were

Turkish citizens, including five Romani, eight Kurds and 23 of Turkish origin.

- Eight of the interviewees are homemakers and five are retired. The others have very different occupations, including a waste collector, a textile worker, a photographer, a jewellery designer, four musicians, two engineers, two publishers, two cafe managers, two salespersons and two teachers, among others.
- The respondents came from a broad range of income groups. Among the 54 interviewees, 11 placed themselves in the low-income group, 17 in the medium-low income group, 17 in the medium-high, and nine in the high-income group.

Perception of diversity and 'others' in Beyoğlu

Previous literature has underlined the importance of language, religious and cultural practices, and other symbolic markers related to migrants as important factors in the perception of diversity. In many European countries, otherness is built on the distinction between native *residents* and *immigrants*. However, the definition of otherness in Turkey is intricate and has changed substantially in different periods and differs according to national and urban levels. While ethnic, religious and cultural differences of Turkish citizens dominated the discourses of otherness at the national level, having a rural background or not and socioeconomic differences have been more important in urban areas. In recent years, lifestyle has also come to play an important part in how *others* are defined in Turkish society. The perception of the other's lifestyle is based not only on socioeconomic factors, but also on religious practices, political choices and ideologies (Toprak et al, 2009), as a result of policies intervening both directly and indirectly into the lifestyles of people through the imposition of Islamic and conservative norms.

As several respondents underlined, Beyoğlu is a unique place in which people with different identities and from different socioeconomic and cultural backgrounds live together, including both rich and poor, affluent people and disadvantaged groups, as well as people of different races, cultures and ethnicities. As the findings of the in-depth interviews show, who is considered as *other in such a super-diverse district* varies substantially among the different respondents, being closely linked to their perception of diversity. The interviewees defined four major factors as significant when defining *others*.

First, almost all of the interviewees defined diversity in terms of socioeconomic and occupational attributes, tending to define *others* as people belonging to socioeconomic groups different from their own perceived groups. In Turkey, levels of occupational income and education are important in defining *others* on an equal footing as ethnicity, religion and cultural background (Güvenç and Işık, 1997; Eraydin, 2008), and this was the case for the respondents from different ethnic and cultural groups in their definition of the *other*. One of the respondents (female, age 27, jewellery designer) says:

> 'In our apartment, we live together with two research assistants, an oncologist and a salesperson with a shop in the Istanbul Textile Centre. Across from our building, two people are working in publishing houses, and my aunt also lives there. In our neighbourhood, people have different levels of education and different occupations, including foreigners engaged in various jobs.'

According to her, this is a real indication of the diversity of Beyoğlu.

Second, the way of defining *others* is based on whether they are established or new residents. Those who have been living in the neighbourhood for a long time consider themselves to be the real landlords of the district, perceiving newcomers as the *others* of the neighbourhood. Established residents tend to think of themselves as urbanites, and complain about those who have migrated recently from less-developed parts of Turkey or abroad, criticising them for maintaining their village culture and for not trying to adapt to the urban way of life. They claim that these people do not belong in Beyoğlu.

Third, *others* are defined according to their hometown. Each neighbourhood is home to people who come predominantly from the same town; as evidence in Turkey has shown, people migrating from the same city or village are inclined to settle in the same district, where they maintain most of their old habits and cultural norms (Kıray, 1999). The birthplace of immigrants and compatriots is still important in Turkish society, and is often used in defining *we*, and is used as a determinant of *sameness*, referring to uniformity in culture, attitude, norms, language and ethnic origin. This *sameness* is the primary source of the close relationships and active collaborative networks that help migrants live in cities, although it also prevents them from becoming part of the larger urban society. There is a tendency among migrants to make little effort to adapt to the existing urban conditions, which opens them up to criticism from people who consider themselves as having an *urban culture*: "When people come from their hometowns, they bring with them their cultures and habits. They have difficulty in adapting to local conditions" (64-year-old Romani man). However, just who is the true native resident is not clear. One interviewee (38-year-old actor) voiced his criticism of people who complain about this situation, saying, "Those who complain about the increasing numbers of immigrants are in fact immigrants from the eastern provinces who live in the houses that belonged to the Greeks."

Fourth, when talking about the diversity of their neighbourhoods, some of the respondents said that there were *even prostitutes* in their neighbourhood. Marginal groups are referred to mainly as LGBT or as prostitutes, and are described as *others* by most of the residents of the district. Beyoğlu has a substantial LGBT community (Özakın, 2011), and although some of them have good relations with their neighbours, the attitude of many residents to them is still not very receptive.

These leading factors reveal that ethnic and cultural differences are not important in defining *others*, although these attributes defined by the interviewees are strongly linked to certain ethnic and cultural categories, the fact that most of the new residents with low socioeconomic status (education and income) from south-eastern provinces usually have Kurdish ethnicity. The findings underline that lifestyle is also a prominent factor in the definition of *others*, since socioeconomic and cultural differences are noticeable in people's lifestyles, which is also connected to differences in political ideologies and religious norms.

Attitudes and feelings towards 'others' in a diverse neighbourhood

One of the major objectives in the fieldwork was to identify the attitudes of people living in a diversified district towards *others* and to assess to what extent they affect the feeling of *belonging* within the neighbourhood. Previous studies have shown that people are keen on living among those of the same ethnicity, seeking the sense of community and cohesion of their own group (Clark, 1992). Natives and those belonging to distinct ethnic and cultural backgrounds tend to avoid majority ethnic neighbourhoods for fear of being discriminated against (Havekes et al, 2014). In this regard, residential preferences may be driven by either in group preferences or out-group rejection, such as prejudice or ethnic discrimination (Swaroop and Krysan, 2011). For example, middle-income residents are inclined to leave their neighbourhoods when the numbers of different groups increase (Jackson and Benson, 2014).

In Beyoğlu, almost all of the respondents commented on the diversity of their neighbourhoods as an asset, and two-thirds defined living with *others* as something positive. One community leader stated: "We are here together with people with different languages and beliefs. We know each other, and we have no problems. In other words, we do not exclude anyone based on his or her religion, culture, language or sect. For us, everybody is equal; at least for me" (51-year-old Mukhtar [elected head] of a Çukur neighbourhood). His sentiments were echoed by many of the respondents, although the language used distinguished between *them* and *us*. Furthermore, many of the respondents defined the ability to live together as a significant success, offering the fact that *we are used to each other* as an explanation.

The respondents defined two aspects of living together as positive: the ability to get to know different people and learn about their cultures; and the tolerant atmosphere that exists in the district based on the mix of different people. That said, the highly dynamic character of the district and the changing composition of residents in the neighbourhood were defined as threats to the sustainability of existing relationships. As various studies have illustrated, changes in resident profiles compel long-term residents to leave the neighbourhood (Feijten and van Ham, 2009; Havekes et al, 2014; Eraydin et al, 2016). In this regard, the long-term residents of Beyoğlu believe that the increasing number of poor immigrants decreases the *quality* of the area, referring to cleanliness in physical terms and social relations. Those who were born in the district are particularly nostalgic about the 'good old days' when Beyoğlu was more peaceful and quiet, and believe that the increasing dominance of immigrants has damaged the former image of Beyoğlu as *cosmopolitan and posh*.[6]

Role of networking patterns in living with diversity

As argued earlier, local networks are vital in providing a sense of community and social cohesion in neighbourhoods (Bell and Newby, 1974; Blokland and Nast, 2014), and this is one of the reasons behind the recent efforts of urban policy-makers to create areas of mixed population composition, believing that networks formed among different groups can bring social capital to those in disadvantaged positions (van Kempen and Bolt, 2009; Blokland and Nast, 2014). That said, in networking, with whom one forms relationships and shares information is important. Family-based, ethnic and hometown networks enhance segmentation and *otherness* in a district, while networks with neighbours and friends can mitigate against the perceptions of *others*.

If people tend to connect to people like themselves, the exchange of knowledge, experience and resources may remain weak, and in such cases, neighbourhood diversity may not permit disadvantaged groups to access resources and enhance community structure (Blokland and van Eijk, 2010; Jackson and Benson, 2014). As Putnam (1995) claims, networks among residents do not necessarily lead to the building of social capital, unless one person learns casually about the needs of *others*.

The findings of the interviews reveal that the inhabitants of Beyoğlu have different views regarding the importance of different social networks. Although the outcomes of the fieldwork underline that relationships with family members and relatives are vital for all groups, this is especially true for immigrants and those belonging to minority ethnic groups. Most immigrants have only limited access to the benefits of social security schemes, such as unemployment, permanent disability and old-age benefits, since they do not have regular jobs. These findings support existing literature, which highlights that living close to each other is a key survival strategy, especially when people are unable to access the benefits provided by the existing social security systems. This explains why although Beyoğlu is a highly diversified area, it is possible to see agglomerations of family members and relatives living in the same neighbourhoods of the district.

Interestingly, the perception of *others* is rarely an obstacle to networking among neighbours, unless there are considerable differences in socioeconomic levels and lifestyles. In the fieldwork, several of the interviewees from low-income families underlined the importance of their neighbours in their decision to remain in the neighbourhood and highlighted the importance of knowing each other for a long time. According to these respondents, in community relations, ethnic, cultural and religious backgrounds are not so important, as neighbours may have different ethnic backgrounds and cultures; it is living in the same place that connects them to each other.

A 49-year-old Romani musician, who has neighbours from different ethnic and cultural backgrounds, said, "the reason I prefer to live in my existing neighbourhood is my neighbours." Several other respondents spoke about their neighbourhood relations in positive terms, underlining the importance of knowing each other for a long time:

> 'For us, neighbourhood relations are crucial. In our neighbourhood, not only our fathers but also our grandfathers know each other. Everybody has a nickname. For example, everybody calls me "the son of Çakır Ahmet". I am a child of this neighbourhood. Although the windows

of my house are always open, I have never lost even one
Turkish Lira.' (offal seller, Romani descent)

In contrast, ethnicity is important in building networks among
African and Syrian immigrants. An African respondent stated that he
preferred living together with other people from Africa in the same
neighbourhood for reasons of security (Nigerian textile worker, age
30). According to one of the new immigrants from Syria, the dense
networks of people from the same ethnic background can be attributed
to the hostility shown towards them by the established residents. For
example, one 52-year-old Syrian/Kurdish immigrant claimed that
older residents did not welcome them at all.

While interactions among neighbours are important for low-income
families, working women and older people, several groups maintain
only limited relations with local inhabitants:

• For artists and people with full-time jobs outside Beyoğlu, social
  networks within the neighbourhood are considered less important
  in that they prefer to establish relationships with people from outside
  their place of residence. Some of the respondents emphasised that
  they lacked the time to develop close relations with their neighbours,
  and this was the case particularly among those working in the
  entertainment sector, such as musicians, actors and actresses, and
  those working in service industries.
• Several of the newer foreign residents said that they did not have
  well-established relations with their neighbours, and for these
  groups it is the networks between friends living both in the same
  neighbourhood and in different places in Istanbul that are more
  important, rather than their relations with their neighbours.
• Bachelors/single people have fewer interactions with their
  neighbours and spend most of their time with their friends, for
  which Beyoğlu was stated as an appropriate meeting place.
• Members of the LGBT community tend to have fewer relations
  with their neighbours and maintain a particular network of friends
  with which they socialise.
• The Romani tend to be reluctant to form relationships with other
  residents in the neighbourhood, since they feel that they are not well
  received by existing social networks. For them, problems such as
  social prejudice and repression are not novel issues, as the oppression
  of the Roma/Gypsy populations is deeply rooted in Anatolia and
  has a long history (Toprak et al, 2009).

The findings show that for the interviewees from disadvantaged groups, networks formed with family members and neighbours are of primary importance, while those who have different lifestyles, especially those with higher levels of income, have fewer relations with their close neighbours. Furthermore, a group's networking patterns highlight the different lifestyles and the commonalities in the various neighbourhoods of the same district.

Networking leading to trust and mutual support

Trust-based relations among neighbours are important since they form a zone of comfort and enhance mutual support among inhabitants (Blokland and Nast, 2014). Low-income residents tend to develop good trust-based relations with their neighbours since the support provided by their neighbours and relatives is essential for the sustainment of their lives in Beyoğlu. For example, one of the interviewees, the mother of a child with a physical disability, said that for her, mutual support is vital: "My neighbour Gülsüm is my closest friend. Whenever I need her, she runs to help me. God bless her. My daughter has grown up with her help. Neighbours are vital if you have a disabled child and you have to work for a living." According to the findings, most of the interviewees borrow items from neighbours, including money, and ask for help when they have problems with health, childcare and many other issues. *Giving the key to a neighbour or a friend* is used as a symbol of trust by many interviewees. One interviewee (Turkish working woman, age 49) said that whenever she goes somewhere outside the city, she leaves her key with her neighbours so that they can water her plants and look after her fish.

It should be noted here that trust and a willingness to help also inflicts an element of social control on those people who are in need of support, although this is usually accepted as habitual and positive by those asking for help from others. A single 43-year-old mother, working in a school for children with disabilities, says:

> 'I get support from my two best friends, who look after my youngest daughter when I am at work. My eldest daughter goes to secondary school, and all of the people in the neighbourhood keep a protective eye on her. I ask my neighbours to take care of her, since she is so young and may make mistakes.'

In building trust-based relations and mutual support among neighbours, how many years people have spent in the neighbourhood is important. Most of the interviewees said that living in the same area for many years leads to mutual trust among neighbours, and suggest that ethnic and cultural differences do not matter in the building of trust-based relationships. The social control in the neighbourhood addressed earlier, which was unfamiliar to some foreign immigrants, makes life easier and safer. An English teacher, (American, 27 years old) explains that the support provided by her neighbours is quite valuable and facilitates many things in her life, although it also comes with elements of social control, such as an inability to stay out late at night.

A few of the interviewees stated that they do not trust those of different ethnic or cultural backgrounds. In this respect, Roma people often face problems related to trust with their neighbours. Although they are the established residents of the district, their way of life is not accepted willingly, and relations with Roma people may be less trustful. Syrian immigrants, whose presence in Istanbul has risen astronomically in recent years, are also yet to be accepted in terms of trust, and are still not well adapted to the Beyoğlu way of life. A female Syrian immigrant aged 45 claims that they get no support from their neighbours, aside from those who share their Kurdish descent: "If the Kurds were not here, we would be dead. They are the only people that have helped us." That said, more recently, Syrian immigrants have started to form contacts with established residents.

Conclusion

The research conducted in the Beyoğlu district provided several interesting findings related to the perception of *others* and implications on conviviality and social cohesion. The findings show that although *others* are defined in different ways by diverse groups, the *level of income*, connected to *occupation* and *education*, is often used to define others, besides their ethnic and cultural backgrounds. In Beyoğlu, socioeconomic differences are more important than other attributes when defining *others*, although usually several socioeconomic, ethnic and cultural categories coincide with each other, as is the case in many European cities (see Blokland and Nast, 2014). Moreover, contrary to much of the existing 'otherness' literature in which the emphasis lies on immigrants from different ethnic backgrounds, the findings of the fieldwork pinpoint the increasing *importance of lifestyles* in the defining of *others*. That said, the factors defining whom they classify as *us* and *them* change quite swiftly. As Batur (2001) explains, Beyoğlu is a space in which identities are constructed and deconstructed at great speed.

In relation to the findings of the fieldwork, those belonging to different social groups claim that they are tolerant of *others*, and underline the multicultural character of Beyoğlu, although in discourse they still differentiate between *us* and *them*. Differences in socioeconomic status are also reflected in networking relations and the way of living in a neighbourhood. Strong relationships with family members and relatives are important for all groups, but especially for those with lower incomes. Family networks and those among compatriots are essential for the survival of poor people who live in this district, and they do not act as an obstacle to the development of relations with people from different ethnic and cultural backgrounds. Difficult living conditions and the need for support from others in such matters as childcare and care of older people, and the occasional need to borrow money or foodstuffs, tend to prevent the exclusion of people with different backgrounds. Residents of the district, especially those from the Black Sea region, emphasise the importance of mutual assistance among neighbours in matters related to health and in general, with several interviewees claiming that neighbours will help when necessary. In fact, difficult living conditions make people more tolerant and understanding of others.

Those with a higher socioeconomic status maintain weaker networks than the other inhabitants of their neighbourhoods: they prefer to maintain only loose ties with neighbours, since it gives them a sense of freedom when living in diversified neighbourhoods. It is important here to underline the appraisals of residents with higher socioeconomic status on the diversity of the district, in that they define the cosmopolitan atmosphere as a real asset while underlining the increasing numbers of poor immigrants as a negative factor. The main reason stated for this is the low adaptive capacity of *others* to the cosmopolitan and tolerant way of life in the district. In this regard, *others* are defined as those who are unable to adapt to the image favoured and endorsed for Beyoğlu.

For the interviewees with professional careers and a higher level of education, the cosmopolitan character of the district is essential, and this is their main reason for choosing to live in Beyoğlu. According to these respondents, one of the most important characteristics of Beyoğlu is its protest culture and the sense of freedom it instils, which is supported by the diversity of the inhabitants of the district. Colourful metaphors such as *cultural mosaic*, painting a picture of the harmonious coexistence of different perceptions and worldviews, were used often by respondents of different cultural and ethnic groups, echoing the rhetoric reported in earlier studies (see Cox, 1994). According to the interviewees, individuals with very different lifestyles and social networks opt to live in such a liberal district, and this doesn't represent a problem. The research findings presented in this fieldwork indicate that social interaction is possible in a district where many different social groups live side by side, even when diversified groups are continuously changing. It is worth noting that the composition of the residents and their changing identities make Beyoğlu liveable for so many different types of people, and enables non-conflictual relations among most of them.

However, some residents are afraid that their lifestyles are under threat as a result of the increasingly authoritative policies of the existing central and local governments. Concerned with the rising conservative values in the society,[7] two of the respondents spoke about the increasing dualism in Turkish society and the emergence of opposing lifestyles heralded in with the revival of religious attitudes. Restrictions on pavement cafes in Beyoğlu, bans on the public consumption of alcohol, increasing criticisms of mixed gender socialisation and disparaging remarks made to women deemed to be inappropriately dressed (Kezer, 2015) are just some of the reasons behind the deepening divisions among the different social groups, and discouraging interactions among them. These policies negatively affect the attraction of the district for some groups looking for a multicultural environment and may weaken the tolerance to others.

Notes

[1] Spanning two continents, Istanbul is the largest city in Turkey, and is the country's economic, cultural and historical core. According to 2013 figures, it is home to 14,160,467 inhabitants. Istanbul has experienced rapid growth, particularly during the second half of the 20th century, with its population increasing tenfold between 1950 and 2000. This remarkable growth has been fuelled largely by migrants from different parts of Turkey who come to the city seeking employment and better living conditions. In recent decades, the city has also experienced increasing numbers of foreign immigrants, with 2006 figures showing that only 28% of the city's residents are originally from Istanbul.

[2] On 6-7 September 1955, a large-scale attack organised by several groups in reaction to the existing political conflict between Greece and Turkey targeted Greek, Armenian and Jewish citizens living in Istanbul. Acts of violence were committed in the neighbourhoods in which Istanbul's non-Muslim population was concentrated.

[3] Among the population of the district, 35,461 people (14.7% of the district population) were born in Istanbul (TSI, 2014); the rest came from other Turkish provinces or abroad. Figures (TSI, 2014) show that the largest numbers of people migrated from the Black Sea region (20.1% of the total population), among which

the Giresun province has the largest share. There are also substantial numbers of immigrants from Central Anatolia, especially from Sivas, and from the eastern parts of the country.

[4] These figures do not include the Syrian immigrants who have only very recently migrated to Turkey, and so are new to this district.

[5] The organisations that were important in finding the first samples of the target groups were the Çukur and Bostan Neighbourhood Units, the Turkish-Armenian Minority Schools' Teachers Support Organisation (Türk Ermeni Azınlık Okulları Öğretmenleri Yardımlaşma Vakfı), Hrant Dink Foundation, Istos Publishing House, Beyoğlu Lider Women Cooperative and Müjdat Gezen Arts Centre (MGSM), among others.

[6] This way of feeling has been important in purification efforts in Beyoğlu (Özakın, 2011), although none of the interviewees mentioned these.

[7] Beyoğlu has experienced several attempts to purify the neighbourhood during different periods (see Özakın, 2011).

References

Albrow, M. (1997) *The global age: State and society beyond modernity*, Cambridge: Polity Press.

Amin, A. (2002) 'Ethnicity and the multicultural city: Living with diversity', *Environment and Planning A*, 34(6), 959-80.

Arasyumul, N. (2007) *Kamusal İnsanın Prototipi Pera Levantenleri*, İstanbul: Osmanlı Bankası Arşiv ve Araştırma Merkezi (https://docplayer.biz. tr/6008342-Kamusai-insanin-prototipi-pera-levantenleri.html).

Batur, E. (2001) *Three Beyoğlu's. In a Beyoğlu photo-romance: A monograph on a legend*, Istanbul: Yapı Kredi Kültür Sanat Yayıncılık.

Bell, C. and Newby, H. (eds) (1974) *The sociology of community: A selection of readings*, London: Frank Cass.

Berzano, L. and Genova, C. (2015) *Lifestyles and subcultures: History and a new perspective*, New York: Routledge.

Blokland, T. and Nast, J. (2014) 'From public familiarity to comfort zone: The relevance of absent ties for belonging in Berlin's mixed neighbourhoods', *International Journal of Urban and Regional Research*, 38(4), 1142-59.

Blokland, T. and van Eijk, G. (2010) 'Do people who like diversity practice diversity in neighbourhood life? Neighbourhood use and the social networks of "diversity-seekers" in a mixed neighbourhood in the Netherlands', *Journal of Ethnic and Migration Studies*, 36(2), 313-32.

Bolt, G., van Kempen, R. and van Ham, M. (2008) 'Minority ethnic groups in the Dutch housing market: Spatial segregation, relocation dynamics and housing policy', *Urban Studies*, 45(7), 1359-84.

Clark, W.A.V. (1992) 'Residential preferences and residential choices in multi-ethnic settings', *Urban Geography*, 29(3), 451-66.

Cox, T. (1994) *Cultural diversity in organisations: Theory, research, and practice*, San Francisco, CA: Berrett-Koehler.

Enlil, Z. (2011) 'The neoliberal agenda and the changing urban form of Istanbul', *International Planning Studies*, 16(1), 5-25.

Eraydin, A. (2008) 'The impact of globalisation on different social groups: Competitiveness, social cohesion and spatial segregation in Istanbul', *Urban Studies*, 45(8), 1663-91.

Eraydin, A., Armatlı-Köroğlu, B. and Uzun, N. (2012) 'Importance of social capital in coping with and benefiting from new economic conditions', *Tijdschrift voor Economische en Sociale Geografie*, 103(2), 222-39.

Eraydin, A. Yersen, Ö., Güngördü, N. and Demirdağ, I. (2016) *Fieldwork inhabitants, Istanbul (Turkey)* (www.researchgate/net/publication/323995585_Fieldwork_Inhabitants_in_Istanbul_Turkey_Work_Package_6).

Erkamp, P. (2006) '"We Turks are no Germans": Assimilation discourses and the dialectical construction of identities in Germany', *Environment and Planning A*, 38, 1673-92.

Feijten, P. and van Ham, M. (2009) 'Neighbourhood change... Reason to leave?', *Urban Studies*, 46(10), 2103-22.

Forrest, R. and Kearns, A. (2001) 'Social cohesion, social capital and the neighbourhood', *Urban Studies*, 38(12), 2125–43.

Güvenç, M. and Işık, O. (1997) 'Istanbul'u okumak: mahalle düzeyinde konut mülkiyeti statü farklılaşmasına ilişkin bulgular nasıl genellenebilir?', *Toplum ve Bilim*, 7(2), 153-64.

Havekes, E., Coenders, M. and van der Lippe, T. (2014) 'The wish to leave ethnically concentrated neighbourhoods: The role of perceived social cohesion and interethnic attitudes', *Housing Studies*, 29(6), 823-42.

Hipp, J.R. and Perrin, A. (2006) 'Nested loyalties: Local networks' effects on neighbourhood and community cohesion', *Urban Studies*, 43(13), 2503-23.

Hudson, M., Philips, J., Ray, K. and Barnes, H. (2007) *Social cohesion in diverse communities*, New York: Joseph Rowntree Foundation.

Jackson, E. and Benson, M. (2014) 'Neither "deepest, darkest Peckham" nor "run-of-the-mill" East Dulwich: The middle classes and their "others" in an inner-London neighbourhood', *International Journal of Urban and Regional Research*, 38(4), 1195-210.

Kearns, A. and Parkinson, M. (2001) 'The significance of neighbourhood', *Urban Studies*, 38(12), 2103-10.

Kezer, Z. (2015) *Building modern Turkey: State, space, and ideology in the early Republic*, Pittsburg, PA: Pittsburg University Press.

Kıray, M. (1999) *Toplumsal Yapı ve Toplumsal Değişme*, Istanbul: Bağlam.

Labini, M.S. (2008) *Social capital and the labour market: When is the family at work?* (www.aiel.it/bacheca/BRESCIA/papers/syloslabini.pdf).

Leonardi, R., Nanetti, R. and Holguin, C. (2011) 'The local path to sustainable development: Social capital in Naples', in L. Sacconi and G. Degli Antoni (eds) *Social capital, corporate social responsibility, economic behaviour and performance*, New York: Palgrave Macmillan, 358-79.

Musterd, S. and de Vos, S. (2007) 'Residential dynamics in ethnic concentrations', *Housing Studies*, 22(3), 333-53.

Nanetti, R.Y. (2006) 'Social capital and territorial development in Italy. Conceptual update and empirical analysis', Presented at the Conference on 'Social capital, sustainability and socio-economic cohesion within the EU MLG structure in development policy', SOCCOH Project, London, 29-30 June.

Özakın, E.Ö. (2011) 'Space, identity, and abjection: Purification of Beyoğlu', PhD dissertation, Ankara: Bilkent University (www.thesis.bilkent.edu.tr/0006322.pdf).

Putnam, R.D. (1995) 'Tuning in, tuning out: The strange disappearance of social capital in America', *Political Science and Politics*, 28(4), 664-83.

Putnam, R.D. (2007) '*E. pluribus unum*: Diversity and community in the twenty-first century', *Scandinavian Political Studies*, 30(2), 137-74.

Riano, Y. and Wastl-Walter, D. (2006) 'Immigration policies, state discourses on foreigners, and the politics of identity in Switzerland', *Environment and Planning A,* 38(9), 1693-713.

Sabatini, F. (2008) 'Social capital and the quality of economic development', *Kyklos*, 61(3), 466-99.

Stone, W. (2001) *Measuring social capital: Towards a theoretically informed measurement framework for researching social capital in family and community life*, Research Paper No 24, Melbourne, VIC: Australian Institute of Family Studies.

Swaroop, S. and Krysan, M. (2011) 'The determinants of neighbourhood satisfaction: Racial proxy revisited', *Demography*, 48(3), 1203-29.

Toprak, B., Bozan, I., Morgül, T. and Şener, N. (2009) *Being different in Turkey: Religion, conservatism and otherization*, Research Report on Neighbourhood Pressure, Istanbul: Boğaziçi University.

Turok, I. and Bailey, N. (2004) 'Twin track cities? Competitiveness and cohesion in Glasgow and Edinburgh', *Progress in Planning*, 62(3), 135-204.

van Ham, M. and Clark, W.A.V. (2009) 'Neighbourhood mobility in context: Household moves and changing neighbourhoods in the Netherlands', *Environment and Planning* A, 41(6), 1442-59.

van Kempen, R. and Bolt, G. (2009) 'Social cohesion, social mix, and urban policies in the Netherlands', *Journal of Housing and the Built Environment*, 24(4), 457-75.

Vertovec, S. (2007) 'Super-diversity and its implications', *Ethnic and Racial Studies*, 30(6), 1024-54.

Vranken, J. (2004) 'Changing forms of solidarity: Urban development programs in Europe', in Y. Kazepov (ed) *Cities of Europe. Changing contexts, local arrangements, and the challenge to urban cohesion*, Oxford: Blackwell, 255-76.

Wessendorf, S. (2014) *Commonplace Diversity: Social Interactions in a Super-diverse Context*, Basingstoke: Palgrave McMillan.

Wimmer, A. (2004) 'Does ethnicity matter? Everyday group formation in three Swiss immigrant neighbourhoods', *Ethnic and Racial Studies*, 27(1), 1-36.

5

Nurturing solidarity in diversity: Can local currencies enable transformative practices?

Anika Depraetere, Bart van Bouchaute, Stijn Oosterlynck and Joke Vandenabeele

Introduction[1]

There is continuing ethnic-cultural diversity in Flanders, with more and more people with a migration background[2] living in the cities in particular, but gradually moving out to other parts of Flanders as well. Furthermore, the nature of this diversity has changed: we can now speak of 'super-diversity' (Vertovec, 2007; Maly et al, 2014). As country of origin and ethnicity are no longer sufficient to grasp diversity in society, super-diversity introduces a multidimensional perspective in which attention is given to the internal differentiation of ethno-cultural groups regarding language, gender, social class, migration channels, place of residence, religion, migration status, and so on. This then makes it impossible to speak in terms of 'the' migrant or 'the' foreigner.

In this chapter we analyse the relationship between super-diversity and solidarity. Quite a few sociologists are profoundly pessimistic about the possibility of fostering solidarity in ethno-culturally heterogeneous societies (see, for example, Putnam, 2007), arguing that ethno-cultural diversity impedes the development of solidarity in both informal networks and national structures of redistribution. These kinds of analyses frequently lead to policy pleas for cultural integration and assimilation, in which the idea of *one* territory, *one* community and *one* culture is pushed forward. In this chapter, we argue that solidarity in diversity is possible. We seek this solidarity, however, elsewhere than in the traditional spatial and time registers of the nation-state. Instead of grounding solidarity in a shared history and homogeneous culture, we look for solidarity in the here-and-now of specific practices in particular places.

As a concept, solidarity is strongly linked to the search for social order (Silver, 1994). This raises the question of whether new forms of solidarity in diversity have an integrative or a transformative effect. On the one hand, practices of solidarity imply the integration of super-diverse groups in already existing social structures and relationships, while on the other hand, practices of solidarity can actually lead to a transformation of these social structures and relationships.

We explore the potential of solidarity in diversity based on an extensive case study in Rabot-Blaisantvest, a super-diverse and poor neighbourhood in Ghent. We put forward two research questions. First, we examine if and how a professional intervention in the neighbourhood, namely, the introduction of a local currency system, the *Torekes*, stimulates interpersonal practices of solidarity in diversity. Our research focus is on what the participating residents of the neighbourhood do together, in spite of their lack of shared past and cultural background (Oosterlynck and Schuermans, 2013). Second, we examine the integrative and transformative effects of this currency system. Solidarity practices that arise because of this local currency project tend to confirm the existing social relations and social structures, but we also noticed the potential of this project to challenge these normalised relationships and structures. We discuss this transformative potential in relation to the way the labour market, public space and social cohesion are socially structured and symbolically constituted in the neighbourhood and beyond. For this analysis we make use of Jacques Rancière's post-foundational political thought.

Our empirical analysis is based on a combination of qualitative research methods: document analysis; semi-structured interviews; a focus group discussion; and participatory fieldwork. In a first research phase (September 2013-June 2014) we focused on the development of solidarity in diversity. For this we analysed 33 documents, conducted 10 in-depth interviews and organised one focus group discussion. The document analysis included 'internal communication documents' – reports of the meetings of the Torekes steering committee, consultation reports by the city of Ghent and several planning, reflection and budgetary reports – as well as 'external communication documents' such as (bi-)annual evaluation and planning reports and a diverse range of (social) media (website, catalogue, film, brochures and so on). In addition to this, we interviewed the initiators of the Torekes project, the community workers carrying out the project and their local partner organisations. In order to include the perspective of the 'Torekes participants', we also organised a focus group discussion with eight people. A second research phase (March 2015-June 2016) was planned in order to deepen our understanding of the transformative potential of the currency system. For this we conducted four months of participatory fieldwork on an urban agricultural site where most of the Torekes are earned. Participatory fieldwork is particularly apt for getting a grip on meaning-making processes as they take place in the here-and-now. Through working together in the field, we deepened our understanding of the diverse background of the participants, their varying motives for participating and the meaning they attribute to the currency system. This chapter draws on data from both research phases in order to present an integrated analysis of both the development of solidarity in diversity and its consequent integrative and/or transformative effects.

Stimulation of solidarity in super-diversity through a local currency system

Solidarity in super-diversity

Solidarity regulates the tension between an individual and a collective orientation. Feelings of shared destiny and group loyalty play a central role in this regulation. Drawing on Stjerno's description of the concept (2004), our aim was to analyse those practices where a readiness to share and redistribute material and immaterial resources becomes possible.

Many sociologists consider the growing ethno-cultural diversity in Western society as an important threat to solidarity. They take the view that this growing diversity creates a legitimacy crisis for the welfare state (Kymlicka and Banting, 2006; van Puymbroek and Dierckx, 2011). Studies confirm, for example, that many Western Europeans prefer solidarity with older people, people with disabilities and those who are unemployed over solidarity with immigrants (van Oorschot, 2006). They believe that diversity would also hinder solidarity on a smaller scale. On the basis of research in the US, Putnam (2007) indicates that immigration and diversity can produce cultural and economic advantages in the long run, but that they impair social capital and social cohesion in the short term. In light of these conclusions, some scientists and politicians plead for more cultural integration and assimilation (Brubaker, 2001), emphasising that solidarity in Western European welfare states is strongly based on the idea of *one* territory, *one* community and *one* culture.

This traditional integration model, based on a clear distinction between a *they* minority and a *we* majority, is fundamentally questioned by the evolution towards super-diversity (Blommaert, 2011). In an empirical study in London, Vertovec (2006) introduced this concept in order to demonstrate that the paradigm of the multicultural city[3] falls short in understanding the social and cultural diversity of our contemporary cities precisely because it is only the dimension of origin or ethno-cultural identity that is considered. Where in the 1960s fairly homogeneous groups of foreign workers migrated from a limited number of countries, in the past few decades the number of countries of origin as well as the diversity within the diversity has gradually increased. This has taken place simultaneously with economic globalisation and the expansion of the European Union (EU) after the fall of the Berlin Wall in the 1990s (Vertovec, 2007; Crul et al, 2013; Geldof, 2013). Super-diversity is especially present in the cities, which evolved into *majority-minority cities*, with a majority of residents coming from a broad spectrum of minorities (Geldof, 2013).

In these times of super-diversity, it is utopian to think that migrants will be completely integrated into the culture of the host society, or what is imagined as such (Anderson, 1991). It is likewise an illusion that local communities can be created based on having a similar way of life and identical norms and values. This is why, in our search for new forms of solidarity, we have sought for solidarity elsewhere than in the traditional national registers of the historically developed and homogeneously conceived community. To be able to grasp solidarity in diversity, we shift our spatial register from the national territory to particular places and our time register from historical time, that is, the social connections that have grown and been passed on generation after generation, to the present moment (Oosterlynck et al, 2015). Within this new register, community building still takes place – not through predetermined norms and values but through shared practices, such as the local currency system under study in this chapter.

The Torekes: An extension of solidarity through interdependence

According to a traditional liberal view, solidarity is a product of mutual dependence. It grows from the need for interaction and cooperation in a context of division of labour (Durkheim, 1984). However, the regular labour market offers little perspective on solidarity with groups that are not included as a result of discrimination, lack of education or other reasons. In Belgium, there is a diverse range of labour market-oriented initiatives seeking solidarity with vulnerable groups through, for example, job placement, publicly subsidised employment for specific (often long-term unemployed) target groups and so on. Local currencies are, strictly speaking, not part of these initiatives since they do not directly create labour opportunities. But they do seek to stimulate processes of economic development in districts that attract little external capital investment and with social groups whose skills are not valued in the regular labour market. In places and periods of economic crisis in particular, local currencies are introduced as cooperative and non-profit exchange systems in which people who are time-rich and cash-poor can be socially and economically productive in spite of their lack of official money (De Filippis, 2004). Local currencies are based on an agreement between a group of people and/or businesses to accept a non-traditional currency as a means of exchange. This non-traditional currency does not replace the conventional currency, but supplements it by valuing social functions that the official currency does not prize (Lietaer, 2001, p 33).

The Torekes currency system was introduced in September 2010 in the Rabot-Blaisantvest neighbourhood on the initiative of both Kathleen van Brempt, the former Flemish Minister of Employment and Social Economy, and *Netwerk Vlaanderen* (Network Flanders, now known as FairFin), an organisation that stimulates alternative ways of dealing with money. Rabot-Blaisantvest is a dense and super-diverse neighbourhood in the 19th-century ring around Ghent with 8,230 residents in an area of 0.82km^2 (Stad Gent, 2015). The district has the highest percentage of ethno-cultural minorities and non-Belgians of all neighbourhoods in Ghent. It is also characterised by acute forms of socioeconomic deprivation: the number of people with the right to social security and the pressure of unemployment is one of the highest in Ghent, and the average net taxable income is the lowest of all neighbourhoods in Ghent.

This neighbourhood was chosen as an experimental area for a local currency because of the existing network of community organisations and the potential of under-utilised resources such as residual spaces in the neighbourhood and the capacities of its residents. The local currency could be embedded into a broader already existing project of shared care for public spaces and urban farming in the neighbourhood. At present, the project's most important partners are the City of Ghent and the civil society organisation Community Development Ghent (Samenlevingsopbouw Gent). The City of Ghent subsidised the Torekes as part of its urban renewal project in the area. Through introducing the Torekes, the city wanted to strengthen three pillars of urban renewal: the improvement of the general quality of living in the area, the strengthening of social cohesion and the countering of the rather bad image of the neighbourhood, and the stimulation of local trade and local social economy opportunities. Community Development Ghent is the executing partner because of its experience with projects and activities concerning the quality of community life in disadvantaged neighbourhoods and with strengthening vulnerable groups who inhabit these neighbourhoods.

How, then, does the system of the Torekes actually work? Residents of the neighbourhood can earn Torekes in exchange for acts expressing 'care' for the neighbourhood, their neighbours or the environment. They can earn Torekes through individual activities such as setting up a flower box or a green roof garden or through participating in community activities that make the neighbourhood more pleasant and tidy. These 'Torekes volunteers' can spend the Torekes through local and sustainable consumption such as the purchase of healthy food from local traders, low-energy light bulbs at the Torekes counter, or meals in the social restaurant. There is an exchange rate between the Torekes and the regular Euro system: 10 Torekes have a commercial value of 1 Euro. Because of the intention to stimulate local exchange circles, only the merchants can directly exchange their received Torekes for Euros.

Various reports show that most of the Torekes are earned through community activities, especially the 'working days' or afternoons organised by the community development organisation (Samenlevingsopbouw Gent, 2012, 2013, 2014).

What is striking in Table 5.1 is that the rise in working hours is not accompanied by a rise in the number of participants. Between 2012 and 2013, we can even observe a strong decrease in the number of individual participants while there is a significant rise in the number of working hours. This means that the effort per participant has increased. Community workers confirm that a very committed, stable group of volunteers has been involved in the public space through the Torekes. Most are spent in the local (food) shops. This indicates that many of these volunteers use the Torekes as an additional source of income. In 2014, possibilities for earning Torekes had to be restricted because their expense budget began to increase too greatly. The decrease in the

Table 5.1: Overview of Torekes activity

Year	Total number of Torekes earned in the area	Torekes earned through community services	Number of individual participants	Total number of working hours
2011	50,259	41,589	217	1,664
2012	105,331	99,561	244	3,982
2013	259,973	257,397	117	10,295
2014	No figures available	193,700	No figures available	7,748

number of Torekes earned and the number of working hours performed is therefore not caused by a decreased interest from the neighbourhood's residents. To the contrary, community workers frequently had to send participants away and explain that only a specific number of activities qualified to be rewarded with Torekes.

Solidary in diversity practices in shared areas

Our research focused on new practices of solidarity in diversity in the here-and-now. We looked into specific areas of the neighbourhood where people spend time together, partially stimulated by the Torekes. One of the first things we observed is that the Torekes are grafted into the existing dynamism of the neighbourhood. The currency does not function just by itself; it depends on community workers or other social professionals in the neighbourhood who organise activities that are rewarded with Torekes. The Torekes stimulate the involvement of residents not yet participating in existing, formal and informal activities and networks within the neighbourhood. The currency system strengthens interdependencies in the area through mobilising these new residents and through forging multiple connections between diverse residents, some of whom are already active and some of whom are rather new in their engagement in the neighbourhood. It is this extension and deepening of interdependencies that is the basic source of new forms of solidarity in diversity. Furthermore, the Torekes are embedded in places where these community workers or social professionals actively try to create 'proximity in diversity'.

We will discuss two of these places: the *Site* and the *Witte Kaproenenplein*. The Torekes project, and in particular its income effect, resulted in the involvement of a bigger and more diverse group of people in these places. The project also facilitated experiences of shared responsibility and inclusive appropriation.

The Site is a temporary project on what was formerly an industrial area on the Gasmeterlaan, one of the main roads surrounding the neighbourhood. Awaiting remediation works and housing construction, various neighbourhood organisations transformed this area into a shared neighbourhood project, 'an open space for play and entertainment, culture and relaxation' (Debruyne and Oosterlynck, 2009, p 26). Since 2011 an important part of the Site is used for urban agriculture: private allotments, communal agricultural fields, a greenhouse, a bread oven, and so on. The Torekes played a fundamental role in the development of the Site: you can hire an allotment for 150 Torekes per year, you receive 25 Torekes an hour for working on the communal fields and

Torekes can be used to buy vegetables from these fields. Volunteers who are involved in the various cultural and social activities on the Site, such as the weekly football training, are also rewarded with Torekes.

The Witte Kaproenenplein is a smaller green area that lies between housing blocks in the centre of the neighbourhood. It used to be a typical example of a rather unattractive and user-unfriendly space in a social housing area, unused and uncared for by the neighbourhood. The Studio Basta landscape architecture agency and Community Development Ghent, financed by the city fund for urban renewal, coordinated a participatory project in order to redesign the area and they used the Torekes as motivation to involve residents. Over the course of a year, terraces, benches, a pétanque playing area, flower beds and so on were designed and built. Inhabitants who helped to realise the project were rewarded with Torekes and the maintenance of the square is still being rewarded with Torekes.

People from diverse cultural backgrounds come together in these places. People from the Turkish community, most originally from the agricultural area of Emirdag, are attracted to the allotments and communal agricultural fields, especially since most of them no longer have a garden. A number of older Belgian women organise a give-away shop on the Site. They also work on the communal fields in order to be able to rent their private allotment. Residents in a disadvantaged situation, such as those who are long-term unemployed, are also involved through the efforts and guidance from the community development organisation and because of the currency's effect on their income. Since the introduction of the currency system, more people from more diverse backgrounds come together on the Site and the connection between them is deepened through sustained contact over sustained activities. The diversity of which we speak includes various aspects: age, migration status, gender, religion, language, country of origin, and so on.

> 'A person with a Turkish background who speaks little Dutch, a homeless Belgian man and a Nigerian refugee. These various figures swarm around on the Site, and are linked to each other through the Torekes.' (community worker)

These places, understood as 'small nodes of diversity', offer the possibility of experiencing in a very informal way how we can live with differences. The shared involvement of a diverse group of people can decrease prejudices and make new connections possible (Amin, 2002):

'It used to be each group, each culture relating to itself. They come together here and that's what is so nice about it. Before, those Turkish people, I didn't know them because I don't speak any Turkish. Now it doesn't matter, whether they speak Turkish or whatever.... You learn to communicate with each other, with signs and gestures! Those Turkish people also make an effort to make themselves understandable. We'll get there in the end.' (Site volunteer)

What these people have in common is the place of the Site or the Witte Kaproenenplein where they spend their free time, earn Torekes or simply hang out when the weather is nice. Place can form a basis for solidarity precisely because it is the only factor that we continue to share in super-diverse contexts (Oosterlynck and Schuermans, 2013):

'It is a diverse group, but the fact that they share such an area, and that they all carry out their activities there creates a certain connection, a sense of community. That they know each other and greet each other on the street. It is not realistic to think they will become best friends. Each has their own network and that is not to be found at the neighbourhood level anymore and you cannot try to force.... No, you just work with what is there, a shared involvement in the neighbourhood.' (civil servant)

So, in addition to the network of interdependencies that has taken shape in the neighbourhood, the encounters that occur in these places also nurture solidarity in super-diversity. During the 'working days' on the Site, for example, volunteers picnic together and share their food. If someone who is regularly present doesn't show up for some time, the rest of the group shows its concern. Once a volunteer saved his Torekes in order to be able to treat his fellow volunteers with a meal in the local social restaurant. That same volunteer bought a bike for the son of a fellow volunteer who wasn't able to pay for one himself. Many of these solidarity practices occur among people in a vulnerable situation, such as those who are long-term unemployed, people without legal residency, people with a low pension, and so on:

'Take note, we could identify this solidarity very typically: those who have, giving to those who have not. But here, this is also happening between those who have not. I know people who earn Torekes and I think by myself: "they will make good use of them themselves". But they say "I gave it to this other person because he or she needs it more than I do".' (community worker)

The Torekes are thus important for the development of solidarity between vulnerable residents. In the poorest neighbourhood of Ghent, this system functions as a direct increase in income for people who are time-rich and cash-poor. The work on the Site leads to regular and intensive contacts and a shared vulnerable situation leads to a strong sense of a loyalty (Stjerno, 2004). People in a disadvantaged situation get involved in the project because the currency increases their income and also because of the intensive support offered by community workers who are active, present and easily approachable in the neighbourhood:

'... you get poor by poor people, we help each other, we don't expect anything from rich. Rich people don't know poor people or they don't care, they don't look, turn their head, look around. We take ourselves as brothers, sisters, friends, whatever ... as family, as people, it is unity in diversity.' (Site volunteer)

So, as a provisional conclusion and in response to our first research question, we can now assert that the introduction of the Torekes project generated new, place-based forms of solidarity in diversity. The Torekes extended and strengthened the interdependencies within the neighbourhood, which then made them function more broadly and strongly as a source of solidarity. The network of local interdependencies is further deepened by the diverse encounters in shared public places. Close proximity in itself is, however, insufficient to allow practices of solidarity to develop. The intermediation of the local currency system and the arrangement of specific places, linked with the human effort of community workers and organisations, plays a necessary and stimulating role in these practices of solidarity. Also, the practices of solidarity rest for a great deal on indirect solidarity organised 'at a distance' (Veldboer, 2010). The very recognisable specific forms of warm, interpersonal solidarity stimulated by the Torekes are only possible through a considerable injection of public means from the city of Ghent and other authorities. In what follows we build further on these place-based forms of solidarity in diversity, and question whether they imply an integration or transformation of existing social structures and relations.

The Torekes: Between integration in and transformation of the existing order

Solidarity in diversity and disturbing the existing order

The concept of solidarity has an ambiguous political legacy. Its modern, secularised instantiation was developed in an era of deep social and political upheaval, and was part and parcel of a frantic search for the sources of social order in modern capitalist societies (Stjerno, 2004). Despite this historical association with order and societal integration, the notion of solidarity is also frequently mobilised by a range of social movements to assist calls for societal change and transformation (Featherstone et al, 2012). It is this ambiguity and tension with which the notion of solidarity is imbued to which we want to draw attention in our analysis. This field of tension is of particular relevance for solidarity *in diversity*, given how ethnic and cultural diversity challenges the notion of presumably culturally homogenous nation-states (Oosterlynck et al, 2016). Does solidarity in super-diversity require the disruption of the existing social order, or is it just a matter of integrating culturally diverse groups within the existing sociocultural order?

Rancière's post-foundational understanding of democratic politics can be of use here. Although not specifically concerned with solidarity, Rancière would argue that a proper *politics* of solidarity in diversity can only be transformative. Any social order, regardless of how much solidarity exists within it, disciplines and polices its members by assigning them to specific functions, places and voices. It always has parts that do not fit in and are hence made invisible and inaudible. Politics, then, is about the interruption of the existing and inevitably exclusionary social order to claim a place for 'those who have no part' (Rancière, 2001, p 6). In the context of solidarity in diversity, the question is whether solidarity is culturally framed through an integrationist or transformative perspective. The former sees cultural assimilation (that is, becoming more culturally similar to mainstream society) as a precondition for solidarity, whereas in the latter the confrontation with 'cultural otherness' and the subsequent transformation of the sociocultural order to include other voices and subjects as equals is the very substance of solidarity in diversity. The former requires 'socialisation'; the latter implies subjectification. Socialisation is about getting to know one's place, function and voice in a social order through the learning processes that are implied in becoming part of a group. Socialisation processes, in other words, insert individuals into existing ways of doing and being (Biesta, 2009).

Subjectification, on the other hand, is the process of becoming a subject; it is not about the insertion of newcomers into existing orders, but about ways of being that hint at independence from such orders. If we follow Rancière (1999), subjectification entails the emergence of acting and speaking subjects who, through their acts and voices, transform and dispute their pre-given identities. Subjectification does not create subjects out of nothing; 'it creates them by transforming identities defined in the natural order of the allocation of functions and places into instances of experience of a dispute' (Rancière, 1999, p 36). Emancipatory processes of subjectification are therefore not about the confirmation of one's own sociocultural identity or the expression of specific sociocultural values of a certain group; they concern the forming of a political claim on the basis of the right to be counted as equal (Oosterlynck, 2014).

Based on this approach, we see how the introduction of the Torekes in the super-diverse Rabot-Blaisantvest neighbourhood not only reflects the participants' desire for integration in the existing order but also produces a capacity to challenge this order. As a local currency system, the Torekes calls into question the regular labour market as the prevailing system of recognition in our society. Moreover, the embedding of the Torekes in specific places calls a particular view and design of public spaces into question. The fact that a socially vulnerable group of volunteers is active in the Torekes project challenges the presumptions about this group as well as the position to which they are allocated in society. The interrelation of integrative and transformative practices indicates how the creation of solidarity in diversity forces subjects to navigate within this tension. To be clear, the practices developed around the Torekes are small and limited in reach. In line with Rancière's perspective, our analysis thus focuses on challenges to the *symbolic* constitution of society, rather than to any actual material transformation of, for example, the labour market.

Disrupting what is valued as 'labour'

The implementation of the Torekes and the subsequent involvement of groups that are barely or not taken up into the traditional interdependence of the labour market strengthen an alternative form of interdependence. As a currency system the Torekes project gives the unemployed, and virtually anyone, the opportunity to turn working capacity or work time into purchasing power without the need for an employment contract or the capital required to register as self-employed (Offe and Heinze, 1992). Neighbourhood residents are thus indirectly integrated into the employment and trade system when they convert their time into Torekes that are ultimately re-converted into purchases in Euros through local traders. At the same time, the Torekes have the transformative potential to challenge the idea of the labour market as the dominant system of remuneration and recognition in our society in several ways. For example, the relationship between work productivity and salary is disrupted because the level of remuneration per hour is not linked to the efficiency of the work performed:

> 'People work at different paces. An elderly lady in her 60s who regularly works on the fields, well she works at her pace and he [other volunteer], well, he will probably work ten times as fast but they do earn an equal amount of Torekes and nobody makes a fuss about it.' (community worker)

More importantly however, the Torekes project challenges the taken-for-granted policy logic concerning activation towards the regular labour market. As we showed earlier, a very committed group of volunteers has been working on a regular basis in the public space, at least partially stimulated by the currency. Those people are often the very same that policy-makers and institutions for job placement refer to as 'people we can no longer socially or economically activate':

> 'What I find remarkable is that a lot of these volunteers have stayed over the years. But they are the same people who have been written off by the labour market. According to the VDAB [Flemish Office for Labour Market Mediation and Job Training], they can no longer be activated. But they come here to work for €2.50 an hour, which is a lot less than they would get at any other job.... How come? This is difficult to explain to the outside world...' (community worker)

We found that this striking difference can be explained because activation through the Torekes involves a possibility for redefining labour as a meaningful activity, calling into question the very particular meaning that is attributed to work nowadays. The Torekes participants have considerable autonomy to determine when and for how long they work. The tasks are distributed through mutual consultation and on the basis of what each has to offer, as well as on each participant's wishes. Furthermore, a lot of attention is given to the development of equal, trusting relationships between the participants and with the community workers. And involvement in the Torekes project is experienced as a meaningful activity, giving participants a good feeling about themselves and a sense of recognition in relation to others and the broader neighbourhood. These experiences stand in stark contrast with their experiences in the regular labour market where they either cannot get access to it or if they can, they find little sense of freedom, reciprocity or recognition:

> 'I regularly had jobs but I did not pursue them for a very long time. It was always the same jobs. I have a driver's licence so I got jobs as a furniture remover or in a beverage company. Hard work and quite okay for a while, but there was no challenge. A challenge for me is something in which I can develop myself and that makes me feel as if I'm making myself useful. After a day of moving furniture or carrying around beer vats you feel tired but well, I guess a trained gorilla could also do that.' (Torekes volunteer)

But the Torekes were implemented as a social project, trying to stimulate active involvement in the neighbourhood and not as a labour project. Community workers often stress this by stating that the Torekes project is not paid labour but voluntary work. While there was criticism that existing volunteer work in the neighbourhood would suffer due to the monetisation, in practice, however, it became apparent that new volunteer tasks were taken on by new residents. In recent years, those who are in a vulnerable position have made use of the Torekes in order to supplement their income. They have appropriated this system of voluntary work and use the additional income to purchase basic necessities:

> 'The first time I came here I thought "this is paradise". I love trees, flowers, plants. I come here because I like to work in the nature, to spend my time; otherwise I have nothing to do. And because of the Torekes I can make a small contribution to my family. Even if it is just small money, I can buy bread and water for my family. It is a small revenue.' (Torekes volunteer)

Working in the Torekes project hence feels like working in between voluntary work and paid labour. When community workers express how participants gain self-confidence and can also be trained in their working attitudes through the project, one may conclude they have developed an innovative socioeconomic project aimed at ultimately integrating or socialising participants into the regular labour market. Yet the community workers turn this line of thought around: they stress how the Torekes project challenges the structures of the existing labour market. The project makes the capacities of vulnerable neighbours visible and hence critically questions the regular labour market for not being the place where these capacities are able to flourish.

For the participants, then, the position of the Torekes project in the grey area or twilight zone in between voluntary work and paid labour makes them reflect on their own position. During our first encounter with Torekes participants, one of them interrupted our focus group and stated: "The most important question to ask here is 'Why don't they give us Euros?'" During the fieldwork we conducted afterwards, similar statements surfaced, as some of the participants clearly thought that the remuneration was too low. One of them seriously suggested going on strike in order to get a better wage: "If the city's civil servants can decide to strike, why can't we?" This reflects the strong desire not to be locked into a 'ghetto' with a specific local currency, on the margins of the regular economy. Torekes participants claim to be equal to regular workers.

In relation to labour, the Torekes project is thus caught in a precarious tension between integration and transformation. Neighbours are indirectly integrated into a system of employment and policy-makers often consider the project as a first step of integration into the regular labour market. But, as we indicated, the added value of the project lies in the visibility it gives to the activity of people considered 'inactive'. These people claim equality both through their acts and speeches. Stating the fact that what they do is work, they call into question the idea of activation towards the 'regular' labour market. Their community activity is not accounted for in the world of paid labour, and it is the symbolic constitution of this world that needs to be transformed in order to also value their contribution. This, of course, is not a straightforward process. Within the current neoliberal tendencies associated with the restructuring of the Western welfare state (see Brenner et al, 2010), these type of projects also have to take into account the considerable risk of being absorbed by the ubiquitous logic of labour market flexibility, meaning more flexible jobs with less income security. Community workers recognise the risk that their system can easily be looked on as a way of integrating people into the lowest remaining category of the competitive labour market. A small but necessary supplementary remuneration of €2.50 an hour then helps vulnerable participants with a low income to survive in a poor neighbourhood such as Rabot-Blaisantvest, without having to question the structures and relations that affect their conditions of existence.

Appropriation of public space

Stimulated by the Torekes, residents work in the public space. Having clean streets and squares has always been a policy concern of the city of Ghent, and the Torekes seemed a nice incentive to involve inhabitants in this. And because of the currency some streets and squares do look cleaner; this very fact then seems to convince policy-makers of the added value of this currency system.

But if you take a closer look at the underlying dynamics in these places, another story comes to the surface. The squares and places do look nicer because they used to be 'leftover spaces'. The two places we discussed earlier, the Site and the Witte Kaproenenplein, used to be, respectively, a 'block of concrete' and a 'leftover plot of grass'. Civil servants of the city of Ghent responsible for the development of the area and the community development organisation both noticed the potential of these unused spaces in the very dense neighbourhood and joined forces in order to redesign them. A participatory process was set up in which the Torekes functioned as an incentive for neighbours to get involved. Both places have become useful again through an intensive and experimental process of neighbourhood engagement:

> 'These spaces used to benefit no one and now, through using them for another purpose, they have become something that people can use in different ways. It does not need to be design, you know, it needs to be real.' (community worker)

Inhabitants soon started to feel more connected to the place, not the least because they could codetermine the conditions under which they were supposed to take care of the area. On a local level, the acts and voices of residents fundamentally challenged the existing routines and guidelines of the city's planning and management of green areas:

> 'This is a place that we have claimed, not least because we said "you don't do anything here, you only cut the grass once a month and that's it". When children came to play, there was a sign that read "forbidden to play". The city's maintenance service can't deal with it: "What do we have to do now? Do we still have to cut the grass?" They completely panic. They have about a thousand guidelines

on how a public space should look like, but no guidelines for when a resident says: "I just want to sow some lettuce here".' (community worker)

On a broader level, this 'do-participation', as the community workers define it, disturbs decision-making processes concerning public spaces: a top-down expert model is challenged through a bottom-up approach that focuses on the social value and user-friendliness of the public space for its residents. The emphasis here lies not on the fact that 'inactive' groups have to be involved in the maintenance of public space, but on disturbing existing participatory systems and opening up possibilities to give people in a vulnerable position a voice as equally valuable members of the community:

'There are the traditional channels of participation, such as steering committees, feedback groups, etc. But what we do is "participation by doing". We believe that you can be a citizen by doing very simple things. And by doing a number of things, we succeed in leaving the traditional channels and a certain manner of decision-making behind. The traditional system of "round tables", for example, obliges us to hoist ourselves up to the city level, to the level of the planners. But we say "no, we are not going to join in with this, we are here and we are already doing all sorts of things".' (Community Development member of staff, Ghent)

On the Site, this appropriation process is even clearer. In 2007 this area was claimed by different sociocultural organisations and experimentation opportunities have been abundant ever since: an outdoor cinema was put in place, a bike trail was built, a football area was constructed and so on. The urban agricultural fields established in 2011 were an instant success leading to a series of new and sometimes unexpected activities, some of which we have witnessed taking place during our fieldwork. For example, on a given day, some of the older Turkish ladies started to gather small plants growing near the potatoes on the communal fields. Everyone thought they were weeding, but the next day they arrived back on the Site handing out bread they had baked with this 'weed'. A bread oven was then built and these ladies now organise the baking activities and even give small workshops when class groups from nearby schools visit the area. These women hardly speak any Dutch and before the construction of the urban agricultural fields, they were not that visible within the neighbourhood.

Furthermore, they were often even targeted as being part of a group that has difficulties integrating into 'our society'. Their activities and performances, stimulated by the Torekes project, now strongly challenge this allocation of particular people to particular places and functions (Rancière, 1999).

But the Site is only a temporary experimentation zone, awaiting reconstruction into a residential area, and community workers and residents are now lobbying for the continuation of their activities within the residential project:

> 'We just want a place like this and not only those little allotments where there is no room for us, not even a room for a gardening shed like the one we are sitting in now, drinking coffee, having a chat. For them, this is not design enough, it's not aesthetic, you know what I mean? So now we really have to make an effort and really try, starting from the group here ... even if it's a football pitch or ... we have to have a spot where it's up to us to decide what to do with it.' (community worker)

So in relation to the development of the public spaces, the introduction of a currency system to get neighbours involved within the neighbourhood can easily be thought of as a way to activate (vulnerable) residents in order to take up their role in building a cleaner living environment. Nonetheless, we noticed very clearly a transformative vision in which different spaces are transformed not only in a material way but also in a symbolical way that challenges existing routines of decision-making and whose voices are counted within them.

Disrupting the allocated place in the community

The Torekes project offers residents opportunities through which they can integrate into the existing network of relations within the community, as one of the project goals indicates: 'local residents discover that it is possible to do something for others or for the public space' (Samenlevingsopbouw Gent, 2013). At the same time, working in the public space makes vulnerable residents visible and valued within the neighbourhood:

> 'The people see that those "hooligans" who used to be out on the street are doing something so positive and that brings

about a connection, the perception alters.' (community worker)

'The people in the neighbourhood think the project is great, especially when it concerns people who don't work and who get benefits. They sit at home and actually they should be doing something. So something like: you get support, but you still need to work a couple of hours every so often as volunteer. People who work think it's terrible that others get money without doing anything in return.' (local shopkeeper)

Furthermore, some volunteers explicitly use the term 'integration' when asked about the impact of the Torekes project on their lives:

'It is important in a neighbourhood where a lot of newcomers are arriving that a project like the Site exists. You can try to get involved, know what is going on, you have to interact with other people, it is integrating the people.' (volunteer)

But the kind of integration we see here does challenge the traditional way in which newcomers are expected to integrate into society, for example, via integration courses in formal learning environments and on the basis of clearly defined criteria. For residents who are involved in the Torekes project, there is no top-down authority determining how the integration will take place and what needs to be learned. They can codetermine or reinvent ways in which they can integrate in the neighbourhood, as the above example of the Turkish women has made clear. In this way they dispute their pre-given – inferior – position within the neighbourhood through work that supports their sense of dignity. The football coaches are a good example of this. Two men living in the neighbourhood train youngsters on Wednesday afternoons. Both of them have quite a troubled past and have taken op their engagement as a way to give some of the neighbourhood youngsters the opportunities they themselves did not have when they were young:

'You can say it is only football but I like to think of it as a way to offer them a positive activity during the day. You never know, we have trained many children until now. If we did not do this, I believe at least a few of them would have ended up in specialised youth care. So in a way, we are also taking up our responsibility within society, you know.' (football coach)

Nonetheless, a particular tension persists here. We see that by taking care of the neighbourhood, certain people in the neighbourhood are no longer seen as unwanted and dangerous outsiders who have to be avoided, but are accepted as part of the community. This then runs the risk of accepting the presence of vulnerable groups because these groups themselves demonstrate that they earn this presence. According to this logic only partial integration is achieved in which groups that are considered threatening gain just enough connection with society to ensure that *we* will not be bothered by *them* (see also Tuteleers, 2007). But where we actually situate the transformative potential of this currency system and the practices in which it is embedded is within the possibilities of subjectification it offers to vulnerable residents to step out of their attributed positions within the neighbourhood. As we have argued here, through their active involvement they do not claim to be accepted but they claim to be part. They want to be counted not as a 'partial part' but as part and parcel of this neighbourhood.

Conclusion

The Torekes project demonstrates how solidarity in a super-diverse neighbourhood can develop, not on the basis of *one* community, *one* culture, *one* territory, but on the basis of practices where people commit themselves to spend time in each other's company. The Torekes project is embedded in specific places in the neighbourhood where Torekes are earned or distributed. All sorts of practices and social dynamics were already in play in places such as the Site and the Witte Kaproenenplein. What we have demonstrated in this chapter, however, is how the local currency introduced new activities and stimulated a more diverse group of inhabitants to participate. In this way, the interdependency in the neighbourhood was extended and strengthened, providing the source of new forms of solidarity. Through the shared care for these places, strong feelings of loyalty are created between the participants, as was evident in the specific examples discussed in this chapter. The micro practices of solidarity are most noticeable between volunteers with a low income and a vulnerable social position.

Professionals play a crucial role in all of this. The Torekes is not a bottom-up project of community service and urban agriculture, but consists of practices that are promoted through professional interventions. This is given shape first and foremost through the local currency itself that extends interdependency in the neighbourhood in particular to residents in vulnerable situations, something in which the regular labour market does not succeed. Furthermore, the alternative design and experimentation opportunities of residual spaces are of fundamental importance in giving these residents a place in the neighbourhood. Community workers also organise individual support, group work, mediation and advocacy directed at this vulnerable group. Moreover, the 'warm', interpersonal solidarity is strongly promoted through 'cold' solidarity in the form of funds that are reserved and redistributed to this project. These observations nuance an all-too-romantic approach to practices of solidarity as spontaneous bottom-up processes and indicate the importance of a material and social infrastructure in which place-based forms of solidarity in super-diversity can flourish.

We not only examined whether solidarity in diversity grows through particular practices in specific places, but also whether these practices confirm or transform the existing social relations and social structures. The Torekes project highlights a social reality that questions the 'normalised' order. In one of our first interviews, a community worker pointed at the transformative potential of the Torekes using the following words:

> 'You collide with systems that do not work and the Torekes have a brilliant role here. You can trigger lots of things that would otherwise stay under the surface. We have to tell these stories more often because those are the true stories of the Torekes, and not that there are now six additional flower boxes in the streets.'

The community workers gave a whole range of examples of social exclusion and the limits of different systems that our society has put in place in order to deal with difference, such as alternative sanctions, labour market mediation or integration courses. In this chapter we have analysed how the Torekes project integrates a diversity of people within the neighbourhood. It gives them a place in the neighbourhood but not without questioning their having 'no place' within other systems. We discussed how mainstream assumptions on activation towards the regular labour market are strongly challenged by residents staging their de facto active role in society. These residents state in a variety of ways that they do not want to be put in the margins of society, in a grey zone between voluntary work and regular labour. They claim to be working and in this way bring forward the limits of the regular labour market. We witnessed how residents also get involved with the outline and design of public spaces, not by adapting to the existing models of expertise, but through 'participation by doing'. In this way, they co-create the environment in which and the conditions on which they are supposed to integrate. Although the solidarities that we observed are situated in a particular neighbourhood, they do have the power to blur or even refute the way vulnerable groups fall between clear-cut sociocultural conventions and categories. Residents position themselves as people who are part and parcel of the neighbourhood instead of being attributed to the lowest step of its social hierarchy. What therefore emerges is a practice that is guided by the hypothesis that all people are equal and that all people can be involved in changing or reconsidering the boundaries of what constitutes a community.

Notes

[1] This chapter is based on research that was subsidised through the Strategic Basic Research (*Strategisch Basisonderzoek*, SBO) programme of the Agency for Innovation by Science and Technology Flanders (*Instituut van Wetenschap en Technologie Vlaanderen*, IWT). This research project was called DieGem (*Diversiteit en Gemeenschapsvorming*/Diversity and Community Development) and ran from 2013 to 2016, coordinated by the Centre on Inequality, Poverty, Social Exclusion and the City (OASes), University of Antwerp.

[2] We use the term 'people with a migration background' here to refer to a very diverse group of citizens who have, since the Second World War, and for a variety of reasons, moved to Belgium. We prefer this rather broad term in order to go beyond ethnic-cultural categorisations of people.

[3] The multicultural paradigm is based on the recognition of and respect for collectively and ethno-culturally defined identities that are nurtured by strongly organised communities.

References

Amin, A. (2002) 'Ethnicity and the multicultural city: Living with diversity', *Environment and Planning*, 34(6), 959-80.

Anderson, B. (1991) *Imagined communities*, London: Verso.

Biesta, G. (2009) 'Good education: What it is and why we need it', Inaugural Lecture for the Stirling Institute of Education, 1-12.

Blommaert, J. (2011) *Superdiversiteit maakt integratiebeleid irrelevant*, Sociale Vraagstukken (www.socialevraagstukken.nl/site/2011/10/27/superdiversiteit-maakt-integratiebeleid-irrelevant).

Brenner, N., Peck, J. and Theodore, N. (2010) 'Variegated neoliberalization: Geographies, modalities, pathways', *Global networks*, 10(2), 182-222.

Brubaker, R. (2001) 'The return of assimilation? Changing perspectives on immigration and its sequels in France, Germany and the United States', *Ethnic and Racial Studies*, 24(4), 531-48.

Crul, M., Schneider, J. and Lelie, F. (2013) *Superdiversiteit. Een nieuwe visie op integratie*, Amsterdam: VU University Press.

Debruyne, P. and Oosterlynck, S. (2009) 'Stedelijke vernieuwing in het Gentse Rabot', *Alert*, 35(3), 20-30.

De Filippis, J. (2004) *Unmaking Goliath. Community control in the face of global capital*, New York: Routledge.

Durkheim, E. (1984) *The division of labour in society*, London: MacMillan.

Featherstone, D., Ince, A., Mackinnon, D., Strauss, K. and Cumbers, A. (2012) 'Progressive localism and the construction of political alternatives', *Transactions of the Institute of British Geographers*, 37(2), 177-82

Geldof, D. (2013) *Superdiversiteit. Hoe migratie onze samenleving verandert*, Leuven: Acco.

Kymlicka, W. and Banting, K. (2006) 'Immigration, multiculturalism and the welfare state', *Ethics & International Affairs*, 20(3), 281-304.

Lietaer, B. (2001) *Het geld van de toekomst*, Amsterdam: de Boekerij.

Maly, I., Blommaert, J. and Ben Yakoub, J. (2014) *Superdiversiteit en democratie*, Antwerpen: Epo.

Offe, C. and Heinze, R. (1992) *Beyond employment: Time, work and the informal economy*, Cambridge: Polity Press.

Oosterlynck, S. (2014) 'Over politiek: Gelijkheid als hypothese', in G. Schuermans (ed) *Politieke Ruimte*, Bruges: Die Keure.

Oosterlynck, S. and Schuermans, N. (2013) 'Superdiversiteit. Solidariteit herdenken', *Alert*, 39(4), 13-19.

Oosterlynck, S., Loopmans, M., Schuermans, N., Vandenabeele, J. and Zemni, S. (2016) 'Putting flesh to the bone: Looking for solidarity in diversity, here and now', *Ethnic and Racial Studies*, 39(5), 764-82.

Putnam, R. (2007) '*E. pluribus unum*: Diversity and community in the twenty-first century. The 2006 Johan Skytte Prize Lecture', *Scandinavian Political Studies*, 30(2), 137-74.

Rancière, J. (1999) *Disagreement: Politics and philosophy*, Minnesota, MN: University of Minnesota Press.

Rancière, J. (2001) 'Ten thesis on politics', *Theory & Event*, 5(3) (www.egs.edu/faculty/jacques ranciere/articles/ten-thesis-on-politics/).

Samenlevingsopbouw Gent (2012) *Torekes: Evaluatie – planning 2012 – Suggesties lange termijn*, Internal document.

Samenlevingsopbouw Gent (2013) *Complementaire munt, een innovatief instrument. Tussentijds rapport*, Internal document.

Samenlevingsopbouw Gent (2014) *Verdere uitbouw van de complementaire munt*, Internal document.

Silver, H. (1994) 'Social exclusion and social solidarity: Three paradigms', *International Labour Review*, 133(5/6), 531-78.

Stad Gent (2015) *Gent in cijfers* (www.gent.buurtmonitor.be).

Stjerno, S. (2004) *Solidarity in Europe. The history of an idea*, Cambridge: Cambridge University Press.

Tuteleers, P. (2007) *Sociale activering. Exploratieve studie naar de achtergronden van het concept*, Ghent: Academic Press.

van Oorschot, W. (2006) 'Making the difference in social Europe: Deservingness perceptions among citizens of European welfare states', *Journal of European Social Policy*, 16(1), 23-42.

van Puymbroeck, N. and Dierckx, D. (2011) 'De Gordiaanse knoop van migratie en de (multiculturele) welvaartstaat', in D. Dierckx, J. Vranken, J. Coene and A. van Haarlem (eds) *Jaarboek Armoede en Sociale Uitsluiting*, Leuven: Acco, 285-302.

Vertovec, S. (2006) *The emergence of superdiversity in Britain*, Working Paper 25, Oxford: Centre on Migration, Policy and Society.

Vertovec, S. (2007) 'Super-diversity and its complications', *Ethnic and Racial Studies*, 30(6), 1024-54.

6

Interculturalism as conservative multiculturalism? New generations from an immigrant background in Milan, Italy, and the challenge to categories and boundaries

Eduardo Barberis

Introduction

This chapter analyses the emerging national and local models of incorporating minorities from an international migration background in Italy. It uses Milan as a case study and focuses on second generations from an immigrant background, which are considered a new frontier in public and policy debate (Andall, 2002; Colombo and Rebughini, 2012). Italy might be considered a latecomer – even a backward case of poor relevance for an international audience that has long been debating immigrant policies and generations from an immigrant background as policy targets. However, Italy is also an interesting comparative case in the European arena. Today, Italy has one of the largest numbers of immigrant residents in Europe, and it is at the forefront of some of the most meaningful societal and institutional challenges pertaining to immigrant-related diversity. These challenges include the societal reception and incorporation of super-diversity, along with the layering of very different immigrants groups in terms of length and reason of stay, origin and migration path (including recent humanitarian flows across the Mediterranean Sea), as well as the transformation of national identities to recognise new and future citizens from immigrant backgrounds.

Since migration and incorporation do not necessarily follow a linear path, and the experience of diversity is place- and time-specific, Italy is facing the same post-Fordist, super-diverse migration and minority-building processes that other European countries are facing today. Nevertheless, these processes are taking place with specific features:

- without a policy legacy from the management of 20th-century migration flows – and even without an explicit immigrant policy;
- with a micro regulation that may be considered at the forefront of localising migration policy in Europe, within a trend of rescaling social and immigrant policy (Kazepov, 2010; Glick Schiller and Çağlar, 2011; Barberis and Pavolini, 2015); and
- using an intercultural approach that – as stated in the first point – is not based on a retreat from multiculturalism.

In this respect, this chapter contextualises and stresses the consequences of this implicit intercultural incorporation model by placing it in the frame of recent neoassimilationist policy trends (Joppke and Morowska, 2003; Ambrosini and Boccagni, 2016). The hypothesis is that interculturalism in practice is not a consistent approach, since it includes different ways of framing diversity. In general, interculturalism is often presented as a consistent policy puzzle, which rejects 'traditional' European models of integration, whether assimilationist or multiculturalist, in favour of a 'middle ground'. This middle ground is even considered – both in national policy documents and the literature (Mincu et al, 2011) – to be a specific Italian contribution to the international debate on incorporation policies. My argument here is, however, that the middle ground is not so much in the middle and that it is a form of assimilationism, for example, through an implicit subordination of immigrant rights and life chances via the discourse on 'social cohesion'.

The chapter starts with a description of migration processes in Italy and Milan and then moves on to analyse immigration and immigrant policy, based on a literature review, analysis of policy documents and interviews with policy-makers and stakeholders at national and local levels. In the third section we focus on two local measures targeting new generations from an immigrant background as examples of the resulting piecemeal intercultural incorporation model in Italy:[1] symbolic citizenship and a local dedicated information desk. These examples are aimed at showing how 'second generations' challenge the boundaries of the Italian nation-state and require a rethinking of national and local identity, while at the same time producing local answers that are not particularly consistent. The final section discusses the potential long-term negative consequences for the incorporation of minorities from an immigrant background.

Migration in Italy

Background data at the national level

According to the National Institute of Statistics, Italy had 5 million foreign residents in 2015. If non-resident regular stayers and undocumented migrants are added, an estimate of 6 million foreigners (9% of the population) can be made (ISMU, 2015), while foreigners who have achieved Italian citizenship are estimated to number almost 1.2 million.[2] Foreigners numbered 1.5 million in 2005 and less than 400,000 according to the 1991 census. Even though the economic crisis slowed down new entries, these numbers are the outcome of a steep growth, which in the last 15 years was paralleled in Western Europe only by Spain and Ireland.[3] Migration changed while growing: from temporary stayers during journeys toward Continental Europe to labour migrants; from labour migrants to permanent stayers; and from permanent stayers to naturalised minorities. There has also been a gender rebalancing, partly due to some feminised flows (for example, from Eastern Europe) and partly due to family reunifications: at first, the number of minors grew (they are now one-fifth of total foreign residents) and then also new-borns. More than 60 per cent of non-Italian minors in Italy are born in Italy, and almost 20 per cent of new-borns have a foreign parent (UNAR, 2013). At the same time, the origins of migration flows have changed. In 1991, immigration was mainly from Morocco, Tunisia and the Philippines. Ten years later, Albanians, Romanians and Chinese migrants were top of the list. Nowadays, Romania is the first country of origin, and Ukraine has entered the top five. These trends have resulted in a remarkable diversity of immigrant groups. While new flows arrived, the older ones settled down: nowadays, two-thirds of non-European Union (EU) holders of permits of stay have been in Italy for five years or more (UNAR, 2013).

Immigration to Italy is mostly labour migration, with features that place it within a 'Mediterranean' model (King, 2000): a high share of undocumented stayers and unskilled, precarious and informal labour market insertion,[4] especially in agriculture and services, including family welfare. Yet Italy is in a more advanced phase of the migration transition (Baldwin-Edwards, 2012, p 150) than other Southern European countries, since immigrants in Italy are also employed in industrial small businesses, consistent with Italy's manufacturing specialisation. Immigrant employment has been disproportionately hit by the economic crisis. As a reserve army of labour, immigrants have been the first to be expelled from the labour market and from standard jobs. The crisis had more of the same effect, with further vulnerability accumulating in labour conditions. This has significantly widened the gap between immigrants and natives in terms of poverty and material deprivation. Eurostat shows that Italy is among the EU countries with the highest share of adults at risk of poverty and social exclusion – both for nationals (25.8%) and for foreigners (48.2%) – and also has one of the widest gaps between the first and second groups.[5]

At the same time, Italy is an important Mediterranean entry door for refugees and asylum-seekers, especially when sociopolitical crises and wars hit surrounding areas: this happened during the Balkan crises in the 1990s, and is happening now. Over 150,000 migrants have been arriving annually in Southern Italy in the last three years from countries like Syria, Eritrea, Somalia, Nigeria, the Gambia, Mali and Egypt (SPRAR, 2015). Even though labour and refugee flows can be separated from an analytical and policy point of view, they overlay and blur in the public and political debate, setting the tone of emergency and security-based responses.

...and at the local level: Milan

The research presented here focuses on the city of Milan, one of the first, largest and most diversified immigration hubs in the country, with a long tradition of policy initiatives (not rarely with an assimilationist stance) and multicultural grassroots activism (IRER, 1994; Alietti, 1998; Caponio, 2010). This city currently has 3.2 million inhabitants in the metropolitan administrative area and 1.3 million in the municipality. Of them, 13.1 per cent of residents in the metropolitan area and 17.4 per cent in the municipality are non-Italian citizens who have come from many different countries. The Philippines, Egypt, China, Peru, Sri Lanka, Ecuador, Ukraine and Morocco are the top eight countries of origin, totalling 70 per cent of all foreign residents in the municipality. This migration-related diversity is changing quickly, as data from the municipal civil registry show:[6] in recent years, the share of naturalised foreigners has grown substantially.[7] Almost 30 per cent of new-borns have foreign parents and one foreign resident out of four is a minor. A relevant share of new foreign residents is actually made up of Italy-born children whose parents do not have Italian citizenship. In addition, 45 per cent of foreign residents in Milan have been living there for 10 years or more.

The crisis has also hit some groups hard in Milan, starting with migrants and youth: the unemployment rate among foreigners was just 6 per cent in 2007, but grew to 20 per cent in 2012-13 (Menonna and Blangiardo, 2014). The youth unemployment rate skyrocketed to 34.5 per cent in 2013 (it was well under 20% in the mid-2000s). Thus, youngsters from an immigrant background combine two highly vulnerable conditions. This issue has become increasingly relevant due to the rise of generations of hyphenated, 'new' Italians (Andall, 2002; Colombo et al, 2009): people from immigrant backgrounds who were born and/or grew up in Italy, yet who are often excluded from Italian citizenship due to a restrictive naturalisation law (Pastore, 2004; Tintori, 2013). 'Italians without citizenship' (to use the name of an activist group of youth from an immigrant background) are struggling to gain public and institutional recognition (Parati, 2005; Ricucci, 2015).

Immigration policy in Italy

Compared to other national models of integration – which are well known in the academic literature – the Italian incorporation policy model can be defined as late and blurred. Many scholars (Calavita, 2005; Caponio and Graziano, 2011; Peixoto et al, 2012) maintain that it is based more on the accumulation of inconsistent practices than on a clear design. This also leads to implementation problems and to an inadequate legal framework in which to grant rights.

Immigration was not really an issue in the Italian political debate until the 1990s. From then on, it became a hot political cleavage: a heated debate resulted in emergency solutions rather than a long-term, shared immigration agenda. The political and media discourses towards immigration are often blaming and exclusionary, usually associated with media hype over undocumented migration and/or crime, and influence law enforcement and the actual practices related to diversity and immigration. For instance, when the most important Italian immigration law was passed in 1998, naturalisation norms and voting rights were left out as a response to a criminalising media campaign (Zincone, 2011). Thus, policies for recognition – and, not rarely, policies for equity – have often been limited by a control agenda (Grillo and Pratt, 2002). At the same time, the policy agenda has also been steered by an advocacy coalition that focuses on humanitarian claims (expressed by non-governmental organisations [NGOs], the Catholic Church and trade unions) and on functionalist perspectives (carried by pro-business social and political actors) (Zincone, 2011). Civil society and market actors have contributed to incorporation practices by providing support, inter-group contact and (subordinate) labour market participation.

Incorporation policies have been affected by a general weakness in the structuring of the Italian welfare state. The access of foreigners to social rights had already been granted in the 1980s and was reaffirmed with the Immigration Law 1998. Migrants and citizens were equalised in their access to the labour market, education, health and (contributory) subsidies; however, in practice, equal access did not follow. Scant expenditure on welfare services, together with territorially variable provisions, affected newcomers in welfare, while a nativist approach prevailed in the institutional regulation and practice (for example, in access to many cash allowances for families and individuals with disabilities as well as in access to public sector jobs). The effort to exclude migrants from some welfare provisions – dismissed by many courts – has been revived in unlawful but poorly contrasted practices enacted by national and local welfare institutions (Bracci and Valzania, 2015). The outcome of this institutional regulation is a system that considers migrants temporary in terms of immigration policy, while granting them formal rights in some welfare fields, although with a limited and territorially variable implementation. This is a veritable denizenship, also given the difficult naturalisation regulations.

Does this comprise an Italian model of integration? If we think about the grand narratives dominating the European debate (British race relations, the French *intégration républicaine*), the answer is probably no. However, we can see a 'mode' consistent with Italy's political culture and welfare state making: national measures are implemented inconsistently and common features develop more by chance than by design, through the accumulation of (assumedly) successful local practices, EU influences and court judgments. As a consequence, this 'mode' can be defined as implicit and indirect (since it is not based on clear rights and shared principles) as well as subaltern (since it does not prioritise incorporation into the agenda for an immigrant policy) (Ambrosini, 2001; Calavita, 2005; Caponio and Graziano, 2011). The lack of proper institutional management underlies an incorporation process taking place at the micro level through local interactions. As the state has often left local authorities alone in facing migration-related challenges, local policy networks have acquired a relevant role (Campomori and Caponio, 2013). Hence, local arenas are the main context for incorporation policy and practice, along with poorly coordinated and ineffective multilevel governance (with poor chances for local initiatives to 'scale up' and poor top-down implementation of national measures).

Representations of diversity: Policy discourses and practice between national and local levels

Methodology and data

In this section the representations of immigrant-related diversity portrayed in the national and local policy-making arenas are analysed. The inconsistency of the Italian mode of incorporation – assumed above – will be tested first by analysing discourses on diversity at the national and local levels, as well how this informs initiatives in the field of migrant incorporation. To reduce the complexity of reconstructing the whole discourse on immigrant-related diversity, the focus is on a specific issue: the incorporation of new generations from an immigrant background. The choice of this issue is due to its growing relevance in the public debate (at the beginning of this chapter) and its prospective features, as a discourse that may influence the incorporation and future chances of a relevant share of youth living in Italy.

The analysis presented here is based on two sets of data (Barberis and Kazepov, 2012; Barberis et al, 2017), which include policy documents and interviews with stakeholders. Policy documents refer to the documents released by policy-making institutions and stakeholders. They were selected by browsing the websites of relevant institutions and by asking relevant stakeholders. I analysed 125 documents (including policy strategy documents, media documents, specific projects and expert policy analyses). For a more thorough analysis, eight were selected as particularly relevant.[8] Interviewees were selected among relevant policy-makers, experts and stakeholders at the national and local levels. I used 35 interviews (25 interviewees operate at the local level and 10 at the national level), which included 9 key officials, 16 policy-makers (including managers of public and private local initiatives) and 10 other stakeholders and experts (mainly from civil society organisations).

I analysed the research data using critical discourse analysis, whose focus is on how problems are defined and addressed, which solutions are considered, and within which ideological frameworks. Such a focus is aimed at disentangling the mechanisms that produce and reproduce unequal social relations, and at connecting agents and underlying social structures (Fairclough, 1992; Jessop et al, 2008).

The 'intercultural' buzzword

The lack of an explicit diversity agenda – a feature of the Italian mode of incorporation mentioned earlier – is quite clear in the multiple representations of diversity provided by the relevant interviewed stakeholders. Considering Syrett and Sepulveda's (2012) types of diversity policy agendas, we can find almost every approach to diversity being conflated in the 'intercultural' policy discourses.[9] For example, I focus on two of the most explicit strategic documents issued by Italian governments – 'The Italian way for intercultural schools and the integration of foreign pupils', issued by the Ministry of Education in 2007 under a centre-left government, and the 'Plan for integration within security. Identity and encounter', released in 2010 under a centre-right government. They both distance the Italian way from international assimilationist and multicultural models – or at least, from a stereotypical and simplified version of such models that is not based on specific examples, in which assimilationism is equated to cultural conformity and multiculturalism (especially in the second document) is referred to as a 'juxtaposed coexistence' of cultures living side by side with limited contact. Nevertheless, the arguments in the two documents differ partially – the first is more integrationist, the second is more assimilationist:

> Choosing an intercultural perspective means we limit ourselves neither to assimilation strategies nor to targeted measures for immigrant pupils.... The Italian way to interculture keeps together the ability to recognize and appreciate the differences and the search for social cohesion, with a new idea of citizenship fitting the present-day pluralism, where a special attention is given to building up a convergence towards common values. (document 6)

> We are suspicious of a cultural approach where the encounter takes place among social, ethnic and religious categories, ideologically freezing out individual responsibility in being responsible for the encounter with the other.... To build up a long-term civic engagement, in a context of growing social pressures, we can just rediscover in our past its basic conditions, revaluing our roots.... This vision, which we call Open Identity, ... overcomes, on the one hand, the multicultural approach (according to it, different cultures can live together by staying juxtaposed and perfectly separated)

and, on the other hand, the assimilationist approach, which aims at neutralising traditions in the society, in favour of the hosting one. (document 1)

The literature has quite a shared definition of assimilation – a model 'separating persons from qualities' (Alexander, 2001, p 243), in which group identities are denied and individuals are included as long as they get rid of their (minority) backgrounds. Yet it is often clear that assimilation is not a way of accommodating diversity in practice, and that it must to be mixed with other models of incorporation (Castles, 1995). The definition of multicultural/pluralist models is much more articulated (see, for example, Hartmann and Gerteis, 2005; Koopmans et al, 2005). Usually, they are based on the recognition of minority groups and cultural difference, if in different manners: models are defined according to factors like the role of the state, the rules on citizenship as a proxy of belonging principles and the political stance they assume (for example, the debate on liberal and communitarian multiculturalism that involved authors like Parekh, 2000 and Kymlicka, 1995).

In these models, interculturalism was often not clearly defined, and the debate focused more on how much it is influenced by multicultural or assimilationist models (Taylor et al, 2012; see also the debate following Meer and Modood, 2012 in the same issue of the *Journal of Intercultural Studies*).

For the purposes of this chapter, and considering that the reference documents that made the Italian 'intercultural' model more explicit are from the educational field, I utilise the taxonomy of multiculturalism and multicultural education suggested by Kincheloe and Steinberg (1997), namely, the features of the Italian model resemble their description of 'conservative multiculturalism', which is aimed at incorporating minorities without challenging the power structure in society, implicitly defining an invisible norm that reaffirms the hegemonic position of national majorities. Social cohesion and majority cultural transmission are considered a prominent value. Diversity is admitted and tolerated, but is considered as an add-on to the dominant culture (McLaren, 1995, p 49).

The literature on conservative multiculturalism helps to critically consider both the acknowledgement of diversity as well as its asymmetries, and the apparently contradictory mix of non-policy, culturalist connotations and pluralist stances. Framing interculturalism as conservative multiculturalism helps in challenging interculturalism as a middle ground. Two issues are relevant here. On the one hand, diversity is accepted and accommodated in the public space, with the aim of avoiding culturally based conflicts.[10] On the other hand, political anxiety about security and law and order issues leads to punitive and revanchist measures (for example, local regulations to contrast immigrants' gatherings, business and the like; see Ambrosini, 2013), with the aim of reducing the visibility of diversity in public spaces (Briata, 2014). In particular, most governmental actors see diversity as a social risk to avoid. Perceived social cohesion problems (for example, the isolation and inequality of immigrant groups, nuisance and deviance in neighbourhoods with a high share of immigrant inhabitants) and the risks of ghettoisation – as mentioned by most interviewees – are considered the results of diversity that need to be addressed through an intercultural approach. That is, diversity can find room in the public space (as in multicultural models) but mainly as an individual stance, while the visibility of group diversity has to be attuned with the concerns (and cultural characteristics) of mainstream society (as in assimilationist models). For example, mainstream media and policy-makers often consider the requests to build mosques or *paifangs* (Chinese-style arch gateways) and the visibility of minorities from an immigrant background (Chinese or Arab store signs, Muslim prayers in public spaces, and so on) to be worrisome. To summarise, diversity is accepted if it is not too much (too visible, too diverse, too disadvantaged…):

> 'Diversity is a problem beyond certain thresholds. There's an effort to look at immigration as an opportunity, but it causes problems that cannot be kept hidden.' (key official, housing policy area, Municipality of Milan)

> 'The Italian solution is not a multiculturalism in the Anglo-Saxon way, that would allow a Chinatown. The Italian intercultural way doesn't love ghettoisation; it's more about interaction in diversity than about a multiculturalism that doesn't cross breed.' (key official, international affairs area, Municipality of Milan)

Different discourses on diversity do not build up an explicit policy strategy, instead swaying between multicultural and assimilationist leanings. Nevertheless, a 'consistent inconsistency' emerges incrementally: even though the interviewees may have complained about the lack of a national or local strategy of incorporation and found it hard to define a clear position, most of them shared common references. These were visible in the quotes mentioned earlier, in the refusal of other national models of incorporation as well as in the ambivalent acknowledgement of diversity and attention to social cohesion.

Such a model can have some pros, as maintained by scholars who are starting to consider interculturalism in a more positive way, as a pragmatic correction of multiculturalism (Taylor-Gooby and Waite, 2014). Its strength lies in the flexibility of arrangements (cherry picking from international models) and in the compression of conflicts (thanks to local accommodations and adaptations). An example can come from measures concerning the Islamic veil. Italy had its *affair du voile* – even more than one (concerning pictures in documents, veils in public and private workplaces, for example). None of them peaked in national debates: they were managed locally – in cases by tribunals – and were later assumed with regulations ranking low in the hierarchy of sources in the national law (see Lorenzetti, 2010). That is, they were not discussed in Parliament.

Yet the lack of consistency between assimilationist and multicultural stances may also be considered a weak point. One of the main risks of the Italian intercultural model is its inconsistency. As underlined by Bertolani and Perocco (2013), assimilation and multicultural elements in the Italian intercultural model lack congruent measures. A functional assimilation usually requires policies to contrast discrimination and inequalities (including naturalisation rules), so that minorities 'giving up' their identity can become part of the majority (Castles, 1995) – and this is not the case of Italy, which has weak and young anti-discrimination and equality policies as well as a tough citizenship law (see Huddleston et al, 2015). On the other hand, pluralist models usually recognise minorities: even though ethno-national labelling is frequent in Italy (Calavita, 2005), this is not matched with extensive recognition policies for immigrant groups (Barberis et al, 2017).

The rescaling of immigration policy adds up to this weakness: the territorialisation process has turned into a local fragmentation of incorporation measures.[11]

> 'A municipality can hardly affect issues concerning rights: from an administrative point of view, we can just act as a stopgap; from a political point of view we can just lobby on the competent institutional level.... At the national level, nothing happens. There's something going on in some cities.' (key official, social policy area, Municipality of Milan)

The devolution of policy regulation supports a differentiated treatment of diversity, not only through the classical national channel of access to citizenship, but also through local regulations of denizenship pertaining to labour, welfare and housing, and cultural rights. We can call this a postcode-based civic stratification. Morris (2003) defines civic stratification as an unequal and nationally variable system of rights based on a formal and informal differentiated granting of rights per category of individuals. Among the informal national dimensions of civic stratification, the intranational variation of rights is relevant. As a consequence, local initiatives and practice have a relevant role in framing national approaches to migration – in the intersection between economic (for example, housing and labour markets) and institutional processes (for example, in agenda setting and the accessibility of rights).

The 'intercultural' buzzword: The intercultural model at the local level

Based on the analysis discussed earlier, Italy is characterised by an implicit conservative multiculturalism that is mostly produced at the local level. The incremental dimension of this model is also visible in the case of Milan: even though it has been dealing with migration and incorporation issues earlier than most municipalities in Italy, there is still an unclear definition of diversity- and immigration-related policy targets.

For example, the pluralisation and diversification of society via migration have not been thematised in local policy documents or by the interviewed key informants. Therefore, the local strategy has emerged implicitly – not from strategic plans but from the undeclared priorities in small-scale initiatives. The interviewed key officials and policy-makers found it hard to build up an explicit and reflexive discourse on diversity. Most of them were keener to present projects and exemplary cases rather than to define a broad set of priorities in diversity relations and management. This approach has had ripple effects on implemented initiatives (including the ones analysed later): the lack of an explicit strategy is matched with limited prioritisation and resources (Grossmann et al, 2015):

> 'Local policies do not grasp reality, they are just announced.... Politics seems to use a discourse open to diversity now, but has no intention of putting its money where its mouth is.' (stakeholder, policy strategist, social policy area, Milan)

Interviews at the city level confirm the use of a range of different discourses on immigrants' incorporation. Even though the interviewed policy-makers and stakeholders often shared a view of interculturalism being more pluralist than national counterparts, they usually consider diversity as a social risk that can also carry some opportunities. The risky side includes inequality and the concentration of disadvantaged groups. Opportunities are related to the contribution that diversity can make to social cohesion and the local economy in mixed neighbourhoods: "In the new local government diversity is not contrasted to normalcy. The multiplicity is a richness that contributes to the sense of belonging to the urban community" (policy-maker, cultural policy area, Municipality of Milan).

Nonetheless, we can also see elements of conservative multiculturalism among local policy-makers and stakeholders. When neighbourhood diversity is considered too 'visible' in the public space, it is considered more as a danger than as a challenge. The key informants predominantly and implicitly supported a model in which diversity is accepted but not encouraged. Pluralism should be tempered by an attention to social cohesion – and social cohesion usually and implicitly refers to the worries of natives and to the need to blend minority specificity by mixing minorities with the majority (even though not usually to the point of supporting assimilation):

> 'We wondered whether to do specific initiatives targeting this issue [cultural diversity] or not; and whether to give money just to immigrant firms or not. And our answer is: immigrants in Milan have equal opportunities. They can access all the calls we do.' (key official, innovation policy area, Municipality of Milan)

> 'Emphasising the ethnic features of a neighbourhood is risky; our bet for the future is to avoid spaces of belonging of individual communities but have mobile and intertwined communities.' (policy-maker, cultural policy area, Municipality of Milan)

> 'We may see two options: one is the ethnicisation, creating a Chinatown. But this option was not appreciated by the inhabitants of the neighbourhood, neither Italian nor Chinese. Perhaps the latter just wanted to avoid conflicts, and self-censored themselves? Don't know'. (key official, international affairs area, Municipality of Milan)

In this respect, even though this research was carried out after a relevant local political turn (the municipal elections were won by a leftist coalition after 18 years of centre-right administrations, which had quite an exclusionary vision; see Foot, 1999; Verga, 2016), local initiatives and relevant stakeholders maintained their adherence to ambivalence to the Italian intercultural model outlined earlier, contributing to its micro-level 'inconsistent consistency':

> '… the commitment was to revamp integration policy through participation about what to do for integration and how to do it. One year of work, many ideas.… The problem is that it didn't become actual policy, since at a given point we understood that there was no money. This means that the administration doesn't consider it as a priority.' (stakeholder, policy strategist, social policy area, Milan)

The interviewed policy-makers and stakeholders often associated ethnicisation[12] with 'ghettoisation', while *mixité* and the promotion of dialogue were to be supported. The frequent use of the concept of 'ghetto' was not so much associated to poverty and stigmatisation as it was with an 'unrelated diversity'. Interestingly enough, as already noted by Koopmans et al (2005) in other national contexts, claims from minority members also tend to share this common frame. Key informants from an immigrant background showed that the conservative-multicultural discourse is quite pervasive, even when entailing a subordination of minorities. Examples include the interviews with the Milanese branches of two well known and emerging organisations of new generations from an immigrant background – the G2 Network and Associna (Zinn, 2011; Marsden, 2014). The interviewed 'second generations'[13] representatives saw themselves as key actors in building a new representation of diversity in Italy. For instance, they challenged the idea that diversity is related to immigration, since they are not immigrants themselves, having grown up in Italy.[14] Nevertheless, their pluralist concept of diversity took on conservative-multicultural elements, by trying to balance minority and majority identities while focusing on social cohesion through social contact: "Second generations are a kind of bridge, having social circles larger than kinship groups: the city, the society as a whole, the media … avoiding isolation is a primary goal" (vice president of an advocacy association of second generations' advocacy associations, Milan). In this respect, their campaign for citizenship reform is not just about rights, but about belonging: "*Ius soli* is necessary not because now you are limiting my rights but because you are limiting my sense of belonging. The state doesn't allow you to feel Italian; it denies you" (member of an advocacy association of second generations' advocacy associations, Milan). Hence, even for actors praising the recognition of minorities, the visibility of diversity should be subordinated to social cohesion: accommodation can take place if diversity is limited and faded in with native identities. In line with the conservative-multicultural approach, they complain about the lack of social cohesion more than they do the lack of recognition.

An example: Measures for the social participation of second generations

Two examples of local initiatives targeting second generations are now analysed, showing the inconsistencies and contradictions of both the intercultural frame (as outlined earlier) and the multilevel governance of immigrant policies. The focus is on two initiatives: (1) the issuing of symbolic citizenship at the local level (as a way to argue against the exclusion from naturalisation of new generations from immigrant backgrounds); and (2) the G.Lab, a liaison office that targeted new generations from an immigrant background in Milan, to acknowledge and recognise their role in local society. These two initiatives are interesting because they involve multilevel governance – the first one lobbies for a national reform, while the second was funded with European resources managed by the national government – and target the transformation of immigrant-related diversity, by promoting new social positions for 'second generations' through their naturalisation and inclusion in the national and local identity, and by making them visible as a specific social group.

Symbolic citizenship

Access to citizenship has recently become an issue in the Italian political debate as well as in relation to a national campaign promoted by trade unions, advocacy associations and immigrant communities. The campaign is called '*L'Italia sono anch'io*' ['*I'm Italy too*'] and is aimed at easing the naturalisation of new generations from an immigrant background (Degler, 2014). The appointment of the first black Italian minister, Cécile Kyenge, attracted attention to this issue, as did the racist backlash to the increasing visibility of Italians from minority backgrounds (Merrill, 2015). Their visibility in the public space has received mixed public attention. The city of Milan, together with 245 other Italian municipalities, grants honorary or symbolic citizenship to children from immigration backgrounds who do not meet the requirements for naturalisation. This symbolic measure was supported by UNICEF Italy and the National Association of Municipalities, and was enacted by city councils and advocacy groups to raise public and political awareness of the denizenship situation of many minors and to lobby for the approval of a new citizenship bill at the National Parliament. Even though this initiative may be contested as potentially raising expectations of naturalisation that cannot easily be met, it is an example of a local recognition policy aimed at changing the national political and public agenda on migration. As two interviewees put it: "The symbolic value is what it is – our participation [as a second generations' advocacy association] was just aimed at refocusing public attention to achieve a more concrete result [the reform of the citizenship law]" (member of an advocacy association of second generations' advocacy association, Milan); "We made a campaign called 'A time window for your rights': all of the entitled 17-year-old persons received a letter to inform them about the naturalisation requirements. Milan was a trailblazer in this, because now a decree compels municipalities to do this" (key official, social policy area, Municipality of Milan). The former mayor of Milan, Giuliano Pisapia, has also been the national spokesperson for the '*I'm Italy too*' campaign to reform the citizenship law, "and Milan is the city that collected the highest number of signatures in Italy to support this reform" (key official, social policy area, Municipality of Milan).

For our general argument, it is interesting that such a pluralist recognition measure can also been reconnected with a conservative-multicultural perspective, with the refusal of targeted ('ghettoising', as most of our interviewees would perceive it) initiatives. In this respect, a key official in Milan's Social Policy Department stated:

> '… we considered the issue: is symbolic citizenship an "exclusionary inclusion"? You separate those with immigrant backgrounds from the others. Therefore, we decided to call them all [including Italian classmates] in a public event. There's a risk in dividing groups, and our goal is always cultural – supporting open mindedness and shared participation.' (key official, social policy area, Municipality of Milan)

An office for the second generations: The experience of G.Lab[15]

G.Lab was conceived as an information desk for 'second generations'. G.Lab was opened by the Municipality of Milan in collaboration with the G2 Network (mentioned earlier), thanks to European funds managed by the national government.[16] The municipality provided facilities, while G2 Network provided the staff. G.Lab started in March 2013, and the experiment came to an end in December 2013, although with the intention to extend its duration. As a front office, it was aimed at supporting youth and families from immigrant backgrounds, teachers, social workers and other relevant stakeholders. The goal was to provide information and guidance, and improve the access of 'second generations' to city offices and services (for example, youth initiatives, study and job opportunities) and to support them in naturalisation procedures.

As a lab, its aim was to promote diversity and social mix as a value, that is, by providing a place to discuss and share the condition of having a mixed identity and strengthening the collaboration between the municipality and G2 Network in organising events, projects and initiatives. G.Lab was located within the Informagiovani (Youth Information Centre) in the very heart of the city, to avoid "ghettoising targeting" and to provide a "symbolic impact, giving a new life and a new image" to Informagiovani itself (as stated by an interviewed key official from the Mayor's Office). This initiative was aimed at strengthening social cohesion by acknowledging and legitimising the public role of new generations from an immigrant background, to support their naturalisation and the value of their diversity as a positive social transformation. In this respect, it was also a space of democratic engagement, since the two partners behind G.Lab – the Municipality of Milan and the G2 Network – campaigned together for a more inclusive national law on citizenship and naturalisation.

G.Lab was based on the idea that diversity should be a constitutive part of the national and local identity – from both legal (support for naturalisation) and social points of view (support for intercultural initiatives). It promoted the naturalisation and recognition of those who are 'Italians de facto, even though not de jure' (Comune di Milano, 2013a, b). G.Lab portrayed one perspective recognising minorities; it is worth emphasising that it did not acknowledge any specific ethno-cultural background. It was not about Albanian-Italians, Moroccan-Italians, Chinese-Italians or the like, but about acknowledging a generational diversity of youngsters from immigrant backgrounds and accommodating their identity within the Italian national and local identities. According to the interviewees, the success of G.Lab was due to its effectiveness in answering the unmet needs of the target population (for example, supporting naturalisation). While it operated, G.Lab was an effective aid for the Municipal Register Office, which was not prepared to provide support to manage the increasing inflow of youths asking for naturalisation. The interviewees maintained that its effectiveness came from two main factors – peer support and a close relationship with the local administration – that increased accessibility and eased problem-solving.

Nonetheless, the interviewees were disappointed since the project came to an end in a way they considered a failure, as the targeted needs persist and were supposed to be met on a long-term basis. Highly promoted and advertised, G.Lab created expectations of long-term, enduring support, yet it was connected to short-term funding and projects: "The problem is the economic sustainability, in a context of retrenchment that affects social initiatives overall. The municipality is relying very much on participation, activism and volunteering – even too much" (member of an advocacy association of second generations' advocacy association, Milan).

This means that the coverage and duration of the service was largely unpredictable, which may sound discouraging: political backing for new generations has not always been matched with the actual prioritisation of resources. Thus, the project can be considered innovative because it provided recognition of new generations from an immigrant background through their direct participation, and promoted mixed identities as part of the local and national identity. This boosted accessibility to rights and the effectiveness of the local administration in answering a need for information and guidance that was largely unmet before. However, the evidence of low prioritisation may be considered a failure – consistent with the informal conservative multiculturalism characterising the national and local immigration policy-making mentioned earlier – since it interrupted the minority recognition process.

Discussion and conclusion

The local initiatives mentioned earlier have a limited scope, as a consequence of limited prioritisation and a lack of explicit, strategic discourses on diversity. In the frame of a conservative multiculturalism, the visibility of diversity is somehow disturbing, and the relations with minorities are ambivalent. The swaying discourse on diversity has produced short-term measures unable to cope systematically with minorities' needs, with the risk of producing disillusion and social detachment among minorities.

The local and national intercultural discourses I have analysed show an implicit consistency in their focus on social cohesion concerns: minorities have to adapt and lower their expectations of equal participation, especially when their diversity is too 'visible'. Diversity seems to be considered acceptable when it is not related to public visibility and inequality. Rarely is there an appreciation of minorities. While often presented as a pragmatic and sympathetic welcoming policy strategy, interculturalism may legitimate exclusion and subordination.

This inconsistency is magnified by weak coordination between national and local policy: claims from new generations from an immigrant background have found a (feeble) voice at the local level, but have found it hard to scale up, institutionalise and find room in the national policy arena. The two case initiatives mentioned earlier show that the targeting of emerging diversity issues is inconsistent and short term. When relevant and new stances – such as those mentioned earlier, expressed by new generations from an immigrant background – come to light, intercultural answers look particularly inconsistent. Local responses are not enough to manage emerging issues, and national responses are weak due to low prioritisation and the ambiguity between assimilationist and multicultural positions.

In this respect, the intercultural approach – at least in the form of conservative multiculturalism, as implemented in the Italian case – may not be the positive solution to the problems of assimilationist and multicultural models that some scholars and practitioners maintain it to be. As a policy implication, a more aware intercultural approach should probably not dismiss assimilationist and multicultural practices, and it should refocus its attention on encounters, dialogue and intergroup contact along with a critical assessment of the conditions favouring contact, including equality and anti-discrimination tools.

Notes

[1] The research published here is based on funding received from the European Union's (EU) Seventh Framework Programme for research, technological development and demonstration under Grant Agreements No 243868 (GOETE) and No 319970 (DIVERCITIES). The views expressed in this chapter are the sole responsibility of the author and do not necessarily reflect the views of the European Commission.

[2] This estimate has been produced by the author, based on naturalisations surveyed from the 2011 census (Istat, 2013) and updated with yearly data from municipal registries (available on the website demo.istat.it).

[3] Author's own calculation based on Eurostat indicator migr_pop2ctz.

[4] Foreign workers in Italy account for more than 10% of the workforce but 35% of unskilled workers; see Saraceno et al (2013).

[5] See the EU-SILC-based indicators ilc_peps05 and ilc_peps06 at http://ec.europa.eu/eurostat/data/database

[6] See demo.istat.it and dati.comune.milano.it

[7] In 2015, some 2.7% of foreign residents in Milan became Italian citizens – a quite relevant share given the strong legal constraints to naturalisation and the much lower figures in previous years.

[8] (1) 'Plan for integration within security. Identity and encounter', issued by the Ministry of Labour and Welfare, the Ministry of Interior and the Ministry of Education (August 2010); (2) 'Framework agreement for the implementation of measures concerning social integration of migrant people', issued by the Ministry of Labour and Welfare and the Italian Network of Intercultural Cities (September 2013); (3) 'Programme Roma, Sinti and Travellers 2012-2015. Guidelines for a proposal', issued by the Municipality of Milan (July 2012); (4) 'Plan for the welfare development of the Municipality of Milan 2012-2014', issued by the Department of Social and Health Policy, Municipality of Milan (September 2012); (5) 'Programme of the candidate for Mayor Giuliano Pisapia', issued by the Committee Pisapiaxmilano (May 2011); (6) 'The Italian way for the intercultural school and the integration of foreign pupils', issued by the Ministry of Education (October 2007); (7) 'Instructions and suggestions for the integration of the pupils without Italian citizenship', circular letter 2 issued by the Ministry of Education (January 2010); and (8) 'Parliamentary inquiry on the problems related to the inclusion of non Italian pupils in the Italian education system. Final document', issued by the Chamber of Deputies – Commission VII (Culture, Science and Education) (January 2011).

[9] A partial exception is education. Interculturalism in Italy was first theorised in the field of education. As an institution in which diversity has become more visible (due to the significant increase in pupils from immigrant backgrounds, especially in the 2000s), the educational system has been at the forefront of the debate on an Italian model of incorporation, and is one of the few fields in which explicit strategic documents have been released (Favaro and Luatti, 2004; Liddicoat and Diaz, 2008).

[10] A recent example comes from the European debate on banning Islamic veils. Then Italian Minister of the Interior, Angelino Alfano, argued against the ban, considering it a 'provocation that strengthens extremists' and as contrary to the freedom of worship (*La Repubblica*, 18 August 2016).

[11] This is part of a general problem of coordination in the Italian multilevel governance (see Kazepov, 2010).

[12] That is, the ascription of social phenomena and individual behaviours to 'othering' categories; see Murji and Solomos (2005).

[13] I use 'second generations' in the plural and in inverted commas since this is the more common use in the Italian scientific and public debate. Hence, I use it as an emic concept. Differently from the main strand of international literature, in Italy the concept is used in the plural to acknowledge its internal diversity. Without specification (none of our interviewees or policy documents uses 'second generation immigrants' or 'second generation of immigration') and in inverted commas it is used to acknowledge that the concept is contested and that 'second generations' are not immigrants, but at the same time they are not fully included in other categories, like 'New Italians' or 'first-generation Italians', since many of them are

excluded from citizenship. In this respect, the concept is also used by advocates of citizenship reform as a working concept, with a caveat about its inaccuracy.

[14] Therefore they are dissatisfied with the label 'second generations' and are trying to spread a new self-representation, for example, as 'new Italians' or 'first-generation Italians'.

[15] 'G' stands for Generations and refers to new generations from an immigrant background.

[16] G.Lab was funded by the Ministry of Labour and Welfare within an experimental programme agreed with the National Association of Italian Municipalities and the Municipalities of Rome, Milan and Prato. The aim was to assess immigrants' needs, produce good practices to meet them, and build a kit to transfer good practices to four other 'test' municipalities. Youth from immigrant backgrounds were identified as one of the target groups (Ministero del Lavoro e delle Politiche sociali, 2012-14).

References

Alexander, J.C. (2001) 'Theorizing the "modes of incorporation"', *Sociological Theory*, 19(3), 237-49.

Alietti, A. (1998) *La convivenza difficile: coabitazione interetnica in un quartiere di Milano*, Torino: l'Harmattan Italia.

Ambrosini, M. (2001) *La fatica di integrarsi*, Bologna: il Mulino.

Ambrosini, M. (2013) '"We are against a multi-ethnic society": Policies of exclusion at the urban level in Italy', *Ethnic and Racial Studies*, 36(1), 136-55.

Ambrosini, M. and Boccagni, M. (2016) 'Urban multiculturalism beyond the "backlash"', *Journal of Intercultural Studies*, 3(1), 35-53.

Andall, J. (2002) 'Second-generation attitude? Africa-Italians in Milan', *Journal of Ethnic and Migration Studies*, 28(3), 389-407.

Baldwin-Edwards, M. (2012) 'The Southern European model of immigration', in M. Okólski (ed) *European immigrations*, Amsterdam: Amsterdam University Press, 149-57.

Barberis, E. and Kazepov, Y. (2012) *National Report for WP7 – Italy*, GOETE Deliverable, 15.

Barberis, E. and Pavolini, E. (2015) 'Settling outside gateways', *Sociologica*, 2.

Bertolani, B. and Perocco, F. (2013) 'Religious belonging and new ways of being "Italian" in the self-perception of second-generation immigrants in Italy', in R. Blanes and J. Mapril (eds) *Sites and politics of religious diversity in Southern Europe*, Leiden: Brill, 93-114.

Barberis, E., Angelucci, A., Jepson, R. and Kazepov, Y. (2017) *DIVERCITIES: Dealing with urban diversity. The case of Milan*, Utrecht: Utrecht University.

Bracci, F. and Valzania, A. (2015) 'Hidden selectivity. Irregular migrants and access to socio-health services in a heated local context', *Cambio*, 5(10), 141-8.

Briata, P. (2014) *Spazio urbano e immigrazione in Italia*, Milan: Franco Angeli.

Calavita, K. (2005) *Immigrants at the margins*, Cambridge: Cambridge University Press.

Campomori, F. and Caponio, T. (2013) 'Competing frames of immigrant integration in the EU: Geographies of social inclusion in Italian regions', *Policy Studies*, 34(2), 162-79.

Caponio, T. (2010) 'Grassroots multiculturalism in Italy: Milan, Bologna and Naples compared', in T. Caponio and M. Borkert (eds) *The local dimension of migration policymaking*, Amsterdam: Amsterdam University Press, 57-84.

Caponio, T. and Graziano, P.R. (2011) 'Towards a security-oriented migration policy model? Evidence from the Italian case', in E. Carmel, A. Cerami and T. Papadopoulos (eds) *Migration and welfare in the new Europe. Social protection and the challenges of integration*, Bristol: Policy Press,105-20.

Castles, S. (1995) 'How nation-states respond to immigration and ethnic diversity', *Journal of Ethnic and Migration Studies*, 21(3), 293-308.

Colombo, E. and Rebughini, P. (2012) *Children of immigrants in a globalized world*, Basingstoke: Palgrave Macmillan.

Colombo, E., Leonini, L. and Rebughini, P. (2009) 'Different but not stranger: Everyday collective identification among adolescent children of immigrants in Italy', *Journal of Ethnic and Migration Studies*, 35(1), 37-59.

Comune di Milano (2013a) 'Cittadinanza. Al via G-Lab, lo sportello delle seconde generazioni di Milano', Press release (http://goo.gl/FFa2aV).

Comune di Milano (2013b) 'Cittadinanza. Assessore Majorino: "Nuove generazioni, milanesi e italiane a tutti gli effetti"', Press release (http://goo.gl/edXeZT).

Degler, E. (2014) *Citizenship campaigns and voter mobilization in Europe. Five case studies*, Brussels: Migration Policy Group.

Fairclough, N. (1992) *Discourse and social change*, Cambridge: Polity Press.

Favaro, G. and Luatti, L. (eds) (2004) *L'intercultural dalla A alla Z*, Milan: Angeli.

Foot, J. (1999) 'Immigration and the city', *Modern Italy*, 4(2), 159-72.

Glick Schiller, N. and Çağlar, A. (eds) (2011) *Locating migration. Rescaling cities and migrants*, Ithaca, NY: Cornell University Press.

Grillo, R. and Pratt, J. (eds) (2002) *The politics of recognizing difference: Multiculturalism Italian-style*, Basingstoke: Ashgate.

Grossmann, K., Barberis, E., Winther Beckman, A., Kullmann, K. and Skovgaard Nielsen, R. (2015) 'Governance arrangements targeting diversity in Europe. How new public management impacts on work social cohesion in different contexts', Paper presented at the RC21 International Conference 'The Ideal City', Urbino, Italy, 27-29 August.

Hartmann, D. and Gerteis, J. (2005) 'Dealing with diversity: Mapping multiculturalism in sociological terms', *Sociological Theory*, 23(2), 218-40.

Huddleston, T., Bilgili, O., Joki, A.-L. and Vankova, Z. (2015) *Migrant Integration Policy Index 2015*, Barcelona/Bruxelles: CIDOB and MPG.

IRER (1994) *Tra due rive. La nuova immigrazione a Milano*, Milan: Angeli.

Ismu (2015) *XXI Rapporto sulle migrazioni in Italia*, Milan: Angeli.

Istat (2013) *Gli stranieri al 15° Censimento della popolazione*, Rome: Istat.

Jessop, B., Fairclough, N. and Wodak, R. (eds) (2008) *Education and the knowledge-based economy in Europe*, Rotterdam: Sense.

Joppke, C. and Morowska, E. (eds) (2003) *Towards assimilation and citizenship*, Basingstoke: Palgrave Macmillan.

Kazepov, Y. (2010) 'Rescaling social policies towards multilevel governance in Europe', in Y. Kazepov (ed) *Rescaling social policies: Towards multilevel governance in Europe*, Farnham: Ashgate, 35-72.

Kincheloe, J.L. and Steinberg, S.R. (1997) *Changing multiculturalism*, London: Open University Press.

King, R. (2000) 'Southern Europe in the changing global map of migration', in R. King, G. Lazaridis and C. Tsardanidis (eds) *Eldorado or fortress?*, London: Macmillan, 3-26.

Koopmans, R., Statham, P., Giugni, M. and Passy, F. (2005) *Contested citizenship*, Minneapolis, MN: University of Minnesota Press.

Kymlicka, W. (1995) *Multicultural citizenship*, Oxford: Oxford University Press.

Liddicoat, A.J. and Diaz, A. (2008) 'Engaging with diversity: The construction of policy for intercultural education in Italy', *Intercultural Education*, 19(2), 137-50.

Lorenzetti, A. (2010) 'Il divieto di indossare "burqa" e "burqini". Che "genere" di ordinanze?', *Le Regioni*, 38(1-2), 349-65.

Marsden, A. (2014) 'Chinese descendants in Italy: Emergence, role and uncertain identity', *Ethnic and Racial Studies*, 37(7), 1239-52.

McLaren, P. (1995) 'White terror and oppositional agency: Towards a critical multiculturalism', in D.T. Goldberg (ed) *Multiculturalisms*, Cambridge: Blackwell, 45-74.

Meer, N. and Modood, T. (2012) 'How does interculturalism contrast with multiculturalism?', *Journal of Intercultural Studies*, 33(2), 175-96.

Mennona, A. and Biangiardo, M. (2014) *L'immigrazione straniera in Province di Milano*, Milan: ISMU-ORIM.

Merrill, H. (2015) 'In other wor(l)ds: Situated intersectionality in Italy', in H. Merrill and L.M. Hoffman (eds) *Spaces of danger*, Athens: University of Georgia Press, 77-99.

Mincu, M.E., Allasia, M. and Pia, F. (2011) 'Uneven equity and Italian interculturalism(s)', *Policy Futures in Education*, 9(1), 88-95.

Ministero del Lavoro e delle Politiche sociali (2012-14) 'La sperimentazione locale. Roma – Milano – Prato' (http://goo.gl/4lMM5n).

Morris, L. (2003) 'Managing contradiction: Civic stratification and migrants' rights', *International Migration Review*, 37(1), 74-100.

Murji, K. and Solomos, J. (2005) 'Introduction. Racialization in theory and practice', in K. Murji and J. Solomos (eds) *Racialization*, Oxford: Oxford University Press, 1-27.

Parati, G. (2005) *Migration Italy*, Toronto, ON: University of Toronto Press.

Parekh, B. (2000) *Rethinking multiculturalism*, Basingstoke: Macmillan.

Pastore, F. (2004) 'A community out of balance: Nationality law and migration politics in the history of post-unification Italy', *Journal of Modern Italian Studies*, 9(1), 27-48.

Peixoto, J., Arango, J., Bonifazi, C., Finotelli, C., Sabino, C., Strozza, S. and Tryandafillidou, A. (2012) 'Immigrants, markets and policies in Southern Europe', in M. Okólski (ed) *European immigrations*, Amsterdam: Amsterdam University Press, 107-48.

Ricucci, R. (2015) *Cittadini senza cittadinanza*, Torino: SEB27.

Saraceno, C., Sartor, N. and Sciortino, G. (eds) (2013) *Stranieri e diseguali*, Bologna: Il Mulino.

SPRAR (2015) *Rapporto annuale SPRAR. Sistema di Protezione per Richiedenti Asilo e Rifugiati*, Rome: Anci – Ministero dell'Interno.

Syrett, S. and Sepulveda, L. (2012) 'Urban governance and economic development in the diverse city', *European Urban and Regional Studies*, 19(3), 238-53.

Taylor, C., Ferrara, A., Kaul, V. and Rasmussen, D. (2012) 'Interculturalism or multiculturalism?', *Philosophy & Social Criticism*, 38(4-5), 413-23.

Taylor-Gooby, P., and Waite, E. (2014) 'Toward a more pragmatic multiculturalism?', *Governance*, 27(2), 267-89.

Tintori, G. (2013) *Naturalization procedures for immigrants in Italy*, Fiesole: Eudo Citizenship Observatory.

UNAR (2013) *Immigrazione. Dossier Statistico 2013*, Rome: Idos.

Verga, P.L. (2016) 'Rhetoric in the representation of a multi-ethnic neighbourhood: The case of Via Padova, Milan', *Antipode*, 48(4), 1080-101.

Zincone, G. (2011) 'The case of Italy', in G. Zincone, R. Penninx and M. Borkert (eds) *Migration policymaking in Europe,* Amsterdam: Amsterdam University Press, 247-90.

Zinn, D.L. (2011) '"Loud and clear": The G2 Second Generations network in Italy', *Journal of Modern Italian Studies*, 16(3), 373-85.

7

Bringing inequality closer: A comparative outlook at socially diverse neighbourhoods in Chicago and Santiago de Chile[1]

Javier Ruiz-Tagle

Introduction

This chapter seeks to delve into the theoretical assumptions and political rhetoric of social mix. I start from a simple question – how can social relationships be modified by a change in spatial configurations? Or, in other words, how does intergroup physical proximity trigger other processes of integration (functional, relational and symbolic)? To answer these questions, this chapter is presented as follows. First, I describe the policies intended for integration (historical and current), and some problems in the study of socially mixed neighbourhoods. Second, I analyse the cases of Cabrini Green in Chicago and La Florida in Santiago, in terms of four dimensions of socio-spatial integration (physical, functional, relational and symbolic). Third, I discuss differences and similarities between the cases. Finally, I finish with the major empirical findings, theory and policy implications and some critical approaches to deal with segregation.

Policies and problems in the study of social mix

The origins of the idea of socially mixed neighbourhoods date back to the Victorian era in England (Sarkissian, 1976). The idea then was supported by those who idealised the value of small towns, and by those who felt mixing was a solution to industrial overcrowding, but none of them were worried about decreasing inequality. Different actors in the urban debate considered social mix as a solution from a variety of viewpoints: Ebenezer Howard proposed low-scale segregation for his Garden City as a representation of the whole society; Octavia Hill thought that it would help in a 'spirit of emulation' (similar to W.J. Wilson's role models); and Lewis Mumford maintained that it would allow cross-cultural fertilisation (Sarkissian, 1976). After the Second World War, the idea of social mix was revived with the removal of barriers to opportunities reaching urban planning. Meanwhile, Jane Jacobs celebrated the vitality of heterogeneous neighbourhoods, initiating a new emphasis on social mix from planning and legislation (Sarkissian, 1976). The 1990s were especially important for the US in this trajectory: New Urbanism introduced urban design into the debate, contributing with normative prescriptions to the Hope VI programme, and social mix was established as a new consensual wisdom in planning debates. Today, although the political rhetoric still points to the historic progressive ideals of equality of opportunity, recent applications have been more in line with a neoliberal governance (August, 2008).

Four key concepts have been understood by the literature as the major assumptions for present social mix policies (Joseph, 2006). First, higher-status residents would include lower-status neighbours in their 'social networks', thus providing better access to resources and opportunities. Second, the presence of higher-status residents would lead to behaviours that are acceptable to middle-class standards, thus increasing 'social control'. Third, higher-status neighbours would show themselves as 'role models', thus leading to a generalised assimilation of middle-class values. And fourth, the arrival of the middle class would bring a new market demand and political pressures, thus expanding the 'geography of opportunity'.

Contemporary social mix policies have been applied in the US (Goetz, 2003), several European countries (Bolt et al, 2010), Australia (Arthurson, 2012) and South Africa (Lemanski, 2006), and are now emerging in countries like Chile (Sabatini et al, 2013). The general critique to all these examples points to the wide gap between political rhetoric and the reality of its social outcomes, and to the deficiencies of its theoretical assumptions. The rhetoric of social mix policies, exposed by politicians and supported by some scholars, affirms that simple intergroup physical proximity would create a virtuous circle of benefits for the poor. But several authors (Sarkissian, 1976; Arthurson, 2012) insist that the evidence for such rhetoric is very scant and that social mix relies more on normative pretensions than on scientific certainties.

I affirm that there are three problems crossing segregation and integration studies. First, there is an excessive fixation on the spatial causes of social problems. Here, the literature on poverty concentration and neighbourhood effects leads to an inevitable assumption that the problem is essentially spatial (that is, segregation as a cause for social pathologies), and that solutions should be designed accordingly (social mix for positive social outcomes). Second, there is an individualist bias when accounting for the causes of social problems (for example, role models), which points to individualist solutions and to an under-estimation of power relationships. The assumption is that once intergroup physical proximity is achieved, individual relationships would help the poor in overcoming their own problems, and resources would just trickle down. And third, studies on socially mixed neighbourhoods (either planned or unplanned) present a wide dispersion of foci[2] as a consequence of the variety of goals for which the idea of 'integration' has been intended. Thus, there is no wide-ranging explanation of the complexity of sociospatial integration.

From a more comprehensive viewpoint, then, I conceive sociospatial integration as a relationship comprised of four dimensions (Ruiz-Tagle, 2013): physical: intergroup proximity; functional: access to opportunities and services; relational: non-hierarchical interactions; and symbolic: identification with a common ground. Thus, this study seeks to observe the experience of disadvantaged groups living in proximity to higher-status neighbours in different contexts, and to see how this experience could trigger multidimensional processes of integration.

Social mix in Chicago and Santiago

As examples of socially mixed neighbourhoods, I chose the Cabrini Green-Near North area in Chicago, and the La Loma-La Florida area in Santiago. The focus of the study was on the variegated experiences of integration and on the overlaps of integration and segregation. Figure 7.1 shows the location of both sites in each city, over a map of neighbourhood diversity.

The data for this text was drawn from one year of qualitative research. In each case study I used three types of sources: 50 interviews to lower- and higher-status residents and institutional actors; field notes from 60 hours of observation of public meetings and several spaces of intergroup encounter; and 'spatial inventories' from 20 hours of mapping, in which I located the traces of the symbolic presence of each group (visual markers 'done by' or 'targeted to' each group).

The Cabrini Green-Near North area

Cabrini Green was a huge public housing project within the wealthy Near North side, inhabited by a wide majority of poor African Americans. After decades of concerted efforts of social, economic

Figure 7.1: Location of selected cases, over a map of neighbourhood diversity (racial diversity in Chicago, socioeconomic diversity in Santiago)

Note: Both maps show an Index of Neighbourhood Diversity. Lighter colours show the most segregated areas (either upper- or lower-status) and darker colours show the most diverse.

Source: Self-elaboration from US 2010 census and Chile's 2002 census

and political disinvestment (Goetz, 2013), most of the project has been demolished (generating displacement of many poor blacks), and is being transformed into a diverse area colonised by new urbanist, mixed-income developments. There is also a contested future, since the Chicago Housing Authority (CHA) and the City of Chicago are not clear about the large amount of vacant land in the area. Figure 7.2 shows the limits of the studied area and the location of different types of affordable housing.

At present, holding a population of almost 10,000 people, this area presents different types of diversity. In racial terms,[3] the area is 52 per cent Black and 37 per cent non-Hispanic White. In socioeconomic terms, 54 per cent of households are in the first and second income quintiles of Chicago Metropolitan Area, and 36 per cent are in the fourth and fifth quintiles. But not all Blacks are poor in this neighbourhood; 15 per cent of Black households are in the three wealthier quintiles. And regarding housing, there are a number of situations: public housing projects; Section 8 and other subsidised projects;[4] mixed-income developments with public housing, rental and condo units; and other multifamily and single family housing units. Figure 7.3 shows some of the housing developments and Table 7.1 shows the demographic changes in the last decade.

Figure 7.2: The studied area and the different types of affordable housing

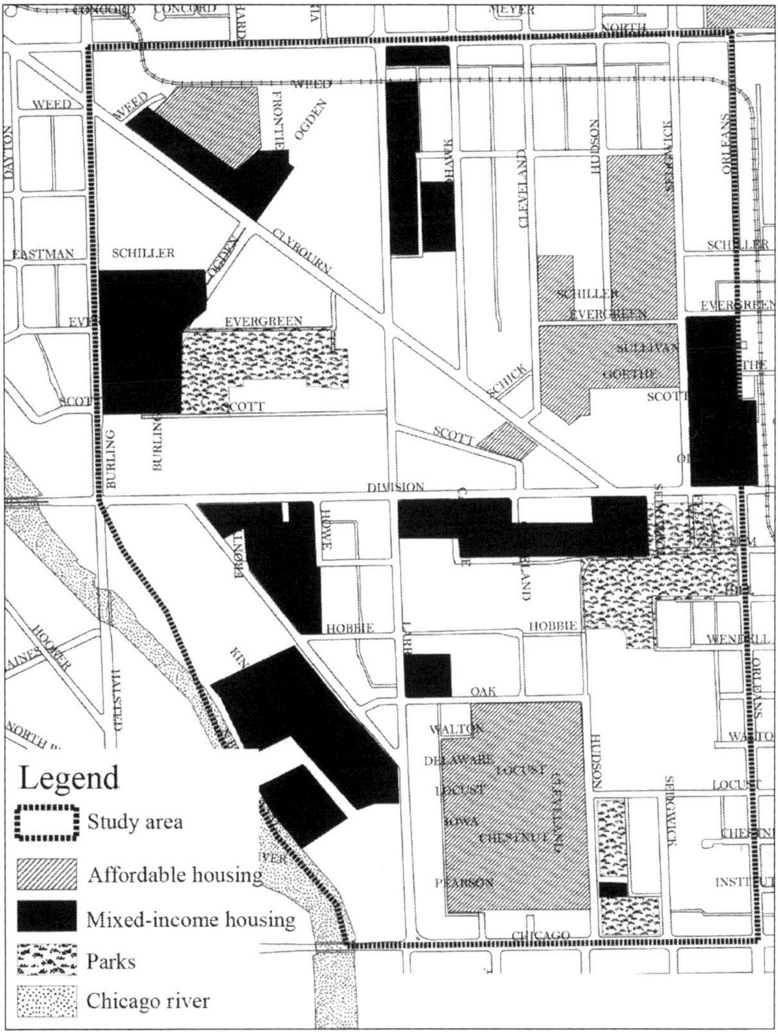

Legend

- Study area
- Affordable housing
- Mixed-income housing
- Parks
- Chicago river

Source: Author

Figure 7.3: The Row Houses (old Cabrini Green, top) and Parkside of Old Town (new mixed-income, bottom)

Source: Author's photographs

Table 7.1: Demographic changes in the Cabrini Green-Near North area

	2000	2010
Total population	10,290	9,645
Percentage black	86.7%	51.7%
Median income (in 2011 dollars)	US$24,450	US$32,500
Percentage with income over US$50,000 (in 2011 dollars)	27.7	44.9
Percentage homeowners	12.1	27.8
Percentage of families that are poor	54.3	42.4

Source: US 2000 Census, US 2010 Census (www.census.gov)

Here I summarise the results based on the mentioned four dimensions of sociospatial integration. In the *physical dimension* the area does not present residential segregation, measured by traditional indexes. Poor blacks live in close proximity to very wealthy neighbours, most of them white. However, the problem of segregation has adopted other, very salient, forms. A first example is local schools. Although most upper-income residents do not have school-age children, most of those who have put them in private, selective enrolment, magnet or charter schools, which have been established in recent years, thus avoiding neighbourhood schools, which are almost 100 per cent black and low income. In the times of Cabrini Green there were five neighbourhood schools receiving local children. Four of them have been closed and their building structures have been converted into private, selective enrolment and charter schools, leaving just a few options for poor residents. A second example is the use of public space and churches. Different groups in this area interact mostly with their own kind. Low-income blacks use public space to socialise and meet new people. On the other hand, high-income people not only avoid poor blacks whenever possible, but also use public space with pre-existing networks of friends coming from their more extended networks. There is also a saturation of churches in the area, all with different congregations and targeting different groups, leading some residents to think of them as "the most segregated institution".

In the *functional dimension* there have been intense changes in this neighbourhood. First, a whole set of upscale private services has arrived: private schools, churches, coffee shops, restaurants, supermarkets, banks, computer stores, fitness centres, and so on. Although they are open to the public, none of them are targeted to poor blacks. Second, several institutions have changed through privatisation of services and more segregation and repression of poor blacks: the public school system has improved through charter, magnet or selective enrolment options; the police force has enhanced safety, working with private security teams; and the CHA has improved the maintenance of units and common spaces, externalising the management to private developers. But the most important of the expected changes (that is, more and better opportunities for the lower-status population) has not yet arrived. The reality could not be further from that. Blacks in the neighbourhood show an unemployment rate of 29.6 per cent (compared to a 1.9% for whites), which has not changed since the arrival of upper-status residents. The majority of the jobs available in the neighbourhood are service industry jobs in the recently established stores. However, the percentage of the workforce living and employed in the area is extremely low (between 2.5 and 4.5%). Keisha, a low-income black resident, describes the low quality of service industry jobs:

> '...for low-income or anyone at this point in the market ... the only jobs that seem to be available are service jobs ... and service, I mean ... at any grocery store, a little restaurant, or something ... are the jobs which would not afford anyone to come up ... the jobs that teenagers used to have as part-time jobs, are now being held by adults, and even elderly ... or just say older workers, so ... no, I don't think, in this area ... anyone to find any really good paying job...'

In the *relational dimension* intergroup relationships are marked by fear, distrust and avoidance. Although there has been a transversal organisation, the Near North Unity Program (NNUP), the general feeling between groups is of a highly distant relationship. Moreover, the middle class has been gaining cohesion and power, putting pressure on the local government to prevent more public housing and low-income population. At the same time, poor blacks have been isolated (physically and organisationally) and are thus losing their power. The proximity between unequal groups is leading to tension and discordance, thus increasing their prejudices against each other. A discussion in a public meeting between Rachel (high-income white) and Aisha (low-income black) summarises this prejudices and mistrust:

> Rachel: 'There's a liquor store that we've been trying to close down ... and they're still dealing drugs and stuff by there ... when you try to get rid of them ... that's an enormous thing that literally took

> years to get rid of that.... Why can't CHA ... do something to get rid of the Row Houses and get rid of the ... to do something that help the police with the crime?'

Aisha: '... the people who are staying in front of the liquor store, of course they're selling cigarettes!!! and not drugs!!! get to know your community a little bit!!!'

The most important outcome of intergroup physical proximity is its utilisation as a mechanism of atomisation and control. Rules and regulations in mixed-income projects are set by developers and then reshaped by owners' associations. And this is where most intergroup problems emerge, with very unbalanced power relationships. Janice, a black public housing resident in a mixed-income building, describes this one-sidedness:

> '... so many rules ... things you can do, things you can't do ... like, I can't barbecue in front of my house ... but you can ... or, if I'm playing loud music, I'm out for eviction ... if you're playing loud music, you'd get a fine ... if the company complains about ... "my neighbour is too loud" ... I'm out for eviction ... you'd get a warning ... if someone leaves my unit and get arrested, and they say he last visited me ... I'm out for eviction, you're not...'

Thus, the unwritten objective of these rules and regulations, and of the severe screening processes for mixed-income projects, is to keep low-income blacks under the strict moral mandates of upper-middle-class residents.

And in the *symbolic dimension* there is a contested and fragmented identity in the neighbourhood. The local community is fragmented between established and newcomers, due to their different times of arrival, but mostly due to their opposed interests. For example, there are different names for the area, depending on which group claims ownership of it. Lower-status groups identify themselves with the entire neighbourhood, but upper-status groups just identify with their spaces, and consider lower status residents as a 'nuisance'. Diversity is said to be positive among most interviewees, with just a few extreme exceptions. The most common reference to diversity is a kind of 'happy talk' (Bell and Hartmann, 2007), which highlights it as a universally positive value. But when discussions go from the abstract to the concrete, that happiness becomes frustration. Upper-class residents are not willing to change their way of life for living in diversity, and think that poor blacks are the ones that have to adjust and "abide by the rules". Their expectations were very different from what they are actually experiencing and they have a feeling of failure for their investment. Poor blacks, on the other side, have a high appreciation for diversity. But the sense of being pushed, screened and controlled everywhere is highly pervasive and unattractive.

The La Loma-La Florida case in Santiago

I selected a case in La Florida district because it is representative of the rapid social, cultural, economic and urban transformations of the last few decades in Chile. La Florida grew fragmented between a south-west sector that received most social housing projects and an east sector, formerly semi-rural, that received middle-class settlements and large real estate projects (commercial, educational, private healthcare, and so on). As an intersection of these two worlds, I chose the area surrounding La Loma. Figure 7.4 shows, on the left, the limits of the selected area and the location of social housing and gated communities, and on the right, the socioeconomic distribution of the population.

The site began to be populated more than 50 years ago. In 1970, the agricultural workers of the area decided to take over the land of La Loma, which was unoccupied, built their own houses and, only in 1995, could install public drinking water and sewage, and obtained property deeds. From the 1980s and 1990s, the expansion of Santiago

Figure 7.4: Social housing and gated communities (left), and socioeconomic distribution (right)

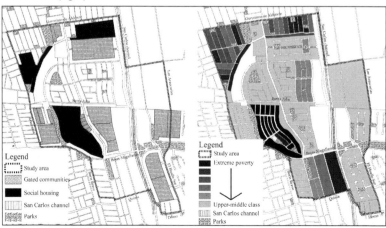

Source: Left, self-elaboration; Right, estimation from 2002 census

arrived into La Loma, with social housing and lower-middle-class developments. And from the 2000s, gated communities and upper-middle-class neighbourhoods were built, changing drastically the quality of public and private local services. At present, with a population of almost 10,000, this area presents a wide socioeconomic diversity: 33 per cent belong to the richest income decile in Chile, and 18 per cent to the four poorest income deciles. Figure 7.5 and Table 7.2 show pictures and a synthesis of demographic changes, respectively.

Figure 7.5: Pictures of different housing situations and services in the area

Source: Author's photographs

Table 7.2: Summary of demographic changes, 2002 and 2013

	2002	2013
Total population	8,871	10,656
Area (hectares)	133.11	
Density (inhabitants/ha)	66.65	80.07
Extreme poverty	3.70%	2.70%
Poor	18.00%	14.80%
Lower-middle class	18.40%	15.90%
Middle class	34.60%	33.70%
Upper-middle class	25.30%	32.90%

Source: 2002 census and estimation from 2013

Again, I summarise the results from the four dimensions of sociospatial integration. In the *physical dimension*, similar to Cabrini Green, there is a high degree of proximity and an almost non-existent residential segregation, according to traditional indexes. As a public official from La Florida municipality described it, there is an "astounding diversity". However, the social mix of this neighbourhood was not created by a mixed-income policy;[5] it was a 'land deregulation accident', in which gated communities colonised a poor area of the periphery. Nevertheless, this level of proximity has its problems as well: most points of contact between social groups are prevented through other forms of segregation. A couple of separation walls have been built and re-built in the neighbourhood, but youngsters from La Loma have torn them down. Several streets have been left as 'cul-de-sacs', even if the Regulatory Plan mandates that they should have continuity. Moreover, gated communities themselves have become areas of restricted access, even for middle-class residents. Eduardo, who has a house outside of the fence of a gated community, but which belongs to the same housing development, explains the situation he has suffered:

> 'There are some that are discriminative ... the ones inside the gated community against the ones facing the street. It's like ... if my son goes to play with them, he's discriminated ... not because we're different, with more or less resources than them ... but they're like ... they do their world apart. They believe the ones inside are different from the ones outside ... when we bought our house, all these squares inside, the playgrounds ... they were for all [of us], they were of the community. Can you see? Then, now if I want to enter, I'd have to have keys or have access...'

A second problem is – again – school segregation, which is very strong in Chile. The majority of residents in the area have their children in 12 establishments that are within or around the studied area. There are four tuition-free municipal schools (with the lowest test scores), five state-subsidised private schools (charging US$50 to US$100 for monthly tuition), and three fully private schools (charging more than US$200 for tuition and with the best test scores).[6] The majority of lower-class children attend municipal schools (tuition-free), and a few attend state-subsidised schools, with a state scholarship. And among middle-class residents, some attend state-subsidised private schools, and most of them, private schools.

In the *functional dimension* there is an important level of exchange of goods and services, as several studies on socially mixed areas in Chile have shown (Salcedo and Torres, 2004; Sabatini and Salcedo, 2007). There are lower-status residents working as maids,[7] gardeners, construction workers and the like in upper-status houses. There are also several small stores, like grocery shops, liquor stores, shoe repairs, and so on, established in lower-status houses. And they have received some of the benefits of an expanded market, with a higher purchasing power. However, there are several nuances to take into account: many domestic workers come from outside the neighbourhood; many domestic workers living in the neighbourhood work outside; there is an important distrust from upper-status residents to hire their own neighbours; many middle-class households do not have domestic service; and the possibility of accessing local domestic service jobs depends on the level of internal cohesion within social housing settlements, which facilitates the circulation of job-related information. In addition, there are grocery stores established near middle-class houses as well, and several middle-class residents prefer to avoid the stores in lower-class areas.

In sum, there are some job opportunities, but the proximity between groups is not a necessary condition for poor residents for finding a job in the neighbourhood. Besides, the available jobs are all low-paid, unskilled jobs, which in material terms maintain economic inequalities, and in symbolic terms maintain subordinated social relationships. This, coupled with the high levels of school segregation, configure a difficult situation for social mobility. In addition, new amenities and private services have arrived, including schools, supermarkets, restaurants, gyms, and so on. However, several low-income residents do not feel the benefits, and sometimes end up using their own self-subsistence commerce, even to the point of affirming that "the neighbourhood would be the same with or without middle-class residents."

In the *relational dimension* intergroup relationships are also marked by fear, distrust and avoidance, mostly from the middle class. There is no relevant relationship beyond the mentioned functional exchanges. While the lower class is established as a cohesive community, middle-class residents are just a set of disconnected individuals who are apathetic, distrustful and not participative. They know too few people and are not willing to expand their local network, they do not trust anybody (even their middle-class neighbours), and show no concern for investing time and resources in the neighbourhood. Lower-class residents (and their spaces) are blamed for every bad event that happens in the neighbourhood, especially crime. Agustina, resident of La Loma, describes this discrimination:

> 'They believe they are exclusive, that they are professionals ... sort of ... owners of cars, owners of this ... then, there is much negative things from them to us ... I mean, they say like "the criminals of La Loma" ... while not all people [are] criminal...'

The distrust of the middle class extends to their own intragroup relationships; they do not know each other, they do not use the neighbourhood and its spaces, and everybody in the neighbourhood could be a potential criminal. Rafael, a resident in a gated community, expressed this isolation:

> 'Neighbours are ... there is no relationship ... let's say it ... like certain activities as group between neighbours, like visiting each other, no, no. Everyone maintains their life independently with its own people ... respecting each other, but there is no social relationship of internal friendship, or instance of communication...'

A second dividing line is the need for social differentiation from upper-status residents. The middle class has historically tended to stress the differences with lower classes. And this has several reasons. In material terms, lower-class residents can look very similar to middle-class ones, given the massive access to consumer goods in the last few decades and the relatively low levels of racial differentiation. In cultural terms, within the history of classism in Chile, hiding one's own social origin has been a strategy used by the middle and upper-middle classes in order to be accepted by the elite. And in institutional terms, from the neoliberal reforms, the state apparatus has implemented targeted policies to attend only the most needed population, generating a sharp fragmentation with the population that is just a few steps above in the social ladder, which creates some resentment. A third dividing line is the lack of relevant institutions or organisations that connect both groups. Social service organisations are non-existent in this neighbourhood because again, the average income is higher than in traditional poor areas. And the state, either by its different centralised agencies or by the municipality, is just worried about the lower class. Thus, the middle class does not have the support of the state and does not have a connecting institution with the lower class.

And in the *symbolic dimension* there has also been an intentional erasure of old community signs. There are no references to the old semi-rural settlements, to the historical landmarks or to the social housing developments. Some say that gentrifying neighbourhoods use 'some' of the old symbolic elements of the area to attract particular segments of the middle class. In socially mixed neighbourhoods like Cabrini Green and La Loma, however, the 'symbolic economy' attempts to erase most references to the past in order to build a new image for a wider middle class. There is also an unclear neighbourhood identity. The lower class feels that changes are not for them, and the middle class feels that the neighbourhood is not totally owned. Both groups have confusing and vague feelings about their own environment, and think their proximity does not generate any symbolic commonality between them. Finally, there are hostile messages sent by the security infrastructure, in particular, fences and their concrete and symbolic effects, for neighbours and passersby. Fences are not only used if owners feel unprotected, but also have a deterrent effect, which sends a hostile messages to all unknown neighbours, either poor or middle class. Figure 7.6 shows different types of fences in middle-class housing:s

Figure 7.6: Different types of fences in middle-class housing

Source: Author's photographs

Differences and similarities

The cases studied here are certainly different, which complicates any effort of comparison. The Cabrini Green-Near North area has been a highly notorious public housing settlement, which was built in an inner-city location of Chicago from the 1950s. Conversely, the La Loma-La Florida area has been a much more silent case of urban development, built in a peripheral area of Santiago from the 1970s. But beyond these general differences, I want to structure the analysis from three structural factors that influence the causes, dynamics and consequences of residential segregation. First, *social stratification systems* mark the causes of segregation in terms of different lines of inequality in each society (race/ethnicity, class, etc), which creates a system of social relationships. Blacks in the US present a particularly interesting example here, since their increasing intragroup distinctions challenges both racial solidarity and assumptions of homogeneity (Pattillo, 2003). The black middle class have a sense of superiority over poor blacks, and have been constituted as a significant interest bloc. Although African Americans are still highly disadvantaged in relation to whites, almost 50 per cent of US blacks are occupationally middle class (Pattillo, 2003). Second, *housing allocation systems* mark the dynamics in which segregation is materialised in terms of residential mobility, the functioning of the housing market, policies for affordable housing, historical practices of segregation, and so on. And third, *welfare systems in space* influence the consequences of segregation in terms of the institutional context that surround neighbourhoods, the administrative division of the state and its jurisdiction on social matters, the funding and management of public spaces, the local police, and so on.

In terms of *social stratification* there are therefore several distinctions. First, there are different race–class intersections. In Chicago, the lower-status group is poor and black, and the upper-status group is wealthy and majority white. In Santiago instead, although there are some differences in skin colour, the main distance is about class. In both cities, both groups have a wide historical social distance, but the overlap of race and class in Chicago makes its social mix much more complicated. Second, there are consequently different forms of discrimination, with racism and classism more predominant in Chicago and Santiago, respectively. Discrimination in Chicago was difficult to unveil among interviewees, but once disclosed, 'the other' was clearly defined. In turn, discrimination in Santiago was much more explicit in discourses, but the definition of 'the other' was less structured. Finally, there is a different role of middle classes and their claims for the neighbourhood in each case. In Chicago, the middle class is highly participative and sometimes shows a significant level of cohesion, which comes from a tradition of (white) middle-class involvement in local issues. In Santiago in turn, the middle class is apathetic, non-participative and disorganised. They have only reacted, very strongly, to stop the construction of more social housing in the area.

The highest differences appear in *housing allocation systems*. Large cities in the US are characterised by what I call a 'continuous/organic' type of neighbourhood change, distinguished by its fast pace, small scale of developments and short term. In Chilean large cities it is the opposite; there is a 'discrete' type of neighbourhood change, with a slow pace, large-scale and long-term character. These differences, applied to the specific cases, have important implications. In Cabrini Green there are higher levels of real estate demand, residential mobility and population turnover than in La Florida. And each of these issues has its consequence: the real estate demand generates exclusionary pressures on the poor population, especially when there is vacant land available; and residential mobility and population turnover complicate the possibilities of establishing intergroup relationships and organisations due to the relatively shorter stay of upper-status residents. A second important difference is marked by the levels of homeownership in each case, which is crucial for lower-status groups. Poor families in La Florida are almost all homeowners, while in Cabrini Green, poor households are all renters. And this represents a double-edged sword, because there are both advantages and disadvantages. The renting situation in Cabrini Green allows maintenance by a management company, which, at present, had the units and housing developments in very good standing. In La Florida instead, with few resources from homeowners, maintenance is very poor. The flip side is that La Florida households are free to occupy their units as they want, even with the possibility of opening small, semi-formal grocery stores in their front gates. In Cabrini Green in turn, there are severe restrictions on the use of public housing units.

And in terms of *welfare systems in space* there are considerable differences. First, there are different levels of territorial conflict for public schools. In Chicago, neighbourhood schools have attendance areas which, depending on the quality, modify the demand for housing in those zones. In Chile instead, schools are open to students from anywhere. Thus it is the demographic make-up of a particular neighbourhood that defines the demand for some of the three mentioned school types. A second point is the level of public investments. Here, the condition of being a planned or an unplanned mixed neighbourhood marks a big difference; while Cabrini Green receives resources for mixed-income housing, for public schools, for parks, for public transportation, and so on, La Florida does not receive any particular investment, excepting a social housing project that has not been built due to the opposition of the middle class. Third, the institutional framework of public spaces is highly different in both contexts, in terms of planning, construction and maintenance. In Santiago, parks are leftovers from the private construction of housing developments and their size is extremely small, while in Chicago, large parks have been planned and built by the municipality. In Chicago there is a Chicago Park District that is in charge of maintenance and recreation activities in each park, while in La Florida there are just some gardeners, hired by the municipality, that mow and water the lawn without any involvement in activities for the neighbours. Both reasons (size and maintenance) explain in part why there is an almost non-existent use of public space in La Florida, especially from upper-status groups. A last point to highlight is the relationship between the state apparatus and the middle class. From the 1980s, targeted policies in Chile concentrated all social protection on the poor population, including education, healthcare and housing, and excluding the middle class, which started to use privatised services. Thus, the relationship with the state, and protection from it, is almost non-existent in Chile. In the US, despite all the neoliberal changes, the state still has a permanent relationship with the middle class, and there is frequent involvement in planning through participatory processes.

Despite the important nuances mentioned above, there are several similarities. In terms of urban development, there is a similar density, socioeconomic change and stability. Both cases have similar levels of residents per hectare, which reaffirms a known claim saying that neighbourhood diversity is somewhat related to density. In addition, both cases have experienced upward socioeconomic change, from homogeneously poor to socially mixed. Finally, both cases present relative stability of their neighbourhood diversity, although through different mechanisms (public property of subsidised housing in Cabrini Green and homeownership in La Florida). In terms of *job opportunities* there are evident similarities. Both cases present limited opportunities, which are almost non-existent in Cabrini Green, and highly subordinated in La Florida. Besides, the few jobs created do not offer effective avenues for upward social mobility: they are characterised by its informality, precariousness, low wages and subordination, preserving the status quo in material and cultural terms.

Regarding *educational opportunities* the stories are similar as well. There is limited access to quality education for lower-status residents in both cases. In addition, there are historical and recent processes of school segregation in both cities. This segregation puts up a strong barrier for poor residents, which is detrimental for their opportunities and for their social cohesion with the middle class. In both cases, but more intense in Chicago than in Santiago, there has been school closings (relocating their students) and privatisations. Regarding *intergroup relationships*, both cases present serious problems. Upper- and lower-status groups feel highly distant from each other; they do not know about 'the other's' life, customs and problems; upper-status groups are afraid of crime coming from their neighbours, and avoid them in public spaces, especially when there are more visual differences (racial traits or class hints). Stigmatisation operates in both cases, but with a different content: while poor black individuals are avoided in Cabrini Green ('human' stigmatisation), the case is against poor spaces in La Florida ('territorial' stigmatisation), given the relatively low racial differences. In addition, several intergroup attitudes have worsened by living in close proximity. There are opposite levels of social cohesion between upper- and lower-status groups, opposite feelings of security and opposite degrees of place attachment. In other words, the *contact hypothesis* has not operated in Cabrini Green and La Florida. It has been all the opposite, which has been called *negative contact*, *environmental spoiling* or *conflict hypothesis*.

Finally, in terms of *housing and political economy*, both cases present exclusionary pressures from real estate entities and the middle class, in order to prevent the construction of more social housing and the increase of a lower-class population. The arrival of the upper classes has brought new amenities, through private investments and institutional changes in public entities such as schools, the police and housing authorities. In fact, one of the few benefits of social mix has been the upgrading of social housing's quality standards, due to the indirect pressures of the middle class for generating an 'acceptable' neighbourhood in which to live. Nevertheless, the amount of social housing units 'accepted' is limited, which in turn generates shortages that have an impact on local and metropolitan housing markets for the poor.

Conclusion

Here I summarise the major findings about socially mixed neighbourhoods:

- Social mix works more as a mechanism of atomisation and/or control than as a policy for diverse and peaceful coexistence, leaving no relevant benefits for the poor.
- The arrival of upper classes brings more amenities and generates institutional changes, but not upward social mobility for the poor.
- Intergroup relationships are marked by fear, distrust and avoidance.
- There is a contested and fragmented identity coming from a higher material and symbolic competition (that is, local resources and place identity).
- Despite the overlap with integration, new forms of segregation emerge and tend to prevail, and thus inequality persists.
- Social mix is a confusing urban arrangement in which the symbolism of physical proximity conceals the persistence of inequality and several active forces maintaining segregation.

There are four areas from which I extract theory and policy implications. First, regarding the *multi-dimensional experience of integration*, some authors have affirmed that socially mixed neighbourhoods perform two civilising roles (Uitermark, 2014): local governments find a way of decreasing the quantity of 'problematic' individuals, which is particularly true in Cabrini Green, and the state uses the middle class as a mechanism of discipline, which happens, to some extent, in the relationship between the middle-class and domestic servants in La Florida. Furthermore, as other authors have demonstrated (Ostendorf et al, 2001), social mix does not reduce poverty. On top of this, local governments are not investing enough resources in poor neighbourhoods and are far more responsive to the claims of the middle class. Moreover, socially mixed neighbourhoods present more tension, discordance and increasing prejudice. Finally, these neighbourhoods could be understood as 'communities without community' (Amin, 2002) – since social networks do not intersect, interactions only occur for some common goods, and there are different levels of place attachment and different cultural customs.

Second, in terms of *experiences and discourses of diversity* there is a wide separation between the political rhetoric and the social reality of socially mixed neighbourhoods, which has been criticised in the last decade (August, 2008; Blanc, 2010; Bolt et al, 2010). All interviewees pass from a 'happy talk' (Bell and Hartmann, 2007) about social mix to an intense frustration with its actual outcomes. As the title of this chapter suggests, social mix makes inequality visible, but it is difficult to say that it is positive by itself. The invitation to create diversity is just a small concession, but it does not touch the roots of what creates inequalities between groups. The idea of diversity, and diverse urban coexistence, clearly conceals power differentials, since the positive language of desegregation hides race and class inequalities.

Third, *neighbourhood effects research* has been intimately related to social mix policies (Kintrea, 2013). The idea of neighbourhood effects implies that additional social problems are (supposedly) generated by the spatial concentration of poverty, and cannot be deducted from poverty itself (Sampson et al, 2002). Thus, is social mix reversing the outcomes of concentrated poverty (that is, positive neighbourhood effects)? The answer is complex, since this is not a question of balanced or unbalanced demographics. Instead, more than demographics, several authors insist that institutions work against social exclusion in segregated neighbourhoods, thus breaking the direct relationship between concentrated poverty and further social problems (Simon, 1992; Dangschat, 1994). Then, without meaningful institutions in diverse neighbourhoods, there are similar levels of exclusion. That is what is happening in Cabrini Green, where poor blacks have almost the same rates of unemployment than before mixed-income projects were built. The problem is therefore not just the concentration of poverty, but also the overlap of different forms of segregation, accumulated stigmatisation and institutional abandonment (Wacquant, 2008).

Finally, there are several things to say about *social mix policies*. As mentioned, socially mixed neighbourhoods are strange creatures of urban development, between the symbolism of desegregation and a context of growing inequalities, or between the progressive rhetoric of social mix and processes of welfare retrenchment and social fragmentation. Given this situation, social mix policies have been highly ineffective in providing more social justice in several parts of the world. Thus, social mix represents a new phase of neoliberal policies, disguised as progressive under the discourse of diversity. First, it produces gentrification and displacement. Second, it leaves affordable housing provision to the market and externalises its management. Third, it carries the implicit belief that opportunities would just trickle down, which is an implicit belief coming from the 'geographies of opportunity' concept. And fourth, it leaves racism unquestioned. In addition, there are two important limitations of socially mixed projects: only one portion of the poor is accepted, and the existing (if any) job opportunities are just a comparative advantage for the poor, but it cannot be used as a policy to decrease general levels of unemployment.

Some decades ago, Lefebvre and Harvey observed contradictions in the capitalist city in terms of the centralisation of power and the decentralisation of poverty (that is, segregation), thus creating the basis for confrontation, making the system unstable and undermining the reproduction of social relations (Saunders, 1986; Harvey, 1989). In present days, however, the current developments of social mix stand as the improvement of those contradictions. As Uitermark (2014) describes it, social mix can be portrayed as a dual policy of rent extraction and social control.

Critical approaches for dealing with segregation

There are two approaches that can be highlighted here: on the one hand, Young (1999) suggests counteracting the persisting disinvestment and lack of resources in poor neighbourhoods; and on the other hand, Marcuse (2006) recommends dealing with inequality and prejudice at a general level, not just in poor neighbourhoods. The first approach deals with territorial inequality, and the second deals with general social inequality and poverty. I think a critical approach should join Young and Marcuse's approaches, and address the mentioned three structural factors of residential segregation: social stratification systems, housing allocation systems and welfare systems in space.

In terms of *social stratification systems*, an overall anti-segregation policy should attack the sources of inequality and prejudice (racism and classism) at a national level. In other words, this implies actions both on the 'material side' (power) and the 'cultural-symbolic side' (status); the first calls for policies of economic redistribution and affirmative action, and the second for serious changes in the educational, cultural and communicational realms. In terms of *housing allocation systems*, an effective policy should prevent and counteract both the concentration of wealth and the concentration of poverty at a metropolitan level. As Marcuse (2006) affirms, policies should not be just directed to poor, conflictive neighbourhoods, but to the whole spectrum of urban life. Finally, in terms of *welfare systems in space*, an overall policy should act at two levels. At a national level the creation of universal systems of protection that reduce the impact of inequality should be promoted. And at a metropolitan level a territorial redistribution of opportunities and resources should be encouraged (that is, moving 'resources to people'; see Young, 1999). The first level attacks general social inequality and the second attacks territorial inequality. Thus, as long as poor areas are improved, and the stay of poor people is assured (that is, no gentrification), this would also attract higher-income families, possibly lowering the levels of segregation. Therefore, by addressing the causes, dynamics and consequences of segregation decisively, and at different scales, more appropriate policies can be built.

Notes

[1] This chapter summarises the doctoral dissertation completed in July 2014 at the University of Illinois at Chicago (UIC), guided by Professor Janet Smith, and winner of the Barclay Gibbs Jones Award for best dissertation in planning given by the Association of Collegiate Schools of Planning (ACSP), and the Outstanding Thesis Award given by UIC.

[2] There are studies on physical impacts (Joseph and Chaskin, 2010), on the overall benefits for poor people (Fraser and Kick), on social cohesion (Arthurson, 2002), and on social interactions (Rosenbaum et al, 1998), to name just a few.

[3] In the US census race is measured as follows: 'An individual's response to the race question is based upon *self-identification*. The Census Bureau does not tell individuals which boxes to mark or what heritage to write in' (emphasis added). Source: US Census Bureau, extracted from www.census.gov/topics/population/race/about.html

[4] Marshall Field, Evergreen and Schiff.

[5] There is an intense academic and political debate about implementing mixed-income policies in Chile, and actually there are a few *proyectos de integración social* (social integration projects) already built. These types of project could have been the best comparison with Cabrini Green, but the projects are too new, not much statistical information was available to collect, and not much literature was available to discuss.

[6] The payment of tuition to these establishments represents between 15 and 40% of household income.

[7] Having domestic service is very common among the middle and upper classes in Chile and in Latin America, due to the low wages of domestic workers.

References

Amin, A. (2002) 'Ethnicity and the multicultural city: Living with diversity', *Environment and Planning A*, 34(6), 959-80.

Arthurson, K. (2002) 'Creating inclusive communities through balancing social mix: A critical relationship or tenuous link?', *Urban Policy and Research*, 20(3), 245-61.

Arthurson, K. (2012) *Social mix and the city: Challenging the mixed communities consensus in housing and urban planning policies*, Collingwood, VIC: CSIRO Publishing.

August, M. (2008) 'Social mix and Canadian public housing redevelopment: Experiences in Toronto', *Canadian Journal of Urban Research*, 17(1), 82-100.

Bell, J. And Hartmann, D. (2007) 'Diversity in everyday discourse: The cultural ambiguities and consequences of "happy talk"', *American Sociological Review*, 72(6), 895-914.

Blanc, M. (2010) 'The impact of social mix policies in France', *Housing Studies*, 25(2), 257-72.

Bolt, G., Phillips, D. and van Kempen, R. (2010) 'Housing policy, (de) segregation and social mixing: An international perspective', *Housing Studies*, 25(2), 129–35.

Dangschat, J. (1994) 'Concentration of poverty in the landscapes of "boomtown" Hamburg: The creation of a new urban underclass?', *Urban Studies*, 31(7), 1133–47.

Fraser, J. and Kick, E. (2007) 'The role of public, private, non-profit and community sectors in shaping mixed-income housing outcomes in the US', *Urban Studies*, 44(12), 2357–77.

Goetz, E. (2003) 'Housing dispersal programs', *Journal of Planning Literature*, 18(1), 3–16.

Goetz, E. (2013) *New Deal ruins: Race, economic justice, and public housing policy*, Ithaca, NY: Cornell University Press.

Harvey, D. (1989) *The urban experience*, Baltimore, MD: Johns Hopkins University Press.

Joseph, M. (2006) 'Is mixed-income development an antidote to urban poverty?', *Housing Policy Debate*, 17(2), 209–34.

Joseph, M. and Chaskin, R. (2010) 'Living in a mixed-income development: Resident perceptions of the benefits and disadvantages of two developments in Chicago', *Urban Studies*, 47(11), 2347–66.

Kintrea, K. (2013) 'Social mix: International policy approaches', in D. Manley, M. van Ham, N. Bailey, L. Simpson and D. Maclennan (eds) *Neighbourhood effects or neighbourhood based problems?*, New York: Springer, 133–56.

Lemanski, C. (2006) 'Desegregation and integration as linked or distinct? Evidence from a previously "white" suburb in post-apartheid Cape Town', *International Journal of Urban and Regional Research*, 30(3), 564–86.

Marcuse, P. (2006) 'The down side dangers in the social city programme: Contradictory potentials in German social policy', *German Politics & Society*, 24(4), 122–30.

Ostendorf, W., Musterd, S. and de Vos, S. (2001) 'Social mix and the neighbourhood effect: Policy ambitions and empirical evidence', *Housing Studies*, 16(3), 371–80.

Pattillo, M. (2003) 'Negotiating blackness, for richer or for poorer', *Ethnography*, 4(1), 61–93.

Rosenbaum, J., Stroh, L. and Flynn, C. (1998) 'Lake Parc Place: A study of mixed-income housing', *Housing Policy Debate*, 9(4), 703–40.

Ruiz-Tagle, J. (2013) 'A theory of socio-spatial integration: Problems, policies and concepts from a US perspective', *International Journal of Urban and Regional Research*, 37(2), 388–408.

Sabatini, F. and Salcedo, R. (2007) 'Gated communities and the poor in Santiago, Chile: Functional and symbolic integration in a context of aggressive capitalist colonization of lower-class areas', *Housing Policy Debate*, 18(3), 577-606.

Sabatini, F., Brain, I. and Mora, P. (2013) *Conciliando integración social y negocio inmobiliario: Seguimiento de proyectos residenciales integrados desarrollados por inmobiliarias privadas*, Boston, MA: Lincoln Institute of Land Policy.

Salcedo, R. and Torres, A. (2004) 'Gated communities in Santiago: Wall or frontier?', *International Journal of Urban and Regional Research*, 28(1), 27-44.

Sampson, R., Morenoff, J. and Gannon-Rowley, T. (2002) 'Assessing "neighborhood effects": Social processes and new directions in research', *Annual Review of Sociology*, 28(1), 443-78.

Sarkissian, W. (1976) 'The idea of social mix in town planning: An historical review', *Urban Studies*, 13(3), 231-46.

Saunders, P. (1986) *Social theory and the urban question*, London: Routledge.

Simon, P. (1992) 'Banlieues: De la concentration au ghetto', *Esprit*, 182(1), 58-64.

Uitermark, J. (2014) 'Integration and control: The governing of urban marginality in Western Europe', *International Journal of Urban and Regional Research*, 38(4), 1418-36.

Wacquant, L. (2008) *Urban outcasts: A comparative sociology of advanced marginality*, Cambridge: Polity Press.

Young, I.M. (1999) 'Residential segregation and differentiated citizenship', *Citizenship Studies*, 3(2), 237-52.

8

Ambiguities of vertical multi-ethnic coexistence in the city of Athens: Living together but unequally between conflicts and encounters

Dimitris Balampanidis and Panagiotis Bourlessas

Introduction

Ethnic diversity in the city of Athens and, relatedly, the coexistence of different ethnic groups constitute relatively recent sociospatial phenomena. During the 20th century, Greece was predominately a country of emigration and thus it rarely received any important inflows of foreign populations (Emke-Poulopoulou, 2007, pp 83-116). Indeed, it was only in the early 1990s that Greece became a destination country for international migrants and asylum-seekers, as well as a transit country for those trying to reach northwestern European destinations.

During the 1990s, the first large migration wave was mostly comprised of people from the Balkans and Eastern Europe, while after 2000 the second significant wave also included people from Africa, Asia and the Middle East. Over the last 25 years, these large inflows have increased the country's migrant presence from 1.6 per cent of the total population in 1991 to 7 per cent in 2001 (ESYE, 2009, p 45) and 8.5 per cent in 2011 (ELSTAT, 2011). Among migrants from more than 200 different countries, Albanians constitute by far the largest migrant population, followed by Romanians, Bulgarians and migrants from the former Eastern Bloc, while those coming from Africa, Asia and the Middle East are less represented. The great majority of migrants in Greece are concentrated in urban areas, primarily in the region of Attica and especially in the municipality of Athens, where they represented almost 17.5 per cent of the total population in 2011 (EKKE-ELSTAT, 2015).

Due to migration being a recent and substantially urban phenomenon, over the last 25 years the population of the large metropolitan areas in Greece, especially Athens, has become increasingly diverse in terms of its ethnic characteristics. This increasing diversity has led to controversial debates regarding the effects of multi-ethnic coexistence, including the spatial relations and social interactions that develop between population groups of different ethnic backgrounds.

In this chapter we focus on a specific and particular manifestation of ethnic diversity in the city of Athens, namely, vertical multi-ethnic coexistence, which refers to the *spatial and social* relationships that develop between different ethnic groups living within the same residential building. The aim of our study is to highlight the various and sometimes contradictory effects of vertical multi-ethnic coexistence, as well as to reveal multiple aspects of ethnic diversity that are less visible and hence often overlooked in both public and academic discourse. The main argument is that, despite high levels of ethnic mix in the neighbourhoods of the city and within residential buildings, crucial inequalities still exist between Greek and migrant residents, while their in-between spatial proximity not only entails relations of tolerance, solidarity and friendship, but also manifestations of racism, mistrust and xenophobia. In other words, we argue that, in the city of Athens, Greeks and migrants live *together but unequally*, and their social relations vary *between conflicts and encounters*.

The chapter begins by discussing certain crucial issues stemming from the global literature. These concern the ambiguous effects of urban diversity, multi-ethnic coexistence and residential segregation, and highlight the complex correlation between sociospatial proximity and distance. Then follow some necessary methodological considerations regarding the means of coexistence between different ethnic groups in the case of Athens. The specific local sociospatial context is presented through a brief literature review. The empirical evidence unfolds in two parts. The first focuses on the spatial dimensions of multi-ethnic coexistence and reveals less visible but still crucial inequalities among households that live together within the same residential building. The second part also examines the social interaction between households of different ethnic origins and reveals both sides of neighbours' social relations. The chapter closes by drawing some general conclusions regarding the complexity of multi-ethnic coexistence and relating them to further reflections on urban policies aimed at addressing diversity.

Urban diversity and residential segregation debated

In the city-related literature, urban diversity has mainly been examined using two different approaches. On the one hand, scholars have focused on the significance of diversity as an urban asset capable of fostering competitiveness, creativity, entrepreneurship and economic growth (Florida, 2002; Bodaar and Rath, 2005; Fainstein, 2005; Eraydin et al, 2010) or contributing to sociospatial cohesion and justice (Sandercock, 2000; Amin, 2002; Fainstein, 2005; Camina and Wood, 2009; Perrone, 2011). Yet, on the other hand, scholars have highlighted how a very optimistic or neutral conceptualisation of diversity may lead to distorted understandings of urban societies; for instance, it may obscure various and crucial social inequalities that actually exist in largely diversified urban environments (Martiniello, 2004; Fainstein, 2005, 2009; Kokkali, 2010; Syrett and Sepulveda, 2011).

In order to further build on the latter approach, it is important to recognise that the explicit link between diversity and inequality is usually missing from urban analyses. Marcuse (2002) reminds us that cities – whether more or less diverse – have always been spatially and socially partitioned, reflecting various types of hierarchies. For this reason, urban diversity cannot be viewed as a neutral condition, since stratified societies tend to convert differentiations into inequalities (Kandylis et al, 2012). Further, when social inequalities meet heterogeneity, urban segregation typically appears as the spatial outcome (Leal, 2004). Following the above reasoning, diversity is inherent in segregation discourse and vice versa. Thus, segregation appears to be a critical parameter in a more complex approach to urban diversity, an approach that essentially considers sociospatial inequalities and embraces all the different aspects, contradictions and ambiguities of diversity.

Similarly to diversity, which can be conceived as both an asset and a difficult challenge for urban life and the coexistence of different population groups, segregation can also be viewed in multiple and ambiguous ways. Indeed, it can be seen not only as a negative, but also as a favourable condition. For instance, segregation typically has a negative connotation in academic and public discourse, since it is related to socioeconomic divisions, racial discrimination, exclusion, marginalisation and the reproduction of hierarchies. From this perspective, public policies often aim at socially and ethnically mixed neighbourhoods with a view to tackling problems such as poverty, racism, weak integration and the lack of a sense of community. However, this prevalent rationale has often been challenged (for a critical overview of social mix policies, see Galster, 2007; Bolt et al, 2010). In many cases, scholars have observed that high spatial concentrations of specific population groups (such as low-income neighbourhoods or ethnic enclaves) do not always have negative effects, but may instead prove beneficial; for instance, they may increase the sense of community, offer mechanisms of mutual support, favour sociospatial integration and so on (Marcuse, 2005). In such cases, urban policies aimed at fostering a social and ethnic mix have been thoroughly criticised for being inadequate and focusing on only the spatial symptoms of social problems and inequalities rather than addressing their origins (Cheshire, 2007).

Nowadays, many scholars agree that the spatial mix and, therefore, the spatial proximity of different population groups is not a necessary and sufficient condition for achieving social cohesion, equality and justice. As argued by Chamboredon and Lemaire (1970) when they studied the case of socially and ethnically mixed neighbourhoods of social housing in Paris, spatial proximity does not necessarily entail social contact. The same argument has been supported in several different northwestern European countries. To offer a characteristic example from German cities, Häussermann and Siebel (2001, pp 73-4) observed that interethnic social contacts in ethnically mixed neighbourhoods should not be taken for granted, since serious interethnic conflicts may arise instead. Similar evidence has been seen in southern European countries after they became the principal destinations for international migrants from the beginning of the 1990s. In fact, despite the low levels of segregation and high ethnic mix seen in many southern European cities, scholars have observed serious housing inequalities between households of different ethnic origins, high levels of migrants' social marginalisation and of neighbourhood deprivation (Malheiros, 2002; Arbaci, 2008; Arbaci and Malheiros, 2009).

To illustrate this contradiction, namely, the existence of crucial social distances despite high levels of spatial proximity, Fujita (2012) discussed cities where people live 'together but unequally'. The city of Athens has also been included in this conceptual category: against a background of increasing ethnic diversity and despite high levels of ethnic mix, social inequalities and distances between Greek and migrant residents subtly exist. This notion has previously been argued in the related academic discourse, and it will be further demonstrated here through our empirical research.

Methodological considerations

To explore the spatial and social effects of the increasing ethnic diversity in the city of Athens, as well as to reveal less visible inequalities and distances between different ethnic groups who live together, the emphasis here is on the micro scale of everyday multi-ethnic coexistence within the city's residential buildings. Our study is based on in situ qualitative research conducted in 10 different yet typical Athenian condominiums (see Figure 8.1) located in various neighbourhoods of the Municipality of Athens (see Figure 8.2). The

Figure 8.1: Typical residential buildings in the city centre of Athens (Patission Avenue)

Source: Authors' photograph

Figure 8.2: Studied residential buildings in 10 different neighbourhoods of the Municipality of Athens

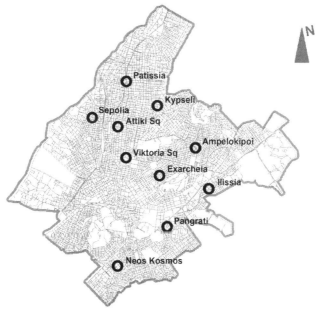

Source: Authors' elaboration

research took place during the period from March to December 2013 and it included two distinct but complementary stages.

During the first stage, the research mostly focused on the spatial relations developed between residents of the same building. For each studied building, we collected data on the residents' social profile (nationality, professional occupation, sex, age, household size) and their apartments' characteristics (floor of residence, apartment surface, occupancy status, rental cost, housing conditions). The aim was to reveal all the possible but not so visible inequalities that exist between neighbours. During the second stage, the research moved beyond spatial relations and further explored the everyday social interactions developed in cases of multi-ethnic coexistence. In all 10 studied buildings, we conducted 27 semi-structured, in-depth interviews with residents of different social profiles. The sample of interviewees included 7 Greek and 20 migrant residents: 11 Albanians, 4 Romanians, 1 Polish, 1 Moldavian, 1 Georgian, 1 Indian and 1 Pakistani. The interviewees comprised 10 men and 17 women, and their ages ranged from 28 to 80. Seventeen of the interviewees were homeowners, while 10 were tenants. The aim of the interviews was to explore the dynamics of everyday interethnic social interactions, not only within the vertically differentiated residential space, but also within all spaces of everyday life, as well as to reveal their multiple and sometimes contradictory aspects and perceptions.

Before proceeding, we would like to make an important clarification. Although the groups represented in this work are primarily defined in terms of nationality, the term 'ethnic' is extensively used in this chapter. In this way we wish to open up to further possibilities for shaping social difference beyond simple lines of nationality, as 'ethnicity' embraces various and complex cultural characteristics. Furthermore, and equally importantly, we recognise that the reference hereafter to national-ethnic categories as '*the* Greeks', '*the* Pakistanis', '*the* Albanians' and so on may appear, in a sense, essentialist. We definitely acknowledge the problematic and contested nature of such terms; group identities should not be seen as homogeneous and definitive but the individual's role and interactions must be considered (Abdallah-Pretceille, 2006). However, the use of these categories here echoes the way the latter have been used by our research participants during interviews. In this way, we seek to show as clearly as possible how national-ethnic categories are reproduced and become essentialised in every day discourse.

The primary research presented here takes into account the specific and particular local context of Athens, and it follows the scientific debate that has already developed around the multiple effects of multi-ethnic coexistence in both the neighbourhoods and the residential buildings of the city. Thus, a short literature review, closely related to the main questions of this chapter, precedes the detailed presentation of our empirical findings, which add to the related discussion.

Sociospatial effects of multi-ethnic coexistence in Athens

In order to contextualise our research, this section briefly describes the evolution of multi-ethnic coexistence in Athens. In the first few years after their arrival, migrants mostly concentrated in the city centre and experienced precarious residential conditions, including homelessness in public squares and metro stations or overcrowding in old hotels and abandoned buildings (Psimmenos, [1995] 2004). However, fairly soon, most of them managed to access housing, mostly through the private rental market (Petronoti, 1998; Vaiou et al, 2007), while a few years later, a significant percentage of migrants even had access to homeownership (Balampanidis, 2015). Overall, in a relatively short period of time, the majority of migrants in Athens followed upward residential trajectories, gradually improving their occupancy status (for instance, from homelessness to homeownership) and their housing conditions (moving to apartments with more living space per person, a higher floor, better household equipment and so on).

The migrants' residential trajectories took place in many different neighbourhoods of the city, neighbourhoods that were socially, ethnically and culturally mixed. Mapping the horizontal distribution of migrants (both tenants and homeowners) in Athens reveals a dual geography (see Figure 8.3). On the one hand, it is possible to notice high ethnic concentrations around the north and west of the very central Omonia Square, that is, in the most deprived and affordable central neighbourhoods of the city. Yet, on the other hand, a significant dispersion of migrants across almost all the city of Athens is also evident, even in the more expensive neighbourhoods to the east and south.

According to many quantitative and qualitative studies of migrants' settlement and spatial distribution, Athens appears to be a relatively homogeneous and cohesive city that is socially, ethnically and culturally mixed, with low segregation levels, not only horizontally (at the neighbourhood level) but also vertically (at the building level) (Maloutas, 2007; Vaiou et al, 2007; Maloutas et al, 2012). Regarding the vertical mix in particular, it has been possible, thanks to a certain peculiarity of typical Athenian residential buildings that offer various apartment types for a wide range of prices and, therefore, for a wide spectrum of different incomes. More spacious and expensive apartments for middle- and upper-class households are found on the upper floors, while smaller, darker and thus cheaper apartments for middle- and working-class households are located on the lower floors (Leontidou, 1990; Maloutas and Karadimitriou, 2001). Thus, the spatial distance between different groups may decrease, although social distances may come to the fore.

Figure 8.3: Concentration of migrants per census tract, Municipality of Athens, 2011

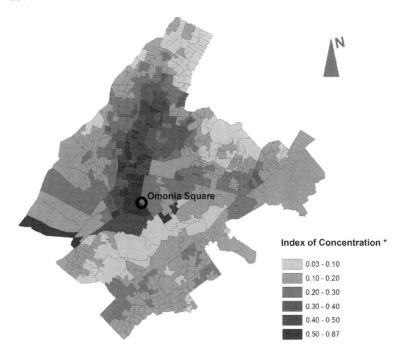

Index of Concentration *

0.03 - 0.10
0.10 - 0.20
0.20 - 0.30
0.30 - 0.40
0.40 - 0.50
0.50 - 0.87

Note: * Index of Concentration = number of migrants/number of residents

Data source: 2011 population census, map edited by the authors

Despite the relatively low levels of segregation observed in the Municipality of Athens (both horizontally and vertically), crucial sociospatial inequalities and distances subtly survive. In fact, Greeks and migrants may share the same neighbourhoods and residential buildings, but they enjoy unequal housing conditions (Arapoglou, 2007; Maloutas, 2008; Arapoglou et al, 2009). Vertical social differentiation in particular, while considered to be an 'alternative to community segregation' (Leontidou, 1990, p 12), offers good examples of the inequalities that exist at the building level. For instance, Maloutas and Karadimitriou (2001) observed a close correlation between income, educational level and nationality on the one hand, and floor of residence on the other, concluding that the micro-scale diversity at the building level 'is hardly the image of social coexistence that the tourist gaze expects' (Maloutas and Karadimitriou, 2001, p 715). The spatial mix between households of different ethnic origins living within the same residential building may obscure not only inequalities such as those described above, but also significant interethnic social distances (Kokkali, 2010), which implies not a substantial but rather a 'shadow integration' of migrant residents (Kandylis et al, 2012, p 269). In fact, Greek and migrant residents sharing the same residential buildings develop a wide spectrum of social relations, including all aspects of human interaction; for instance, not only interethnic contacts, friendship and solidarity (Kambouri, 2007, pp 206-41; Vaiou et al, 2007, pp 167-72), but also interethnic distance, racism and xenophobia (Arapoglou et al, 2009; Kandylis and Kavoulakos, 2010).

Ambiguities of vertical multi-ethnic coexistence in Athens

Drawing on the aforementioned academic discussion, and considering the existing research findings, our study adds empirical evidence at a scale best suited to revealing the many 'shadow' aspects of multi-ethnic coexistence in central Athens. Focusing on the micro scale of everyday experience within typical Athenian residential buildings and beyond (in the neighbourhood, at the workplace, the school or university) can be helpful in understanding the sociospatial dynamics of urban diversity, with the latter being situated in its particular local context.

Together but unequally... Evidence from a typical Athenian residential building

In order to exemplify our evidence, one of the 10 studied residential buildings is presented here. Before that, an important clarification needs to be made. The use of one sole case study does not claim any absolute generalisation; rather, it seeks to provide the readers with an illustrative, comprehensible example of a condition that is considered typical for central Athenian neighbourhoods. We would like to stress, then, that the aim here is not to re-present the (vertical) space of the condominium as a 'neutral grid' (Gupta and Ferguson, 1992, p 7) on which each group distinctively occupies *its own place*, which takes here the form of apartments. On the contrary, we believe that the production of social difference (be it ethnic, in our case) is a process involving numerous, not isolated, but certainly interrelated spaces (Gupta and Ferguson, 1992; see also Amin, 2002), something that becomes evident in the chapter's following parts.

Throughout the basement of the residential building, the ground floor and the five floors above, 13 dwellings are found, two for each level from the basement to the fourth floor and one final apartment on the fifth floor. The included cross-section illustration of the building (see Figure 8.4) summarises the described evidence by illustrating the spatial pattern found across the floors and among households of different social and ethnic backgrounds. The overall sociospatial condition corroborates the broader findings on Athenian vertical social differentiation described by Maloutas and Karadimitriou (2001). Four general points have to be noticed here. First and foremost, Greeks and non-Greeks coexist vertically, with the latter being absent from the upper floors, while the former are very weakly represented in the lower floors. Second, the floor of residence appears to be correlated with its residents' presence in the city: the most recently arrived migrant households, for example, the Bangladeshi households, have settled in the basement and ground floor, while the Filipino households, who have been settled in Athens for a longer period, reside on the higher floors. Third, nationality is strongly correlated with occupancy status: Greek residents are all homeowners while migrant residents are all renters. Fourth, apart from one unemployed resident in the basement, Greek residents belong to higher socioeconomic categories, while their foreign neighbours belong to lower ones. In other words, the nexus between floor of residence, social status and integration is complexly reflected in the households' composition, occupations, occupancy status and nationality.

Regarding the building's vertical residential pattern, nationality and floor of residence are strongly interrelated. Greek, Filipino and Bangladeshi are the nationalities that appeared in this vertical pattern. Migrants are overrepresented on the bottom floors, while Greek households gradually become separate on the upper ones. No natural light reaches the basement's common hallway, which is the only way to access the two flats. A one-person Greek and a four-person Bangladeshi household are located in the basement. Each apartment is $30m^2$, with no separate bedroom and one single window facing the street; moisture was evident on the walls during the field visit. Both the ground floor apartments are rented by Bangladeshi migrants. Filipino households reside in the first floor's two apartments, while the second floor houses a Greek and a Filipino family. Only Greek families dwell on the following three floors, namely, the third, fourth and fifth. It is on these floors, and on the last floor especially, that good illumination and ventilation are accompanied by an ample view over the city and significantly reduced street noise. Filipino families settled in the building before any other foreign residents; "they were the first ones to arrive", a Greek resident stated, "even before the Albanians", another added. The Filipino migrants inhabited the then empty apartments of the building's lowest levels. After upgrading their economic conditions and social integration, they ascended in spatial terms too, by moving upwards. As far as occupancy status is concerned, another distinction is evident: all the Greek households live in self-owned apartments, while all their foreign neighbours live in rented ones.

Figure 8.4: Cross-section of a typical Athenian residential building

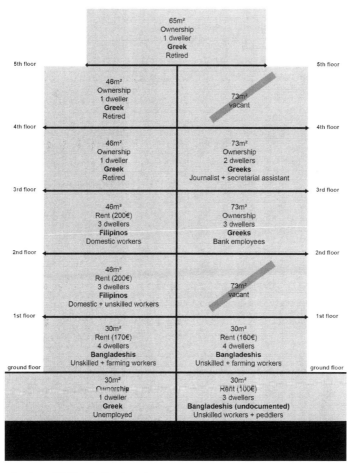

Source: Bourlessas (2013), edited by the authors

In terms of the residential space per capita, discrepancies were found: $10.7m^2$ accounts for each foreign dweller, while the equivalent average for the Greek households is more than three times higher. Nevertheless, investigating the non-Greek group in detail highlighted further complexities. For Bangladeshi households, the average domestic space drops to $8.2m^2$, while for Filipino households, the number almost doubles to $15.3m^2$. This fact could perhaps relate to the specific economic conditions that often lead migrants to form collective households; on the contrary, Greeks may opt for single-person households (age can be an important parameter here). Furthermore, some gendered nuances of the building's sociospatial pattern are evident: migrant women are underrepresented in the basement and ground floor (with Indians and Bangladeshis being predominant), while they are more prominent on higher floors (with Filipinos and Albanians being predominant). Here, we can draw links to the male or female character of migration, depending on the country of origin; for instance, migrant groups from India are male-dominated, those from the Philippines are female-dominated, while the groups from Albania and other countries of the former Eastern Bloc follow family migration patterns (Arapoglou and Sayas, 2009; Kandylis et al, 2012).

...between conflicts and encounters: The social dynamics of vertical multi-ethnic coexistence

As the above exemplary case has shown, diversity at the micro scale may enclose a multiplicity of considerable inequalities, ranging from the residents' different socioprofessional and ethnic profiles to their occupancy status and housing conditions. Diversity is thus translated into a complex plexus of spatial relations that can be expressed vertically. This section marks the passage from these spatial relations to the social dynamics of vertical coexistence, with the latter being explored through interviews with both Greek and migrant residents, since within the spatial interethnic proximity, crucial social distances and proximities may dynamically manifest themselves through the formation of a complex spectrum of interethnic social relations. These very relations, presented below, remind us that diversity is not just reflected in a pre-given and static space, but is rather shaped and understood within numerous dynamic and interrelated spaces of everyday life.

Despite the context of ethnic diversity and mix, some of the interviewees described the social relations between Greek and migrant neighbours as distant or even non-existent. The reasons for this may be purely 'practical', such as the general lack of time that people spend at home, especially in the case of migrants, who usually work for many hours and in many different jobs. As Eda explained:

> 'To be honest, we don't have many relations with our neighbours in the building. Just a "good morning" and "good afternoon". Because I work all day and my husband works overtime … we lack time…, we don't even see our children … I even work on weekends. There is no time for friendships.' (Eda, Albanian, female, age 46)

Similarly, Evi, a Greek resident, attributes the overall lack of communication between herself and her neighbours to the general absence of families in the building and, instead, the dominance of single-person households:

> 'There are no families here any more, everybody lives alone…. When the Kyriakou family lived next door, I used to visit them very often. We were always helping each other. Once they had a problem and knocked on my door at three o'clock in the morning, I supported them.' (Evi, Greek, female, age 79)

However, beyond such 'practical' reasons, the interethnic social distance may also derive from a general sense of reluctance, suspicion and fear among neighbours (both Greeks and migrants), as well as from a general climate of alienation and fear in large metropolitan cities. For instance, Mimi's words indicate that family can play a completely different, perhaps opposite, role to the one described by Evi above. Instead of an opportunity for social contact, family calls for protection and enclosure:

> 'Neighbours here don't visit each other at home. Because, you know, when you are alone and you have no one, you have to protect your family. It's not easy to invite someone into your place. And if you have children, you can't…. And in a foreign country, you are afraid.' (Mimi, Albanian, female, age 38)

A focus on the interviews conducted with Greek residents results in a composed discourse in which common linguistic patterns prove crucial to the verbal manifestation of social distances. More specifically, many Greek residents utilised racial and ethnic classification devices.

Words and phrases such as 'foreigners' or 'immigrants' accentuated the migrants' non-Greek origins by occurring repeatedly in stories referring to migrant residents. Similarly, physical characteristics such as 'the dark ones', 'the black ones' or others that accentuate conditions of negative appraisement emerged several times: migrant neighbours are the ones "starving and exhausted". Additionally, this differentiation sometimes became explicit; for instance, "foreigners are not included" in the community, as one interviewee mentioned.

Moreover, occupancy status appeared to be crucial to the distance between Greek and foreign residents. More specifically, homeownership marks another line of division according to some Greek interviewees. One Greek resident stated that "seven out of the 13 owners ... are a kind of community", before later underlining that homeowners are "a group with common goals". Consequently, homeownership may function as a prerequisite for social contacts between residents. Indeed, one interviewee mentioned that "the ones who are mainly in contact are the homeowners", while another said that she "only [knows] the names of the homeowners, not the tenants."

Further specification techniques were also deployed. On the one hand, Greek residents were mentioned in the interviews by their name or surname, while on the other hand, foreign residents were mentioned merely by their nationality rather than by their name: "Bangladeshis and Pakistanis are all the same", one interviewee stated. However, it is worth mentioning here that to the Greeks the 'different' status was based not only on foreign background and physical characteristics, but also on the floor of residence. Phrases such as "those from the basement" and "the ones below" were used in order to label the migrants living on the lowest floors. Furthermore, the 'different' may sometimes appear as unknown or vague; for instance, a Greek resident repeatedly asked herself during the interview whether her neighbours from the basement "are from Bangladesh or not".

Negative representations of foreign neighbours often appear in the stories in an explicit manner too. Thus, migrant residents are sometimes blamed for having annoying habits: "they don't pay the rent" and they "cause damage". Community problems within the building are sometimes attributed to them: "we don't have bonds because we have the foreigners". Future narrations were used with a similar tone: "they will stop paying rents ... they will cause damage" and they "will definitely sub-rent it", a Greek stated when referring to his migrant neighbours. Furthermore, the non-Greeks may have annoying habits because "they speak too loudly" and "their food smells bad sometimes". Undesired feelings could also be provoked;

for example, one interviewee noted that he is "afraid of them". Clear statements of xenophobia were also present, with phrases such as "I dislike the immigrants who live here", "I would bar [them] from my country" and "here is not an asylum" exemplifying this tendency.

It is remarkable, however, that the discriminatory discourse used by the Greeks was also appropriated by some migrant interviewees. An Indian stated that he "might need to live in a basement one day" given his foreign background, while a Bangladeshi said that, if he got involved in any trouble with Greeks, he would think: "I am a foreigner, so you are right". Further, the discourse appropriation was sometimes explicit, with foreign residents making statements against 'other' migrants who are viewed as the reason for the neighbourhood's deprivation. For example, Adela explained:

> 'Our best man was living in this neighbourhood. And I was asking him: "How can you live here?"... This neighbourhood seemed to me dangerous and dirty.... And I didn't like it. When I was coming by trolley, you know, it was full of ... migrants ... me too, I'm a migrant, but ... you know, black migrants.... I don't have a problem with them ... but the trolley was smelling bad, stinking, always....' (Adela, Romanian, female, age 42)

The social distance, lack of contact and familiarisation, and racist and xenophobic attitudes described above do not foster interaction among different ethnic groups despite their vertical spatial proximity. Instead, they seem to favour in-group enclosure according to ethnic origin and floor of residence, and offer the ground for essentialist attitudes towards the social and spatial 'other'. The social contacts of the Greek residents who live on the upper floors appeared remarkably limited to their co-ethnics – whom they used to refer to by name – while they excluded their migrant neighbours – whom they used to mention by nationality. At the same time, a similar counter-cluster seemed to develop at the condominium's lowest pole. Entering one of the condominiums on a late afternoon revealed another space of intra-ethnic interaction, this time of another ethnic group: the doors of the ground floor apartments remained open and Bangladeshi residents were moving from one residence to the other, using the building's common entrance hall as a space for in-group communication.

Nevertheless, the discourse and existence of social distance, xenophobia and racism constitute only one side of the interethnic social interaction. Both Greek and non-Greek interviewees also described interethnic relations of mutual help, collaboration, solidarity and friendship. These positive social contacts need time to develop through repeated everyday habits and routines that should not be underestimated. Meeting at the entrance to the building and in the common corridors, exchanging visits at home or playing in the backyard offer opportunities for encounters through a process of familiarisation, tolerance and mutual trust:

> '... in the building where we live ... people used to leave us the keys to their apartments so that we take care and answer phone calls. And they would show trust ... there were kids in our building ... and they would often play downstairs and therefore families became closer and got to know each other. They used to play downstairs, in the entrance hall. This building also had a big courtyard. Kids would play there as well.' (Joseph, Polish, male, age 63)

Interethnic encounters go beyond the space of home and the residential building, and they also develop, for example, in the neighbourhood between residents and shopkeepers, in the workplace between employers and employees, as well as at school or university among schoolmates or students from different ethnic backgrounds. Eda offered an example of friendly relations developed in the workplace between migrant women working in domestic or personal care services and Greek female employers:

> 'In the neighbourhood of Kypseli, I met Katerina and Dina. I clean their office ... two amazing women who helped me a lot and I will never forget.... We visit each other at home ... our friendship became closer ... I also clean Katerina's house. We go for coffee, we talk, she is my best friend....' (Eda, Albanian, female, age 46)

As for the school space, Mimi provided an example of social relations developed among schoolmates: "At school, children come from all countries of the world, Bulgaria, Romania, Albania, Pakistan.... Children manage to get along easily, easier than parents.... My children have mixed friendships. I never told them: 'Don't hang out with him or her'.... They solve their own problems" (Mimi, Albanian, female, age 38).

Overall, within all the different everyday life spaces, the quality and degree of interethnic social contacts depend on the way people spend their free time. They also differ according to age or professional occupation, and are gender-related. To offer a characteristic example, the mothers' responsibility for childcare and taking their children to the local square or park creates a 'common place' for Greek and migrant women to develop relations of contact and friendship. As Lorena explained: "I have good relationships ... with other mums and the friends of my daughter ... Greeks and Albanians.... In the neighbourhood, thanks to the children, when we are going out, I make friends.... Tomorrow, my daughter's friend has a birthday party and we are going..." (Lorena, Albanian, female, age 28).

Last but not least, it is remarkable how often the process of familiarisation and social approaching depends on the way people, especially migrants, embody 'normality': migrants who speak fluent Greek, integrate common practices or become homeowners are more easily accepted by their Greek neighbours than migrants who still clearly embody ethnic and social 'otherness'. "... Our neighbour is very nice, she comes from Albania.... I visit them at home, I like it there ... because they are peaceful, clean, follow a schedule in their life. They don't make a mess... they never cause problems" (Nick, Greek, male, age 68).

Embodying 'normality' as a prerequisite for interethnic social contact is sometimes even appropriated by migrant residents who are disturbed by the presence of 'other' migrants in their neighbourhood or their building. For instance, homeownership occurs again as a prerequisite, appropriated this time by foreign residents. As an example, Mimi from Albania, after many years living in Greece, is today a homeowner in a building where other migrants, when living there as tenants, are not welcome:

> 'In the building we are all homeowners. There are not many of us [the foreigners]. And there are no tenants.... And we don't put foreigners in the apartments. We are trying to maintain a certain quality in the building. We only have foreigners who are homeowners, on the third floor from Romania and on the fifth from Albania.' (Mimi, Albanian, female, age 38)

All the evidence presented above highlights the complex social dynamics that can unfold within buildings where Greek and non-Greek residents coexist. Two points need to be underlined here: that such social dynamics vary widely from social proximities to social distances; and that the micro scale of the building as a scale of analysis, in addition to its various methodological benefits, should not prevent us from expanding our views to the numerous urban spaces where social relations are dynamically developed.

Conclusion: Diversity as complexity

By accentuating the micro-scale manifestations of urban diversity, this study revealed multiple contradictory and ambiguous effects of multi-ethnic coexistence. In typical Athenian residential buildings, people may live *together but unequally* and *between conflicts and encounters*. The chapter has sought to clearly demonstrate that, in the case of Athens, low segregation levels – both horizontally and vertically – and spatial proximity between different population groups do not necessarily result in spatial and social justice and cohesion.

The building scale offers an opportunity for enhanced insight into urban diversity and its dynamics of sociospatial proximities and distances. Within instances of vertical socio-ethnic mix, various less visible but still crucial inequalities may exist concerning the residents' social profile (for example, nationality, professional occupation, sex, age) and their housing conditions (for example, floor of residence, square metres per capita, occupancy status). Additionally, in this particular context of spatial proximity, interethnic social interaction may embrace a wide spectrum of relations, ranging from conflictual tensions to more harmonious contacts. By and large, the development of interethnic social contacts, along with their quality and degree, constitutes a long, dynamic, complex and porous process that occurs in multiple spaces (at home, in the apartment building, in the neighbourhood, at the workplace, at school or university and so on) and differs by nationality, socioprofessional profile, sex, age or the way people spend their spare time and shape their everyday life habits and practices.

The multiple, contradictory and ambiguous sociospatial effects of vertical multi-ethnic coexistence should not be underestimated, but should instead be subject to serious consideration when addressing diversity in urban environments that are partitioned in various ways (for example, along the lines of class or nationality) and at different scales (for example, at the neighbourhood or building level), depending on the particularities of the local context. The case of Athens discussed here showed that diversity – when related to segregation – can be interpreted as complexity, as multifaceted sociospatial condition, in contrast to very optimistic or neutral and, therefore, distorting approaches to urban life. A complex perception of diversity can help us to rethink social inequalities and thoroughly understand the multiple social dynamics that it may entail.

Finally, considering the intrinsic complexity and ambiguity of diversity, urban policies aimed at achieving a universal panacea to the 'problem' can be questioned. For example, policies aimed at facilitating ethnic and social mix alone are not sufficient tools for tackling inequality, weak integration and social marginalisation, since there is no linear, clear-cut relation between spatial and social proximity or distance, while both negative and positive outcomes may constantly arise. In any case, one should not forget that any 'togetherness' in terms of space may foster not only social encounters but also social tensions. Due to diversity being a complex condition to address, urban policies should not underestimate the multiplicity and dynamism of contextually dependent sociospatial phenomena and their unpredictable effects, especially within constantly transforming, stratified and conflictual urban societies.

References

Abdallah-Pretceille, M. (2006) 'Interculturalism as a paradigm for thinking about diversity', *Intercultural Education*, 17(5), 475-83.

Amin, A. (2002) 'Ethnicity and the multicultural city: Living with diversity', *Environment and Planning A*, 34, 959-80.

Arapoglou, V.P. (2007) 'Ethnic segregation and housing conditions in Athens: Exposure to prosperity or deprivation?', *Proceedings of the 8th National Geographical Conference*, Athens: Hellenic Geographical Society, vol C, 104-12 [in Greek].

Arapoglou, V.P. and Sayas, J. (2009) 'New facets of urban segregation in southern Europe: Gender, migration and social class change in Athens', *European Urban and Regional Studies*, 16, 345-62.

Arapoglou, V.P., Kavoulakos, K.I., Kandylis, G. and Maloutas, T. (2009) 'The new social geography of Athens: Migration, diversity and conflict', *Contemporary Issues (Synchrona Themata)*, 107, 57-66 [in Greek].

Arbaci, S. (2008) '(Re)viewing ethnic residential segregation in southern European cities: Housing and urban regimes as mechanisms of marginalisation', *Housing Studies*, 23(4), 589-613.

Arbaci, S. and Malheiros, J. (2009) 'De-segregation, peripheralisation and the social exclusion of immigrants: Southern European cities in the 1990s', *Journal of Ethnic and Migration Studies*, 36(2), 227-55.

Balampanidis, D. (2015) 'Access of immigrants to homeownership (2000-2010). Main patterns of "horizontal" and "vertical" ethnic residential segregation in the Municipality of Athens', *Athens Social Atlas* (www.athenssocialatlas.gr/).

Bodaar, A. and Rath, J. (2005) 'Cities, diversity and public space', *Metropolis World Bulletin*, 5 (September), 3-5.

Bolt, G., Phillips, D. and van Kempen, R. (2010) 'Housing policy, (de) segregation and social mixing: An international perspective', *Housing Studies*, 25(2), 129-35.

Bourlessas, P. (2013) 'Spatial proximities and social distances in cases of vertical segregation: Evidence from Athens', Master's thesis, University of Vienna.

Camina, M.M. and Wood, M.J. (2009) 'Parallel lives: Towards a greater understanding of what mixed communities can offer', *Urban Studies*, 46, 459-80.

Chamboredon, J.C. and Lemaire, M. (1970) 'Proximité spatiale et distance sociale. Les grands ensembles et leur peuplement', *Revue française de sociologie,* 11(1), 3-33.

Cheshire, P. (2007) *Segregated neighbourhoods and mixed communities: A critical analysis*, York: Joseph Rowntree Foundation.

EKKE-ELSTAT (National Centre for Social Research-National Statistical Authority) (2015) *Panorama of Census Data 1991-2011* (https://panorama.statistics.gr/en/).

ELSTAT (Hellenic Statistical Authority) (2011) *Population and Housing Census 2011. Table A04. Resident population by nationality, sex and marital status. Country and regions* (www.statistics.gr/el/statistics/-/publication/SAM03/2011).

Emke-Poulopoulou, I. (2007) *The challenge of migration*, Athens: Papazisis.

Eraydin, A., Tasan-Kok, T. and Vranken, J. (2010) 'Diversity matters: Immigrant entrepreneurship and contribution of different forms of social integration in economic performance of cities', *European Planning Studies*, 18, 521-43.

ESYE (National Statistical Service of Greece) (2009) *Population and Housing Census 18 March 2001 (Resident Population)*, Piraeus: ELSTAT, vol 1 [in Greek].

Fainstein, S.S. (2005) 'Cities and diversity should we want it? Can we plan for it?', *Urban Affairs Review*, 41, 3-19.

Fainstein, S.S. (2009) 'Spatial justice and planning', *Justice Spatiale/ Spatial Justice* (www.jssj.org/wp-content/uploads/2012/12/JSSJ1-5en1.pdf).

Florida, R. (2002) *The rise of the creative class*, New York: Basic Books.

Fujita, K. (2012) 'Conclusion: Residential segregation and urban theory', in K. Fujita and T. Maloutas (eds) *Residential segregation in comparative perspective: Making sense of contextual diversity*, Farnham: Ashgate, 285-322.

Galster, G. (2007) 'Neighbourhood social mix as a goal of housing policy: A theoretical analysis', *European Journal of Housing Policy*, 7(1), 19-43.

Gupta, A. and Ferguson, J. (1992) 'Beyond "culture": Space, identity, and the politics of difference', *Cultural Anthropology*, 7(1), 6-23.

Häussermann, H. and Siebel, W. (2001) 'Integration and segregation – Thoughts on an old debate', *German Journal of Urban Studies*, 1, 68-79 [in German] (available in English at www.difu.de/publikationen/integration-and-the-city.html-3).

Kambouri, E. (2007) *Gender and migration. The everyday life of migrant women from Albania and Ukraine*, Athens: Gutenberg, vol 2 [in Greek].

Kandylis, G. and Kavoulakos, K.I. (2010) 'Local anti-migrant action and urban conflicts in Athens', *Geographies*, 17, 105-9 [in Greek].

Kandylis, G., Maloutas, T. and Sayas, J. (2012) 'Immigration, inequality and diversity: Socio-ethnic hierarchy and spatial organization in Athens, Greece', *European Urban and Regional Studies*, 19(3), 267-86.

Kokkali, I. (2010) 'Spatial proximity and social distance: Albanian migrants' invisible exclusions. Evidence from Greece', Paper prepared for presentation at the World Bank International Conference on 'Poverty and Social Inclusion in the Western Balkans' (http://siteresources.worldbank.org/INTECAREGTOPPOVRED/Resources/ikokkalipaperWBWesternBalkans.pdf).

Leal, J. (2004) 'Segregation and social change in Madrid metropolitan region', *The Greek Review of Social Research*, 113, 81-104.

Leontidou, L. (1990) *The Mediterranean city in transition: Social change and urban development*, Cambridge: Cambridge University Press.

Malheiros, J. (2002) 'Ethni-cities: Residential patterns in the northern European and Mediterranean metropolises – implications for policy design', *International Journal of Population Geography*, 8, 107-34.

Maloutas, T. (2007) 'Segregation, social polarization and immigration in Athens during the 1990s: Theoretical expectations and contextual difference', *International Journal of Urban and Regional Research*, 31(4), 733 58.

Maloutas, T. (2008) 'Social mobility and residential segregation in Athens: patterns of segregation under conditions of low residential mobility', in D. Emmanouil, E. Zakopoulou, R. Kaftantzoglou, T. Maloutas and A. Hadjigianni (eds) *Social and spatial transformations in Athens of the 21st century*, Athens: EKKE (National Centre for Social Research), pp 52-3 [in Greek].

Maloutas, T. and Karadimitriou, N. (2001) 'Vertical social differentiation in Athens: Alternative or complement to community segregation?', *International Journal of Urban and Regional Research*, 25, 699-716.

Maloutas, T., Arapoglou, V., Kandylis, G. and Sayas, J. (2012) 'Social polarization and de-segregation in Athens', in T. Maloutas and K. Fujita (eds) *Residential segregation in comparative perspective. Making sense of contextual diversity*, London: Ashgate, 257-83.

Marcuse, P. (2002) 'The partitioned city in history', in P. Marcuse and R. van Kempen (eds) *Of states and cities: The partitioning of urban space*, Oxford: Oxford University Press, 11-34.

Marcuse, P. (2005) 'Enclaves yes, ghettos no: Segregation and the state', in D.P. Varady (ed) *Desegregating the city: Ghettos, enclaves, and inequality*, New York: SUNY Press, 15-30.

Martiniello, M. (2004) *How to combine integration and diversities: The challenge of an EU multicultural citizenship*, EUMC Discussion Paper, Vienna: European Monitoring Centre on Racism and Xenophobia.

Perrone, C. (2011) 'What would a "DiverCity" be like? Speculation on difference-sensitive planning and living practices', in C. Perrone, G. Manella and L. Tripodi (eds) *Everyday life in the segmented city (Research in Urban Sociology*, vol 11), Bingley: Emerald Group Publishing Limited, 1-25.

Petronoti, M. (1998) *Portrait of an intercultural relationship: Crystallisations, cracks and reconstructions*, Athens: UNESCO/EKKE (National Centre for Social Research)/Plethron [in Greek].

Psimmenos, I. ([1995] 2004) *Migration from the Balkans. Social exclusion in Athens*, Athens: Papazisis [in Greek].

Sandercock, L. (2000) 'When strangers become neighbours: Managing cities of difference', *Planning Theory & Practice*, 1, 13-30.

Syrett, S. and Sepulveda, L. (2011) 'Realising the diversity dividend: Population diversity and urban economic development', *Environment and Planning A*, 43, 487-504.

Vaiou, D. et al (2007) *Intersecting patterns of everyday life and socio-spatial changes in the city. Migrant and local women in the neighbourhoods of Athens*, Athens: L-Press National Technical University of Athens (NTUA) [in Greek].

9

Beyond the middle classes: Neighbourhood choice and satisfaction in the hyper-diverse contexts[1]

Anouk K. Tersteeg and Ympkje Albeda

Cities have always attracted diverse groups of people, as they offer work, education, housing, social contacts, facilities and services. However, scholars have recently argued that cities are becoming even more diverse, in terms not only of ethnicity but also of, for example, activity patterns, attitudes and perceptions, and lifestyles (Vertovec, 2007, 2010; Tasan-Kok et al, 2013). In Western European cities, the neighbourhoods that are most diverse are often relatively deprived (Wessendorf, 2014). Low-income groups are thought to be 'trapped' in their neighbourhoods in terms of their residential careers, and their neighbourhoods are associated with crime, vandalism and low-quality housing, public spaces and education (Dekker et al, 2011; van der Meer and Tolsma, 2014). Therefore, these areas are often portrayed in public and political debates as undesirable places in which to live. The negative understandings are reflected in the multitude of sociospatial policy interventions for these areas in Western Europe, for example, to promote the influx of higher-income groups and increase social cohesion and social mobility.

Nonetheless, few scholars or professionals have examined what attracts people to diverse and deprived urban areas and how perceptions of local diversities play a role in this respect. Those who have done so have mostly focused on perceptions of ethno-cultural diversity, particularly among the middle classes. Since the 1990s, studies on social mix, gentrification and the creative class have demonstrated how an appreciation of, for instance, ethnic, lifestyle, gender and sexual diversity has attracted the middle classes to cities or kept them there (Lees, 2000, 2008; Butler and Robson, 2003; Florida, 2003; Hamnett, 2003). The picture has emerged that middle classes choose diversity (Atkinson, 2006; Karsten, 2007), whereas the lower classes are more often trapped in diverse neighbourhoods. Yet the importance of diversity for neighbourhood choice and satisfaction has hardly been studied among non–middle-class residents.

This chapter fills these research and policy gaps by presenting a qualitative study on neighbourhood choice and satisfaction among residents of different social classes in highly diverse neighbourhoods in Antwerp (Belgium) and Rotterdam (the Netherlands). An in-depth approach was adopted to gain insight into how perceptions of neighbourhood diversity had shaped residents' decisions to move to these neighbourhoods, and how the diversity affects their experiences of their neighbourhoods. The study connects the rapidly growing body of literature on highly diverse neighbourhoods to the field of residential choice and satisfaction. The following research questions were formulated to guide the study:

1. To what extent was diversity a motive for residents of diverse and deprived urban areas to move to their current neighbourhoods?
2. To what extent does diversity influence the neighbourhood satisfaction of residents of diverse and deprived urban areas?

The following section provides the theoretical background to the determinants of and mechanisms behind neighbourhood choice and satisfaction in diverse neighbourhoods, demonstrating the need for research on, for example, lower-class and minority ethnic groups, to add to the literature on the middle classes. The research areas, methods and interviewees are then introduced in the third section, on the research design. The research findings section discusses residents' motives for moving to their current neighbourhoods and their satisfaction with their current neighbourhoods. In the concluding section we highlight the particular contribution of our findings to the existing literature on neighbourhood choice and satisfaction and urban policies for highly diverse urban areas.

Living in highly diverse neighbourhoods

Studies on the relation between diversity and neighbourhood choice and satisfaction are scarce. The topic has received most attention in the Urban Studies literature on suburbanisation, gentrification and the creative class. The literature on suburbanisation describes how in the 1960s and 1970s an increase in wealth and car ownership in Western Europe encouraged middle-class households to leave the cities for suburban areas (Jackson, 1985; Loots and van Hove, 1986; de Decker,

2011). The inflow of non-Western migrants to urban neighbourhoods that started in the 1960s further stimulated the suburbanisation. As it was mostly white people who could afford to leave the city, the process has been described as 'white flight' (Frey, 1979; Galster, 1990; Wright et al, 2014). People who could not afford to move away – namely, the poor, older people and immigrants – remained in the city. Although this process was stronger in Belgium than in the Netherlands,[2] the process resulted in population loss in both Antwerp and Rotterdam, as well as a poorer and increasingly ethno-culturally diverse population (Loots and van Hove, 1986; Statistics Netherlands, 2004; Public Affairs Rotterdam, nd). Whereas literature on white flight describes ethno-cultural diversity as a reason for the middle classes to leave the city, literature on gentrification and the creative class describes it as attractive to the middle classes. In the 1990s, these studies started to report the return of middle-class workers and households to cities due to a new appreciation of social diversity and the improved living conditions in the cities (Lees, 2000, 2008; Butler and Robson, 2003; Florida, 2003; Hamnett, 2003; Atkinson, 2006; Karsten, 2007).

Although it has been questioned whether the reappraisal of the city by the middle classes entails an appreciation of the diverse population or the variety of facilities and amenities that are characteristic of urban neighbourhoods[3] (Weck and Hanhörster, 2014), white middle-class households in diverse neighbourhoods are thought to have consciously chosen to live amidst diversity. In addition, diversity is seen as a factor that contributes to their neighbourhood satisfaction (Atkinson, 2006; Karsten, 2007). In contrast, lower-class and minority ethnic households in diverse neighbourhoods are often regarded as being 'trapped' in diversity (Florida, 2005; Lees et al, 2008). Nevertheless, these studies rarely take into account the influence of diversity or perceptions thereof on the neighbourhood choice of lower-class and minority ethnic groups. To get a more comprehensive understanding, the present study therefore explored the importance of diversity for the neighbourhood choice and satisfaction not only of white middle-class residents, but also of lower-class and minority ethnic groups living in highly diverse neighbourhoods. In what follows we discuss what is known from the literature about the ways in which socioeconomic as well as ethnic diversity shape neighbourhood choice and satisfaction.

Class differences

Middle- and upper-class households have more choice when it comes to housing than households in lower socioeconomic positions. The former households living in diverse neighbourhoods can more easily move to less diverse neighbourhoods, of which there are plenty in Western European cities and even more outside cities. Thus, the literature assumes that neighbourhood diversity is attractive to them. Studies show that the middle and upper classes are attracted to different sorts of diversity (Blokland and van Eijk, 2010; Jackson and Benson, 2014; Tissot, 2014). An important point of attraction for middle-class households in diverse neighbourhoods appears to be the heterogeneous facility and amenity structure that characterises highly diverse neighbourhoods (Florida, 2003, 2005; Wessendorf, 2014; Hall, 2015). Nevertheless, studies disagree on the relative importance of this diverse infrastructure compared to traditional push-and-pull factors such as distance to work (Karsten, 2007; van Diepen and Musterd, 2009; Lawton et al, 2013). It also remains unclear why a diversity of facilities might be a pull factor for them.

The literature shows that the middle and upper classes do not choose to settle or remain in highly diverse neighbourhood because of the diverse local social contacts they make or might make. This is because middle-class households generally do not depend on the neighbourhood for their daily activities and social network in contrast to lower-class households (Guest and Wierzbicki, 1999; Blokland, 2003; Dekker and Bolt 2005). Studies indicate that middle-class households living in diverse neighbourhoods have relatively small and homogeneous local networks of neighbours and other local acquaintances in terms of class, culture and ethnicity (Butler and Robson, 2001, 2003; Atkinson, 2006; Karsten, 2007). This is the case even among 'diversity seekers' – residents for whom neighbourhood diversity was a settlement motive (Blokland and van Eijk, 2010).

To the best of our knowledge, few studies have explored the role of urban diversity in the neighbourhood choice and satisfaction of households in low socioeconomic positions. Highly diverse urban areas often offer affordable housing. For lower-class households, affordability is thought to be one of the most important reasons to live in diverse neighbourhoods. Because they might not have chosen to live in a diverse neighbourhood, we might expect them to feel that they are 'stuck in diversity', rather than to appreciate diversity.

The literature indicates that lower-class residents have more local activity patterns and social networks than middle- and upper-class residents. Therefore, the presence of family and friends appears to be more important for their decision to settle or remain in a neighbourhood than it is for the middle and upper classes (Fischer, 1982; Amerigo and Aragones, 1990; Guest and Wierzbicki, 1999; Adriaanse, 2007;

Völker et al, 2013). Yet this preference does not necessarily relate to social diversity, as strong ties with family and friends in diverse contexts mostly develop along lines of ethnicity and class (Putnam, 2000, 2007; Valentine, 2008; Blokland and van Eijk, 2010; Wessendorf, 2014). Contacts with strangers and weak ties with neighbours and other local acquaintances can, however, be highly diverse, due to, for example, the local orientation of lower-class households (Amin, 2002; Wessendorf, 2014; Hall, 2015).

The picture that emerges from the literature is that middle- and upper-class residents in diverse neighbourhoods have chosen to live in such neighbourhoods because they appreciate the specific 'social wallpaper' (Butler, 2003) and the facility and amenity structure of diverse neighbourhoods, whereas lower classes live in these neighbourhoods because they offer affordable housing and enable them to live close to their family and friends. Therefore, we expected to find that middle-class residents in diverse areas experience diversity more positively than lower-class residents.

The role of ethnicity

Middle-class majority ethnic residents in diverse neighbourhoods who moved to the area when it was already diverse are thought to mostly appreciate local diversity (Florida, 2003, 2005). However, the literature indicates that this is different for long-term majority ethnic residents, particularly those with few housing alternatives. For instance, van Ham and Feijten (2008) and van Ham and Clark (2009) have demonstrated that in neighbourhoods with an increasing percentage of minority ethnic groups, more people, particularly white majority ethnic residents, want to leave the neighbourhood because they are becoming more ethnically different from others in the neighbourhood. Part of this group is long-term residents who did not choose to live in a diverse neighbourhood at the time of settlement and lack the means to move away (Feijten and van Ham, 2009). Other long-term residents, however, who lack opportunities to leave, adjust their expectations of the residential environment to reduce residential stress (for example, Brown and Moore, 1970), suggesting that their neighbourhood satisfaction might not be as negative as one might expect.

Compared to majority ethnic residents, minority ethnic residents in Western European cities are more often in low socioeconomic positions and hence have relatively few options when it comes to neighbourhood choice. The literature therefore indicates that minority ethnic groups in low socioeconomic positions settle in diverse, deprived neighbourhoods because of the affordable housing (see also Pemberton and Phillimore, 2016).

According to ethnic enclave theory, minority ethnic groups, regardless of their socioeconomic situation, are thought to settle in diverse areas because they prefer to live close to co-ethnics, who are often spatially concentrated in diverse neighbourhoods (Wilson and Portes, 1980). In this respect they prefer homogeneity rather than diversity. An advantage of living in a neighbourhood with co-ethnics is the presence of specialised facilities and amenities that meet ethno-cultural-specific needs (Logan et al, 2002). In addition, living in the presence of co-ethnics also offers entry points for work, particularly for minority ethnic groups in low socioeconomic positions (Zorlu and Mulder, 2007; Zukin et al, 2016; Saunders, 2010). Furthermore, according to ethnic enclave theory, living among co-ethnics can provide important personal support networks. These networks can further provide protection and security and can contribute to a sense of home (Saunders, 2010; Górny and Toruńczyk-Ruiz, 2014; Pemberton and Phillimore, 2016). However, living among co-ethnics can also cause negative residential experiences, for instance, in the case of too high levels of social control (Dekker and Bolt, 2005). An ethnically diverse neighbourhood could mitigate this, but not if ethnic communities live parallel lives (Forrest and Kearns, 2001; Camina and Wood, 2009). Nevertheless, a growing body of literature shows high levels of everyday social interaction across ethno-cultural differences in highly diverse neighbourhoods. Referred to as, for example, 'everyday multiculturalism', 'corner-shop cosmopolitanism', 'conviviality' and 'light encounters', these exchanges mostly take place between neighbours and other local acquaintances. Inter-ethno-cultural relationships mostly develop between more locally oriented residents in low socioeconomic positions, rather than middle- and upper-class residents (Fincher and Iveson, 2008; Valentine, 2008; Wise, 2009; Hall, 2012; van Eijk, 2012; Wessendorf, 2014).

In sum, one might expect that the white middle classes who settled in diverse neighbourhoods when they were already diverse are attracted to urban diversity and appreciate this, whereas white long-term residents (who are mostly in lower socioeconomic positions, otherwise they would have moved) are more ambivalent about urban diversity because they settled in the neighbourhoods before they were so diverse. Minority ethnic groups might be mostly attracted to neighbourhoods where co-ethnics live, preferring ethnically homogeneous rather than diverse neighbourhoods.

Research in highly diverse neighbourhoods in Rotterdam and Antwerp

The cities of Rotterdam and Antwerp are similar in many respects. The former has about 624,800 inhabitants, the latter 516,000, and both are their country's second largest city. Both are also port cities and former industrial cities, and have relatively high levels of low-skilled workers, unemployment and poor households compared to other large cities in the Netherlands and Belgium. In both cities, urban policies have been implemented in an attempt to turn the tide by attracting more middle- and high-income groups by, for example, stimulating processes of neighbourhood gentrification (Loopmans, 2008; Doucet et al, 2011). Due to their histories as international trade centres, the cities have attracted migrants from all over the world. Migrants have come to work in the docks or, in the case of Antwerp, for instance, as diamond traders. They re-joined their families or formed new families. In 2015, almost half of the inhabitants of Rotterdam and Antwerp (49% and 46%, respectively) were born abroad or had at least one parent who was born abroad (Municipality of Antwerp, 2015; Statistics Rotterdam, 2016).

The present research was carried out in the district of Feijenoord, located on the south bank of Rotterdam, and in three adjacent areas in Antwerp, namely, Antwerpen Noord, Deurne Noord and Borgerhout Intra Muros. Feijenoord has 73,079 inhabitants (as of 2015) and comprises nine neighbourhoods. The neighbourhoods studied in Antwerp have a total of about 95,642 inhabitants (as of 2015). The case study areas are located relatively close to the city centre, in terms of both absolute distance and public transport connections. We conducted our research here because the areas are characterised by an enormous diversity of individuals and households, in terms not only of income, but also of education, household composition, age, ethnicity, attitudes and lifestyles. In 2014, the largest ethnic groups in Feijenoord were Dutch[4] (32%), Turkish (19%), Surinamese (9%) and Moroccan (11%), and in 2015, the largest ethnic groups in the research area in Antwerp were Belgian (32%), North African (25%), East European (10%) and Other West European (6%). Whereas the majority ethnic populations of the Netherlands and Belgium are ageing, the population of the research areas is getting younger: in 2014, 32 per cent of the population of Feijenoord were younger than 25, as were 36 per cent of the neighbourhoods studied in Antwerp. The areas are also deprived: they are characterised by combinations of physical deterioration (low housing quality and badly maintained public places and streets) and a concentration of low-income groups (with relatively high crime rates and large numbers of people who are unemployed and on welfare benefits).

Rather than create a sample that is representative of the population, we interviewed members of as many social groups as possible, paying specific attention to ethnicity, education, income, length of residence and household composition. Interviewees were selected using purposeful sampling to ensure that we spoke with members of the above-mentioned groups (Bryman, 2012). Within this framework, we used two methods. First, we approached local governance arrangements that deal with social diversity on a daily basis, most of which we knew from previous research in the area (see Saeys et al, 2014; Tersteeg et al, 2014), and asked them to introduce us to individuals in the neighbourhood. Second, we asked interviewees to introduce us to other potential interviewees (the snowball method). All interviewees were aged 18 or older and signed a consent form. The interviews were held at people's homes (unless an interviewee preferred an alternative place, such as a community centre, library or cafe) and lasted about an hour. The questions focused on residents' motives for moving to, living in and, where relevant, leaving their current neighbourhoods in relation to local diversity. During the interviews, we also mapped residents' egocentric social networks of family, friends, acquaintances and neighbours, because we expected local social networks to be important for the neighbourhood choice and satisfaction of some resident groups. All interviews were taped and transcribed and then analysed using the qualitative data analysis software NVivo. The interviews were held between September 2014 and May 2015.

In Rotterdam, we interviewed 56 people in eight neighbourhoods in Feijenoord. Most interviewees lived in the neighbourhoods of Feijenoord,[5] Hillesluis, Katendrecht and Vreewijk. In Antwerp, we interviewed 54 people: 21 in Deurne Noord, 16 in Antwerpen Noord and 17 in Borgerhout. The interviewees represented 15 and 17 nationalities in Rotterdam and Antwerp, respectively. The largest ethnic groups represented by the interviewees were Dutch, Surinamese, Turkish and Moroccan in Rotterdam, and Belgian, Moroccan, Dutch and German in Antwerp. In terms of religion, the sample included followers of various forms of Islam, Hinduism and Christianity. Interviewees' duration of stay in the dwellings and neighbourhoods varied from a few weeks to several decades. They represented different age groups (18-88 years old), household types (single, couples, couples with children, single parents) and socioeconomic positions, referring to income and education levels. For an extensive overview of the demographics of the interviewed people, see Albeda et al (2015) and Tersteeg et al (2017).

Neighbourhood choice

We know from the literature on neighbourhood choice that the extent to which residents have a choice when moving to their neighbourhoods and dwellings has important implications for their satisfaction with their neighbourhoods (see, for example, Posthumus, 2013). Before we discuss the most important motives for moving to a diverse and deprived neighbourhood, it is therefore important to note that a few residents felt that the decision to move had not been entirely voluntary and that housing options were limited. A number of interviewees living in social housing in Rotterdam had been forced to switch social rental apartments due to urban restructuring programmes here. Other residents had limited housing options because they had been in urgent need of a dwelling, for instance, because they had been homeless or expecting a child. Nevertheless, the large majority of interviewees felt that they had made a conscious decision to move to their present dwellings and neighbourhoods, and our focus is now on these interviewees.

Availability of affordable housing

Although relocation options were sometimes limited, most interviewees felt that they had chosen to move to their current neighbourhoods. For most residents, however, it was not the diversity they chose: the primary reason to choose the current neighbourhood was the availability of affordable housing. Many of the dwellings in the research areas are the cheapest in the city. In line with the literature, households in low socioeconomic positions[6] (SEP) cannot afford to live elsewhere. Yet, different from what we expected based on the literature, households in medium or high SEP were also attracted to the neighbourhood because of the affordable housing stock. For example, when asked why they moved to their current neighbourhood, Edward (Dutch, medium SEP, Rotterdam, age 43) replied:

> 'We considered [buying a house in] Rotterdam South because of the affordability of the owner-occupied houses. I mean, it saves us €100,000 buying a house four kilometres away [from the city centre]. This [house] was affordable

and large.... I will never get the opportunity to buy such a house for such a low price again.'

Bonds with family and friends

In line with the literature, for interviewees in low SEP and from minority ethnic backgrounds, the presence of family and friends in the neighbourhood was an important settlement motive. These networks provided interviewees with company and support; for example, they shared meals, took care of each other in the case of illness or disabilities, babysat and generally kept an eye out for each other. These strong local ties were mostly homogeneous in terms of SEP and ethnicity. When Usha (Tibetan Belgian, medium SEP, Antwerp, age 27) was asked why he had moved to his current neighbourhood, he responded: "... because all my friends live nearby and I do not know that much about Belgium yet. Therefore, it was important for me to live close to my friends." Likewise, Willemijn (Dutch, low SEP, Rotterdam, age 41) and her son had recently moved to her parents' neighbourhood to be close to them:

> 'It is very nice to have my parents live nearby because they are getting older. They are both 70. I can support them. Of course it is also nice for my son, and convenient for me: when I need to do some shopping, I tell him "Go visit your grandmother".'

A neighbourhood without a majority group

For some interviewees, mostly of minority ethnic backgrounds, the diversity of people appeared important for their neighbourhood choice, as they preferred to live in neighbourhoods that were not dominated by a majority group. Emre (Turkish Dutch, low SEP, Rotterdam, age 21), for instance, reported that the commonality of being a member of a minority ethnic group in his neighbourhood motivates residents to treat each other as equals, despite their differences. It is thus the diversity of the population that was important to these residents, as Salima (Moroccan Belgian, medium SEP, Antwerp, age 38) explained: "I don't think I would like to live in a neighbourhood with only Moroccan people, no. I want some variety, Belgian people, African.... I think [otherwise] it would be boring. Boring, and also everybody has the same opinion, same culture, same religion."

Diversity of the neighbourhood population refers not only to ethnicity, but also to other aspects of diversity, as Rick's (Dutch, medium SEP, Rotterdam, age 45) situation illustrates. He reported that he preferred to live in his current neighbourhood, which was home to diverse types of households, rather than in his previous neighbourhood, which was mostly inhabited by couples with children, because he had just got divorced and lived alone.

Living among diverse ethnic groups or household types thus made the interviewees feel more 'in place' (Cresswell, 1996; Wessendorf, 2014; Pemberton and Phillimore, 2016). Whereas the literature often highlights that minority ethnic groups are attracted to similarity by pointing out that they want to live near friends and family members, our results indicate that minority groups seek not only similarity, but also diversity.

Although for many interviewees diversity was not the main reason to settle in their current neighbourhoods, it did play a role when people had to choose between neighbourhoods with different sorts of diversity. Myrthe (Belgian, high SEP, age 39), for example, preferred Borgerhout to Antwerpen Noord, because people of Belgian origin were a majority in the former and a minority in the latter. Yet, Nel (Belgian, low SEP, age 63) preferred Deurne Noord over Borgerhout because of the perceived concentration of Moroccan people in the latter neighbourhood. She said she liked the diversity in her neighbourhood because no population group was overly numerous or dominant, enabling everybody to feel at home. Nel explained: "We don't have 'clan formation', like Borgerhout, [which] really [has] a concentration of Moroccans.... It is enormously mixed here, and [it all works] without problems." In Rotterdam, too, people from diverse ethnic and socioeconomic backgrounds compared neighbourhoods with different types of diversity when choosing their current neighbourhoods. Hagar (Dutch, low SEP, Rotterdam, age 55), for example, chose to settle in a part of the neighbourhood with few Muslims. She said that she would never want to live near another part (Maashaven) because of the high concentration of Muslims living there.

Neighbourhood satisfaction

To examine the extent to which residents were satisfied with their neighbourhoods, they were asked to elaborate on positive and negative experiences with their residential environments. They were also asked whether they would remain in their neighbourhoods or leave if they had the opportunity, and why.

We found that residents generally experienced their residential environments positively and preferred to remain in their neighbourhoods. In Rotterdam, quite a number of interviewees in low SEP had moved to their current dwellings within the same neighbourhood or from an adjacent neighbourhood. Furthermore, of the interviewees who had moved in from outside the area in Rotterdam, many had chosen to move back to the neighbourhoods they had once lived in. This is in line with the finding of Dujardin and van der Zanden (2014): since the 1990s, at least 35 per cent of those settling in Rotterdam South are local residents, often of a non-Western ethnicity, who moved within their neighbourhood or to other neighbourhoods in Rotterdam South. Although most interviewees in Antwerp came from outside their neighbourhoods, residents were also generally satisfied and did not wish to move out. Whereas for most residents the diversity of people was not the most important reason to settle in their current neighbourhoods, aspects of diversity appear to have contributed to their neighbourhood satisfaction.

Diverse local weak ties

'Strong ties' – social bonds with close family members and friends – were an important motive not only for settling in the current neighbourhoods but also for remaining there, as they provide residents with care and support. Interviewees from different ethnic and socioeconomic backgrounds mentioned this. In line with the literature, local networks of family and friends were generally homogeneous in terms of class, culture, ethnicity and religion. Nevertheless, interviewees from different socioeconomic and ethno-cultural backgrounds also mentioned 'weak ties' with neighbours and other local acquaintances as a factor that contributed to their neighbourhood satisfaction. Unlike the strong ties, these weak ties were diverse in terms of age, culture, ethnicity, gender, religion and household type (see Albeda et al, 2015; Tersteeg et al, 2017). Local acquaintances were described as local people with whom interviewees had become familiar but who were not considered family or friends. Maanasa's story (Hindustani Surinamese Dutch, low SEP, Rotterdam, age 26) illustrates how a diverse network of local acquaintances can positively influence neighbourhood satisfaction. She had recently moved back to the neighbourhood she grew up in: "I meet many people from the old days, whom I grew up with.... When I go outside in the summer, when you go out to buy some bread, it takes at least half an hour to get home because you bump into people and chat with them everywhere." When discussing the people she was talking about, it appeared that they were highly diverse in terms of, for instance, gender, ethnicity, age and household type.

These diverse local networks contributed to a sense of familiarity and provided residents with support. For example, Mouad and Lina (Moroccan Dutch, medium SEP, Rotterdam, ages 45 and 31) said that an important reason for remaining in their neighbourhood was their contact with local acquaintances and neighbours – with diverse ethnic backgrounds, ages and household types – from whom they regularly receive practical support, for instance, when they moved into their current dwelling: "Children, men, everyone helped us."

However, we also came across residents from diverse ethnic and socioeconomic backgrounds who found it difficult to make contact with diverse others. Some interviewees perceived barriers related to class or ethno-cultural differences. For example, Christiane (Colombian Belgian, medium SEP, Antwerp, age 49) reported: "A Belgian on the street would never say, 'Hey, how are you, what is your name?' No. Also not positive or not nice words, but also no bad words. Nothing, nothing, nothing to you." Ethno-cultural barriers are sometimes related to language diversity. Respondents from various ethnic and socioeconomic backgrounds experience a negative impact of language diversity on the social cohesion and social mobility of minority ethnic groups. Some long-term residents, for example, complained that it was difficult to communicate with "foreigners" who do not speak Dutch. Yet some residents of non-Western ethnicities were also bothered. They said that the high local concentration of non-Dutch speakers prevented them from learning Dutch: "I do not have problems with my neighbours, but I have the problem that I cannot learn Dutch. All my neighbours speak another language, for instance, in the local shops. Sometimes I think I live in Turkey or I am in Morocco" (Meriam, Afghan Belgian, low SEP, Antwerp, age 28).

A diversity of experiences and exchanges

Many interviewees said that they valued the liveliness that comes with ethnic, cultural and religious diversity. They enjoyed their neighbourhood because, "there is always something happening" (Nancy, Cape Verdean Dutch, medium SEP, Rotterdam, age 41). Yet we also came across interviewees who complain about this 'liveliness'. They related the presence of "foreigners" to nuisance in public and semi-public spaces, including unauthorised rubbish disposal, spitting in the streets, playing loud music, and talking loudly or yelling. Residents attributed the negative behaviours to "the different cultures" of minority ethnic groups. Interviewees in middle or high SEP often attributed the perceived negative behaviours of minority ethnic groups to their poor SEP, saying, for instance, that the groups' preoccupation with "surviving" prevented them from disposing of rubbish properly.

Many interviewees of diverse ethnicities, SEP and household compositions said that ethnic, cultural and religious diversity offers them new experiences with, for example, different foods and cooking styles, religious practices, and marriage and family cultures. Cheng (Asian Antillean Dutch, medium SEP, Rotterdam, age 30), for instance, said that local diversity enabled intercultural cooking experiences:

> 'I hang out with Turkish and Moroccan [people]. I am always curious. "Hi, how do you cook this, how do you prefer [that]? Oh that is a difference, but I think it is delicious." This way I learn new things from them. I always try, I always ask [them]: "If you would like to learn to cook Chinese, I can teach you." We can help one another.'

Interviewees also often pointed out that neighbours share food, referring mostly to Islamic feasts when they receive food from their Muslim neighbours. Anke (Belgian, high SEP, Antwerp, age 31-45), for example, mentioned that she likes the diversity because, for instance: "I get biscuits from my neighbours during the sugar feast."

A diversity of facilities and amenities

Interviewees of diverse ethnicities, SEP and household compositions in Rotterdam and Antwerp said that they appreciated the diverse local facility and amenity structure. It contributed to their neighbourhood satisfaction and motivated them to remain in the neighbourhood. Residents reported that the facilities met the diverse interests and needs of the ethnically, culturally and religiously diverse population. In both Rotterdam and Antwerp, middle-class residents, mostly of Dutch or Belgian ethnicities, said that they valued the diversity of local shops and restaurants, the extended opening hours of minority ethnic businesses and the liveliness they bring to the streets. According to Julia (Belgian, high SEP, Antwerp, age 63):

> 'What I think is very positive, and I really appreciate, is that the whole world comes together here, for instance, to shop. The exotic supplies are great. The opening hours, the shops

are always open, even on a Sunday evening at 9pm you can buy food, or even a new TV. Some shops never close.'

On the other hand, residents of non-Western ethnicities mostly value the presence of local shops that meet their specific needs. Hannah (Surinamese Dutch, low SEP, Rotterdam, age 62), for instance, said that she valued the local Chinese and Surinamese shops highly because they sold certain Surinamese foods.

Dutch and Belgian long-term residents complained about changes in neighbourhood facilities resulting from the inflow of minority ethnic groups (see also Feijten and van Ham, 2009). These interviewees lived in the area before it became highly diverse. Some had learned to appreciate diversity, but they still missed certain facilities that had disappeared, such as a Dutch bakery. Louisa (Dutch, low SEP, Rotterdam, age 59) lived in the neighbourhood of Hillesluis in which (in 2010) 81 per cent of the residents were not from a Dutch ethnic background. She told us:

'I wish there were more Dutch shops. We do not have a butcher. A Turkish butcher, but not a Dutch one. [We] do not have a bakery.... They [the non-Dutch bakeries] have really nice things, but they are often quite buttery, so that is something that you have to like then.'

A social climate that tolerates differences

Another aspect of local diversity that contributed to the satisfaction of interviewees with their neighbourhood is a tolerant mentality of residents towards cultural differences. Three narratives can be distinguished in this respect. First, for interviewees who were members of minority groups, for instance, regarding ethnicity, household type or lifestyle, the diversity of people was not only a motive to move to the area, but also made them feel at ease in their neighbourhood as they felt they were not the only minority (Wessendorf, 2014; Pemberton and Phillimore, 2016).

Second, several interviewees of Dutch or Belgian ethnicity said that living with diverse income groups, ethnicities and lifestyles had made them more aware and/or tolerant of these differences. Lily (Belgian, high SEP, Antwerp, age 33), for instance, said: "It has definitely opened my mind about how other people live, that it does not all have to be … white middle classes. It has made me less naive about how the world works, and that there is indeed poverty." And Martin (Dutch Belgian, high SEP, Antwerp, age 66) said: "Because there are so many different people living in one street, you do not get large social groups.... People are more tolerant towards one another because everyone is different in some way."

A third narrative about tolerance was mentioned by interviewees in medium or high SEP, mostly parents, who discussed the value of children growing up in diverse neighbourhoods. Vera (Dutch, high SEP, Rotterdam, age 41) said that the advantage of living in a diverse neighbourhood is that she can send her children to ethnically, religiously and socioeconomically mixed schools, where children with diverse backgrounds play together:

> 'I find that a very good thing ... because it [diversity] is just an everyday reality.... One day, they [the children] will jointly have to deal with it in Rotterdam, or somewhere else. The more you know about and understand each other's life world, the more you will be able to make joint decisions on how to handle things.... Just being realistic: this [diversity] is what you grow up with, and later on you will also be part of these people. People with little money, much money, people with high education levels, low education levels, then you will know how to deal with it.'

Yet some parents regarded diversity at schools and sports clubs positively only within certain limits. They said that a low number of ethnic Dutch or Belgian children corresponds with children's language deficiencies, bad behaviour and lower educational performance.

Conclusion

This present research sought to provide an insight into how residents' perceptions of diverse, deprived neighbourhoods affect their neighbourhood choice and satisfaction. The findings show that for most interviewees diversity was not a primary motive to move to a diverse neighbourhood. Instead, the primary pull factor to move to their current neighbourhoods was the availability of affordable housing. Even for middle-class residents, who in the literature are often assumed to move to diverse neighbourhoods primarily for the diversity, affordability was the most important settlement motive. Although diversity was thus not the primary settlement motive, it did influence the decision of a specific group of interviewees. We found that members of minority groups, including minority ethnic groups, were attracted to diverse neighbourhoods because they did not want to be the only person who was 'different'. A diverse neighbourhood allowed them to feel more in place. This does not mean, however, that they did not look for any similarity at all. For low-income residents an important motive to move to their current neighbourhoods was the presence of family and friends, who mostly appeared to be similar in terms of ethnicity and class. Minority ethnic groups appreciated the similarity they found within their strong social ties; however, in this respect they do not differ from majority ethnic and different socioeconomic resident groups. Hence, our study shows that it is not the search for similarity that differentiates minority ethnic from majority ethnic groups, but the desire for diversity. These findings are in sharp contrast to ethnic enclave theory, which suggests that minority ethnic groups are attracted to diverse areas only by the concentration of co-ethnics.

For the majority of residents, diversity appeared to be important once they had settled in their neighbourhoods. Despite the negative discourses about diverse areas in public and political debates, we found that residents in these contexts generally appeared quite satisfied and that diversity contributed to the decision to remain in the neighbourhood – also among the low-income groups. Several aspects of diversity, including a diverse facility structure, the opportunity to have new, intercultural experiences and exchanges, and a social context without dominant majority groups, contributed to the decision to remain. Also long-term residents with limited financial resources were in general positive about the neighbourhood and its diversity. This is not self-evident, because they mostly came to live in a much more homogeneous neighbourhood and hence did not opt for diversity. Negative perceptions among this group are mostly expressed in nostalgic feelings about the past, such as the changing landscape of facilities that meet the diverse needs of the population.

Finally, although we did not find much evidence for diverse social networks of family and friends, the weak ties with neighbours and acquaintances appeared more diverse than we expected on the basis of our literature review. Importantly, among all classes and ethnicities these diverse weak ties appeared to contribute to satisfaction with the neighbourhood. Moreover, for some residents they appeared to be a reason to remain in or move back to the neighbourhood.

The findings show that studies on local social networks in highly diverse contexts should focus not only on strong but also on weak ties. This difference is important, because it can lead to seemingly opposite views on local networks. The findings also show that diversity plays a role in the neighbourhood choice and satisfaction not only of middle-class residents, but also of other resident groups, including households in low SEP and minority ethnic and long-term residents in diverse neighbourhoods. Furthermore, we found that local diversity can positively influence neighbourhood satisfaction, and to a lesser extent neighbourhood choice. Although we also came across negative experiences with diversity, the overall picture is much more positive than the literature suggests.

Notes

[1] This project received funding from the European Union's (EU) Seventh Framework Programme for research, technological development and demonstration under Grant Agreement No 319970 – DIVERCITIES. The views expressed in this publication are the sole responsibility of the authors and do not necessarily reflect the views of the European Commission.

[2] In Belgium, suburbanisation was actively promoted by the government as early as the 19th century as well as after the Second World War (for more information, see de Decker, 2011). In the Netherlands, on the other hand, the government planned new housing estates not only outside but also within urban areas.

[3] Another explanation for the reappraisal of the city is an economic one, described in the rent gap theory. According to this theory, there is a gap 'between the actual capitalized ground rent (land value) of a plot of land given its present use and the potential ground rent that might be gleaned under a "higher and better" use' (Smith, 1987, p 462). Gentrification is seen as an economic process that partly closes this gap.

[4] In accordance with the Scientific Council for Government Policy in the Netherlands, we define 'Dutch' and 'Belgian' as citizens with both parents having been born in the Netherlands or Belgium respectively.

[5] One of the neighbourhoods in the research area, the city district of Feijenoord, is also called Feijenoord.

[6] We define SEP according to the interviewees' education level and household income. A low, medium and high SEP we define as having, respectively: a primary or lower vocational educational degree and a net monthly household income of <€1,670; a pre-university or intermediate educational degree and a net monthly household income of €1,670-€3,300; or a university or university of applied sciences educational degree and a net monthly household income of >€3,300.

References

Adriaanse, C.C.M. (2007) 'Measuring residential satisfaction: A residential environmental satisfaction scale (RESS)', *Journal of Housing and the Built Environment*, 22(3), 287-304.

Albeda, Y.J., Oosterlynck, S., Verschraegen, G., Saeys, A. and Dierckx, D. (2015) *Fieldwork inhabitants, Antwerp (Belgium)*, Antwerp: University of Antwerp.

Amerigo, M. and Aragones, J. (1990) 'Residential satisfaction in council housing', *Journal of Environmental Psychology*, 10(4), 313-25.

Amin, A. (2002) 'Ethnicity and the multicultural city: Living with diversity', *Environment and Planning A*, 34(6), 959-80.

Atkinson, R. (2006) 'Padding the bunker: Strategies of middle-class disaffiliation and colonisation in the city', *Urban Studies*, 43(4), 819-32.

Blokland T. (2003) *Urban bonds*, Cambridge: Polity Press.

Blokland, T. and van Eijk, G. (2010) 'Do people who like diversity practice diversity in neighbourhood life? Neighbourhood use and the social networks of "diversity-seekers" in a mixed neighbourhood in the Netherlands', *Journal of Ethnic and Migration Studies*, 36(2), 313-32.

Brown, L. and Moore, E. (1970) 'The intra-urban migration process: A perspective', *Geografiska Annaler Series B*, 52(1), 1-13.

Bryman, A. (2012) *Social research methods*, Oxford: Oxford University Press.

Butler, T. (2003) 'Living in the bubble: Gentrification and its "others" in North London', *Urban Studies*, 40(12), 2469-86.

Butler, T. and Robson, G. (2001) 'Social capital, gentrification and neighbourhood change in London: A comparison of three South London neighbourhoods', *Urban Studies*, 38(12), 2145-62.

Butler, T. and Robson, G. (2003) 'Plotting the middle classes: Gentrification and circuits of education in London', *Housing Studies*, 18(1), 5-28.

Camina, M. and Wood, M. (2009) 'Parallel lives: Towards a greater understanding of what mixed communities can offer', *Urban Studies*, 46(2), 459-80.

Cresswell, T. (1996) *In place–out of place: Geography, ideology, and transgression*, Minneapolis, MN: University of Minnesota Press.

de Decker, P. (2011) 'Understanding housing sprawl: The case of Flanders, Belgium', *Environment and Planning A*, 43, 1634-54.

Dekker, K. and Bolt, G. (2005) 'Social cohesion in post-war estates in the Netherlands: Differences between socioeconomic and ethnic groups', *Urban Studies*, 42, 2447-70.

Dekker, K., de Vos, S., Musterd, S. and van Kempen, R. (2011) 'Residential satisfaction in housing estates in European cities: A multi-level research approach', *Housing Studies*, 26(4), 479-99.

Doucet, B., van Kempen, R. and van Weesep, J. (2011) '"We're a rich city with poor people": Municipal strategies of new-build gentrification in Rotterdam and Glasgow', *Environment and Planning A*, 43(6), 1438-54.

Dujardin, M. and van der Zanden, W. (2014) *Komen en gaan 2013 [Coming and going 2013]*, Rotterdam: Municipality of Rotterdam.

Feijten, P. and van Ham, M. (2009) 'Neighbourhood change... Reason to leave?', *Urban Studies*, 46(10), 2103-22.

Fincher, R. and Iveson, K. (2008) *Planning and diversity in the city: Redistribution, recognition and encounter*, Basingstoke: Palgrave Macmillan.

Fischer, C. (1982) *To dwell among friends: Personal networks in town and city*, Chicago, IL: University of Chicago Press

Florida, R. (2003) 'Cities and the creative class', *City & Community*, 2(3), 3-19.

Florida, R. (2005) *Cities and the creative class*, New York: Routledge.

Forrest, R. and Kearns, A. (2001) 'Social cohesion, social capital and the neighbourhood', *Urban Studies*, 38(12), 2125-43.

Frey, W. (1979) 'Central city white flight: Racial and nonracial causes', *American Sociological Review*, 44(3), 425-48.

Galster, G. (1990) 'White flight from racially integrated neighborhoods in the 1970s: The Cleveland experience', *Urban Studies*, 27(3), 385-99.

Górny, A. and Toruńczyk-Ruiz, S. (2014) 'Neighbourhood attachment in ethnically diverse areas: The role of interethnic ties', *Urban Studies*, 51(5), 1000-18.

Guest, A.M. and Wierzbicki, S.K. (1999) 'Social ties at the neighborhood level: Two decades of GSS evidence', *Urban Affairs Review*, 35, 92-111.

Hall, S. (2015) 'Super-diverse street: A "trans-ethnography" across migrant localities', *Ethnic and Racial Studies*, 38(1), 22-37.

Hamnett, C. (2003) 'Gentrification and the middle-class remaking of Inner London, 1961-2001', *Urban Studies*, 40(12), 2401-26.

Jackson, K. (1985) *Grabgrass frontier. The suburbanization of the United States*, Oxford: Oxford University Press.

Jackson, E. and Benson, M. (2014) 'Neither "deepest, darkest Peckham" nor "run-of-the-mill" East Dulwich: The middle classes and their "others" in an inner-London neighbourhood', *International Journal of Urban and Regional Research*, 38(4), 1195-210.

Karsten, L. (2007) 'Housing as a way of life: Towards an understanding of middle-class families' preference for an urban residential location', *Housing Studies*, 22(1), 83-98.

Lawton, P., Murphy, E. and Redmond, D. (2013) 'Residential preferences of the "creative class"?', *Cities*, 31(2), 47-56.

Lees, L. (2000) 'A reappraisal of gentrification: Towards a "geography of gentrification"', *Progress in Human Geography*, 24(3), 389-408.

Lees, L. (2008) 'Gentrification and social mixing: Towards an inclusive urban renaissance?', *Urban Studies*, 45(12), 2449-70.

Lees, L., Slater, T. and Wyly, E. (2007) *Gentrification*, London: Routledge.

Logan, J., Zhang, W. and Alba, R. (2002) 'Immigrant enclaves and ethnic communities in New York and Los Angeles', *American Sociological Review*, 67, 299-322.

Loopmans, M. (2008) 'Relevance, gentrification and the development of a new hegemony on urban policies in Antwerp, Belgium', *Urban Studies*, 45(12), 2499-519.

Loots, I. and van Hove, E. (1986) *Stadsvlucht? Een eeuw demografische ontwikkeling in het Antwerpse* [*Urban flight? A century of demographic development in Antwerp*], Leuven: Acco.

Municipality of Antwerp (2015) 'Percentage allochtonen (herkomst ouders meegerekend) 2015' [Percentage immigrants (based on origin parents) 2015] (https://stadincijfers.antwerpen.be/databank/).

Pemberton, S. and Phillimore, J. (2016) 'Migrant place-making in super-diverse neighbourhoods: Moving beyond ethno-national approaches', *Urban Studies*, Online first: 5 July, doi:10.1177/0042098016656988

Posthumus, H. (2013) *Displacement myths: The real and presumed effects of forced relocations resulting from urban renewal*, Utrecht: Utrecht University Repository.

Public Affairs Rotterdam (no date) 'Bevolkingscijfers van Rotterdam vanaf 1868' ['Population statistics as of 1868'] (www.stadsarchief.rotterdam.nl/bevolkingscijfers-van-rotterdam-vanaf-1868#groei-door-annexaties).

Putnam, R.D. (2000) *Bowling alone: The collapse and revival of American community*, New York: Simon & Schuster.

Putnam, R.D. (2007) '*E. pluribus unum*: Diversity and community in the twenty-first century', *Scandinavian Political Studies*, 30(2), 137-74.

Saeys, A., Albeda, Y., Oosterlynck, S., Verschraegen, G. and Dierckx, D. (2014) *Governance arrangements and initiatives in Antwerp (Belgium)*, Antwerp: University of Antwerp.

Saunders, D. (2010) *Arrival city*, New York: Pantheon Books.

Smith, N. (1987) 'Gentrification and the rent-gap', *Annals of the Association of American Geographers*, 77(3), 462-5.

Statistics Netherlands (2004) 'Bevolking grote steden verandert in hoog tempo' ['Population of large cities is changing rapidly'] (www.cbs.nl/nl-NL/menu/themas/bevolking/publicaties/artikelen/archief/2004/2004-14/9-wm.htm).

Statistics Rotterdam (2016) 'Feitenkaart. Bevolkingsmonitor januari 2016' ['Factsheet. Population monitor January 2016'] (https://rotterdam.buurtmonitor.nl/documents/Bevolking).

Tasan-Kok, T., van Kempen, R., Raco, M. and Bolt, G. (2013) *Towards hyper-diversified European cities: A critical literature review*, Utrecht: Utrecht University, Faculty of Geosciences.

Tersteeg, A., Bolt, G. and van Kempen, R, (2014) *Governance arrangements and initiatives in Rotterdam, The Netherlands*, Utrecht: Utrecht University, Faculty of Geosciences.

Tersteeg, A., Bolt, G. and van Kempen, R. (2017) *DIVERCITIES: Dealing with urban diversity. The case of Rotterdam*, Utrecht: Utrecht University, Faculty of Geosciences.

Tissot, S. (2014) 'Loving diversity/controlling diversity: Exploring the ambivalent mobilization of upper-middle-class gentrifiers, South End, Boston', *International Journal of Urban and Regional Research*, 38(4), 1181-94.

Valentine, G. (2008) 'Living with difference: Reflections on geographies of encounter', *Progress in Human Geography*, 32, 321-35.

van der Meer, T. and Tolsma, J. (2014) 'Ethnic diversity and its effects on social cohesion', *Annual Review of Sociology*, 40, 459-78.

van Diepen, A. and Musterd, S. (2009) 'Lifestyles and the city: Connecting daily life to urbanity', *Journal of Housing and the Built Environment*, 24(3), 331-45.

van Eijk, G. (2012) 'Good neighbours in bad neighbourhoods: Narratives of dissociation and practices of neighbouring in a "problem" place', *Urban Studies*, 49(14), 3009-26.

van Ham, M. and Clark, W. (2009) 'Neighbourhood mobility in context: Household moves and changing neighbourhoods in the Netherlands', *Environment and Planning A*, 41(6), 1442-59.

van Ham, M. and Feijten, P. (2008) 'Who wants to leave the neighbourhood? The effect of being different from the neighbourhood population on wishes to move', *Environment and Planning A*, 40, 1151-70.

Vertovec, S. (2007) 'Super-diversity and its implications', *Ethnic and Racial Studies*, 30(6), 1024-54.

Vertovec, S. (2010) 'Towards post-multiculturalism? Changing communities, conditions and contexts of diversity', *International Social Science Journal*, 61(199), 83-95.

Völker, B., Mollenhorst, G. and Schutjens, V. (2013) 'Neighbourhood social capital and residential mobility', in M. van Ham, D. Manley, N. Bailey, L. Simpson and D. MacIennan (eds) *Understanding neighbourhood dynamics*, Dordrecht: Springer, 139-60.

Weck, S. and Hanhörster, H. (2015) 'Seeking urbanity or seeking diversity? Middle-class family households in a mixed neighbourhood in Germany', *Journal of Housing and the Built Environment*, 30, 471-86.

Wessendorf, S. (2014) *Commonplace diversity: Social relations in a super-diverse context*, Houndmills: Palgrave Macmillan.

Wilson, K. and Portes, A. (1980) 'Immigrant enclaves: An analysis of the labor market experiences of Cubans in Miami', *American Journal of Sociology*, 86, 295-319.

Wise, A. (2009) 'Everyday multiculturalism: Transversal crossings and working class cosmopolitans', in A. Wise and S. Velayutham (eds) *Everyday multiculturalism*, Basingstoke: Palgrave Macmillan, 21-45.

Wright, R., Ellis, M., Holloway, S. and Wong, S. (2014) 'Patterns of racial diversity and segregation in the United States: 1990-2010', *The Professional Geographer*, 66(2), 173-82.

Zorlu, A. and Mulder, C. (2007) 'Initial and subsequent location choices of immigrants to the Netherlands', *Regional Studies*, 42(2), 245-64.

Zukin, S., Kasinitz, P. and Chen, X. (2016) *Global cities, local streets. Everyday diversity from New York to Shanghai*, New York: Routledge.

10

Living with diversity or living with difference? International perspectives on everyday perceptions of the social composition of diverse neighbourhoods

Katrin Großmann, Georgia Alexandri, Maria Budnik, Annegret Haase, Christian Haid, Christoph Hedtke, Katharina Kullmann and Galia Shokry

Introduction

Living with social differences and all the encounters, conflicts and transgressions this entails is a constituent part of urban living (see, for example, Amin, 2002; Massey, 2005). With increasing regional and global migration, the level and complexity of social differences seems to have reached a new height, as has been highlighted by work claiming that urban societies have become super- or hyper-diversified (Vertovec 2007; Tasan-Kok et al, 2014). Identities have become more fluid and urban social compositions more complex. The experience of living in large cities and metropolises constitutes the background of a new emphasis on engaging with difference from a diversity perspective.

If this quality is new, does it generate a new normality of living together? Is any notion of this multiplicity of social characteristics present in how people see and judge the social composition of their neighbourhood? Drawing from qualitative interviews with inhabitants in three European cities – Athens, Paris and Leipzig – we aim to understand how people live with diversity in less privileged neighbourhoods. Empirically, we examine how people describe the social groups in their area along two guiding questions:

1. What categories or combinations do inhabitants use to construct social groupings and their relation to place?
2. Which normative assessments about a group's presence in the neighbourhood are accepted and which are contested?

We employ a social differences perspective inspired by intersectionality theory to interpret these data and to understand how inhabitants of such increasingly heterogeneous neighbourhoods perceive, describe and judge their social environment. We show that in all three cities inhabitants' perceptions are replete with stereotypes of intersecting social group identities. Distinctions first and foremost lie at the intersection of characteristics (like income, ethnicity, age and gender), which serve as the basis for expressions of closeness, distance and stigmatisation. In our view, the intersectionality approach offers a strong starting point for their analysis, although it gives less consideration to the variety of differences such as orientations, values or the duration of residence in a neighbourhood.

Social difference from a conceptual perspective

Terms and concepts addressing social heterogeneity

In theories on social inequalities various paradigms have been employed to make sense of social heterogeneity. Heterogeneity – as opposed to homogeneity – is a descriptive term conveying that there are differences between people. Inequalities research makes use of a variety of categories such as income, gender, ethnicity, educational levels, and so on to describe such differences. Differences, as is repeatedly stressed in the literature, are not inequalities per se, but can be turned into inequalities through societal structures, and through power and discriminatory regimes (see, for example, Kreckel, 1972; Therborn, 2013). Thus, there are differences that mark unequal participation and status such as income or education, and there are differences that through discrimination may lead to different life chances such as gender, age or sexual orientation.

In urban studies some scholars concerned with social cohesion in cities use the term 'social differences' referring to a range of contrasting characteristics such as race, ethnicity, gender or sexual orientation (Amin, 2002; Bannister and Kearns, 2013; Valentine, 2013; Anthias, 2016). Their interest is to discuss the intergroup relations living in close proximity. 'Othering' is a concept developed in the larger landscape of postcolonial theory that describes the construction of a marginalised, essentialised 'other' in contrast to the more powerful majority. Such discursive othering is characterised by the construction of a homogeneous 'they', a group of demonised character, with no internal differentiations made (see also Ashcroft et al, 2013).

'Social diversity' highlights the existence of multiple differences, explicitly pointing to the (growing) variety of the social characteristics of people. In the academic debate, a widely recognised milestone was Vertovec's (2007) assertion of a new 'super-diversity' in Western cities referring to increasing ethnic diversity[1] and increased demographic and socioeconomic diversity between and within these ethnic groups. Using the term 'hyper-diversity', Tasan-Kok et al (2014) conceptualise the plurality of social groups and identities as even more complex. They emphasise that besides ethnic, demographic and socioeconomic terms, differences also exist with respect to lifestyles, attitudes and activities.

Lately, critical diversity perspectives argue that the term is well suited to neoliberal and post-political policy-making (see, for example, Vormann, 2015; Wrench, 2015). As Anthias (2013, 2016) points out, diversity is often used to mark an illusion of 'let's happily and successfully live together'. In policy terms, it is used together with economic needs for human capital; it speaks about talent rather than disadvantage. It individualises social injustices and avoids speaking about structural inequalities and power relations (see also Allemann-Ghionda and Bukow, 2011 for Germany or Bell et al, 2014 for the US). With regard to the US context, Michaels (2006, p 4) shows that a 'commitment to diversity became superficially associated with the struggle against racism' and attention needs to return to economic inequalities (see also Faist, 2009, pp 171, 185; 2010, p 299).

In social inequalities analysis, the intersectionality approach explicitly grapples with the multiple mechanisms of subordination and discrimination at the crossroads of differences. In other words, discrimination not only arises from being a woman or being black, but at the intersection of such characteristics. Crenshaw, who is often referred to as a forerunner of such thinking, points to the discriminating effect 'of the interaction between two or more axes of subordination. It [intersectionality] specifically addresses the manner in which racism, patriarchy, class oppression and other discriminatory systems create background inequalities that structure the relative position of women, races, ethnicities, classes and the like' (cited in Lutz, 2014, p 3).

In our chapter, we explore to what extent a focus on differences, othering, diversity or intersections of different identities are helpful to understanding how residents of socially heterogeneous and underprivileged neighbourhoods perceive and construct the social environment around them.

Living in socially heterogeneous urban environments

Urban research has a long tradition of engaging with the relations of heterogeneous populations. The engagement with heterogeneity has seen shifting foci. Valentine (2013, p 76) summarises that research in the 1970s and 1980s was concerned with tension and conflict and the fear of others, while the 1990s brought attention to practices of inclusion and exclusion, of housing market mechanisms and their discriminatory effects, leading to spatially segregated cities. In the 2000s, in light of an increasing global mobility, the debate started to look at living with difference as a positive if at least normal experience of urban life, and envisioned hybridised cultural mixing and cosmopolitanism (for a summary, see Valentine, 2013, p 77).

Lately, this optimism appears to be fading. Even before the upswing of populist and nationalist political positions in Europe and the US, scholarly work engaged in how this civility and cosmopolitanism would emerge raised doubts about the effect of mere co-presence and superficial contact. In 2002, Ash Amin had already pointed to newly evolving conflicts, how material deprivation fuels ethnic resentments, especially in deprived communities. He suggested that only regular and more intense contact in micro-publics like sports clubs or schools could foster meaningful contact or cultural transgression, as he put it. In a similar vein, Nast and Blokland (2014) show that supportive contact across social differences is rare, but that it can occur, for example, in schools, when the common interest of children is at stake. Fincher and Iveson (2008) highlight the role of encounter as intentionally shaped opportunities and spaces for people of different origins to meet and communicate. Bannister and Kearns (2013) distinguish between (growing) intolerance, passive tolerance, a superficial acceptance of the presence of others, and dynamic tolerance that acknowledges the other as a legitimate subject. Even more sceptical, Valentine argues that 'tolerance is a dangerous concept' (2013, p 80), civility is a superficial attitude and meaningful contact is rare: 'Spatial proximity can actually breed defensiveness and the bounding of identities and communities' (Valentine, 2013, p 79). Amin (2002) points to the influence of socioeconomic deprivation on prejudices and growing intolerance. Given this context, we aim to look at the social positions in more detail and explore further what characteristics and positions of people create which kinds of perceptions and attitudes towards other groups in the neighbourhood.

Case studies, data and methods[2]

We chose the three cities because (1) they represent different histories of diversification and (2) they have experienced societal disruptions and dynamic change: post-socialist and short-term diversification since the political change in 1989 (Leipzig); short-term diversification through its location and role in the European refugee challenge and the impacts of the Euro debt crisis since 2008 (Athens); and a long-term migration history and high levels of sociospatial segregation and polarisation (Paris).

Within these cities we focused on diverse and disadvantaged neighbourhoods. They are all inner-city locations and represent low-income areas with an image of being among the more socially troubled areas of the respective cities. This work uses the 'comparative gesture' (see, for example, McFarlane, 2010; Robinson, 2011) employing different cases and contexts to explore the research questions posed, deliberatively acquiring a relational, comparative perspective (Ward, 2009).

In each city, 50 interviews with residents of deprived neighbourhoods were carried out according to a common guideline including questions on perceptions of the neighbourhood, its development and social composition, and inhabitants' social networks. We aimed to represent in our sample the main groups living in the neighbourhood respecting variation in terms of duration of residency, ethnic backgrounds, age, gender and economic resources.[3] Interviewees were approached through existing contacts, local associations and key people in the neighbourhoods. To set the scene for this, the following section provides key contextual information on the neighbourhoods.

Leipzig is a post-socialist city with a recent history of population diversification. During state socialism, the population was comparatively homogeneous in terms of income and ethnicity. After 1989/90, many young, educated residents left Leipzig for the suburbs or left the region entirely. Poverty rates were high, with the average age increasing rapidly. Out-migration resulted in high housing vacancies in certain districts. Since 2010, Leipzig has grown significantly, by about 2 per cent each year (City of Leipzig, 2015). The composition of the population now has a growing share of young, international and financially better-off inhabitants. This is also mirrored in our case study area. Leipzig Inner East is an inner-city former working-class neighbourhood characterised by pre-Second World War residential housing, much of which is currently in redevelopment through both private and public investment. The area is currently witnessing a strong growth in numbers of both international migrants and German youth who are mostly students, while less privileged households increasingly face difficulties in finding suitable housing. This is leading to rising levels of segregation.

Until the 1990s, Athens was depicted as a homogeneous city consisting of a mainly Greek population. With the fall of the Iron Curtain, the city received successive waves of immigrants from Eastern Europe, culminating in the recent reception of war refugees from Africa and the Middle East. Due to lack of social housing, migrants settled in the most deprived inner-city areas, renting apartments in the private sector. Since 2010, austerity policies have caused severe impoverishment, with migrant and Greek families increasingly affected by debt. Our research focuses on Akadimia Platonos, a deprived mixed neighbourhood towards the southwest of the city. The housing stock consists mainly of antiparochi[4] buildings, where low rents and prices encouraged homeownership for the Greek population and access to affordable rents for the migrant and Roma population.

Paris has long been a site of social, economic and ethnic diversification processes to which various populations from other French regions and overseas territories, European countries and former colonies have migrated. The city tends to be divided along socioeconomic lines between the wealthier western neighbourhoods and the lower-income eastern districts. Our research focuses on three adjacent and historically working-class neighbourhoods of Paris' northeastern 18th and 19th districts, La Chapelle, Goutte d'Or and Flandres (Lelévrier et al, 2015). Housing stock consists of a mix of lower rent, mostly deteriorated buildings: some Haussmannian style, some high-rise social housing estates, but also several former warehouses recently converted to mixed-use facilities. Classified as 'priority neighbourhoods' for public subsidies, intensive urban regeneration is underway. As rents increase throughout the city, the area has attracted new, relatively better-off residents, with some of the hallmarks of gentrification in Paris: wine shops, hamburger eateries, artisanal beer makers and organic groceries.

Living with whom? Categorisations and assessments of people's social environments in the neighbourhood

In the following section the interview material elucidated which characteristics residents in Leipzig, Athens and Paris use to describe and assess the social composition of the diverse neighbourhoods in which they live.

Leipzig

Descriptions of the social environment

People in Leipzig Inner East describe residents according to characteristics such as age, gender or ethnicity. Distinctions are made via a range of different dimensions such as social status, income, poverty, lifestyle, educational background, mentality, country of origin and so on. Moreover, distinction and distance to groups are expressed spatially ("no-go streets"). These spaces, however, are perceived as closely related to specific groups that are less favoured. In most cases, generalised terms are applied when talking about others, and usually others are grouped along single dimensions such as "the foreigners", the "migrants", the "Germans", the "socially weak people", the "youngsters", or multiple characteristics such as "young disadvantaged mother" or "old and poor people". Taking an (often implicit) homogeneous group identity as their position, they talk about "the other" groups, indicating that they are different from themselves.

Constructions of normality: the good mix

The perception of residents is influenced by the general dynamics of the neighbourhood. This becomes clear in reference to what residents call the "normal" composition of the neighbourhood. The term 'normal' is either applied in relation to the current composition of the population or to reflect how the neighbourhood has changed: "It was so normal before academics and young folks moved here" (Emma and Max).[5] This quote highlights two aspects of change. First, the length of residency – long-term inhabitants are seen as representing the normal and 'regular' composition of the neighbourhood. Second, it also highlights change in terms of socioeconomic status – references to "the normal working class" (Malte) help describe change from the former – normal – situation to the present.

Often, the 'normal' also marks a safe environment, a spatial and social comfort zone. Samia, a 21-year-old low-wage-earning migrant woman, distinguishes spatially between quiet, clean areas with "normal people" in contrast to an area she describes as troubling and dirty: "Well, yeah, obviously there is always a lot of waste around there; but that's just how it is. Well, the houses, they just look like they are, but the people around there!" Others, however, associate normalcy with a balanced mix of migrants and poor inhabitants, indicating that the over-presence of a certain group leads to an imbalanced composition of the neighbourhood. 'Normal' is often used as a category of distinction, yet the speaker determines what it means. Distance (and degradation) is often expressed by a rhetoric of 'us and them' without a clear description of who is signified. Nevertheless, in relation to the context in question, migrants are frequently associated with 'them'.

Different perspectives on migrant residents

Migrants are often described in terms of race, age, gender and nationality. Each characteristic implies a different prejudice, which either leads to positive or negative discrimination. Marie (40+, German, female, with a secondary school diploma, with a household income of €3,000 per month for herself, her partner and their seven children) highlights the attributes ascribed to certain nationalities:

> 'Syrians and Turks live here; Russians and "Fidschi"[6] are quiet, there we hear nothing; within the house and back house many immigrants, but you avoid those as much as possible.... Foreigners dump their rubbish in the neighbourhood.... Many [German] unemployed people, also second generation, that is heavy here.'

In her quote, Marie addresses common racist stereotypes and distinguishes between different groups of migrants who are either tolerated or avoided, depending on the public discourse. Furthermore, the quote about dumping rubbish implies conflicts in terms of imagined overall cultural differences between migrants and non-migrants. To express a strong social distance, a more detailed stereotype of the problematic migrant is formed by intersecting age, migration background and gender: "young, migrant men" is a common group construction, typically associated with being afraid of this group, a group evoking fear in public space and predominantly employed by female residents regardless of their ethnic background.

Distancing and distinction towards deprived residents

Interestingly, different distinctions are drawn for Germans and migrants. While migrants are often differentiated along ethnic categories, Germans are differentiated along class. Poor Germans are stigmatised as a socially (and spatially) distant German underclass. Although, for example, Marie herself is positioned at these intersections of being German, poor and a woman with children, she nevertheless distinguishes herself as a working person, different from other white Germans who do not work.

Erika (German, and a woman in her 30s with a university degree and a monthly income of between €1,000 to €1,500) offers a similar perspective. She had only recently moved to the neighbourhood and lives in a housing project.[7] From her educated middle-class perspective, she appreciates the diversity of her neighbourhood, especially with respect to the presence of immigrants and thus different cultural backgrounds. However, she is less tolerant towards other groups and sets migrants in contrast to the group of "socially weak" long-term (German) residents who are believed to be less educated and those who are long-term unemployed:

> 'Visible are many, many … veiled women with their kids. There are almost tour groups travelling every morning to the kindergarten and back again. That is a fantastic picture.… And, what I really recognise is such socially weak young families. I mean Germans. They rather brutally handle their children and there is a lot of violence in their language and action. I really see that. And also alcohol addicts. Socially weak, in many ways.'

Intolerance towards "socially weak" Germans is a pattern we found in other interviews as well. Perceptions of deprivation include older long-term residents, and those who are unemployed, including their families and children. Moreover, people speak about drug- and alcohol-addicted people as impoverished people who are ill. 'Deprived' does not simply mean 'poor' but also socially excluded and frustrated (as Marie says, "since they lack the money"). Some interviewees speak of "underclass" and "neglect", while others relate deprivation to violence and crime. Most of the interviewees express a clear distance from deprived people, sometimes accompanied by regret or disgust (Budnik et al, 2016).

Athens

Descriptions of the social environment

Similar to the Leipzig findings, most interviewees in Athens used rather concrete categorisations such as age, gender, ethnicity, educational level and employment status to describe their neighbours. More affluent residents, active in cultural initiatives such as traditional dancing and singing activities or in the neighbourhood assembly, used more generic 'soft' terms, for example, "migrants" and "unemployed". Other interviewees, after pointing out their lack of acquaintance with a neighbour, continued their description on the basis of their daily observations from the street or the building level (for example, the neighbour's economic and social status). More deprived and elderly Greeks used the word *xenos*, which means 'stranger', to refer to migrants. In the dominant discourse this word has acquired a hostile interpretation, referring negatively to the 'one who is not like us'.

Reference to the Greek population (by Greeks) is accompanied by the word 'we', indicating the ethnic affiliation of a common/familiar origin, many times implying the common destiny of impoverishment caused by austerity. Descriptions used for Roma population link to perceptions such as "irritating", "dirty" and "robber". Similar distinguishing terms are used by migrants to differentiate themselves from Greeks and other ethnicities (for example, "we Albanians" versus "Greeks" or "Romanian"). The presence of Roma is also negatively perceived, usually accompanied by expressions of fear. Quite distinctively, Roma interviewees discussed neighbours positively, especially the ones who supported them with clothes and work opportunities, while negatively characterising homeowners who wanted their eviction.

Fear of the 'other'

Social groups, besides cohabiting in the same space, share little in their quotidian lives. This is especially reflected in the use of public space. Many Greek interviewees agreed that living conditions in the area started deteriorating with the arrival of the *xenos*. Indicating the existence of three chief social groups, "elderly, working-class Greeks and migrants", the *xenos* is portrayed as a "dark", "dangerous" male roaming in public spaces, keen on delinquency, especially robberies and attacks. Older people claimed that they were confined to the private space of their home explicitly due to the presence of *xenos*. Similarly, parents indicate the constant need to monitor their young children, in fear of being driven away by the *xenos*. For example, Athina (a low-income 41-year-old cleaning lady) expressed that:

> 'It is a matter of security. We cannot leave our children to play on their own in the playground as someone has to watch over them constantly, as we are afraid that something bad will happen to them, that they will steal from them ... and there are gangs of Albanian children.'

The need for constant surveillance is a clear indication of fear of the 'other', an expression of superiority justifying the perception of the migrant as a criminal. Interviewees with more radical ideas clearly stated that such 'others' must leave the area and return to their country of origin.

Moreover, feelings of fear arise between the various low-income, male, immigrant groups. For instance, Munawar (a 40-year-old low-income and by education a carpenter from Pakistan) narrated how his friend had been attacked by Roma, and later the same month, by Greek neo-Nazi supporters:

> '... it is full of Gypsies ... we don't go to the square; when they see us they start swearing and shouting at us.... The other that makes me feel scared is the Golden Dawn[8] ... and the police controls all the time. I am okay. I have papers, but....'

Other migrant women expressed similar fears when crossing public spaces where Roma people stroll. Likewise, Greek households' fear of the 'other' restricts the migrant population to the private sphere of the home, where there is a stronger feeling of safety.

Overcoming fear through interaction and a common destiny

Interestingly enough, interviewees with young children or those who were active in local initiatives constructed positive perceptions of neighbours of a similar age, educational and professional status. Spaces mainly used by children, such as the park, become places where encounters turn into amity. People from diverse ethnic backgrounds gather while children play. It is in these spaces that prejudices against the 'other' decline and people cross barriers of fear. Ahmet (a 32-year-old high school graduate, unemployed, second-generation Egyptian) narrated how through his daughter's classmates he became friends with their Bulgarian neighbours:

> 'Last year, two Bulgarian girls joined my daughter's class at school. They live next door.... I never believed that we could become friends with their parents ... last summer ... we were all the time together, we took our children to the square, we walked back home together, we did stuff together ... now when there is a school holiday, we arrange that they either come to my house or my daughter goes to them for the day.'

The downward spiralling of the local economy has gravely affected all households dealing with long-term unemployment and lack of welfare support. This impoverishment across educational, professional and ethnic status has decreased previous economic and social distances, and is either expressed as anger against otherness, or contrarily, it has led to the development of a kind of unity among affected groups. Many locals aware of common challenges posed by austerity embrace solidarity to combat the crisis (see Arampatzi, 2016).

Such solidarity is expressed through daily interaction (for example, food and clothing exchange) or self-organised initiatives at neighbourhood level (supportive school classes). It is expressed through microstructures that are created daily, for example, among neighbours who live next to each other (spatial microstructures), or people getting acquainted through their children (social microstructures) or through neighbours who are active in the cultural and social activities around Akadimias Park (activist microstructures). In particular, people participating in local cultural initiatives stress that social solidarity dynamics have bridged a former distance, indicating, however, that migrants are still not that receptive to solidarity, due to fear and enclosure. As Matina (a 50-year-old average-income journalist) indicated:

> '... migrants, especially if they have families are very closed to themselves ... they construct their own communities and they don't allow you to approach....'

Paris

Descriptions of the social environment

Interviewees in northeastern Paris tend to characterise their neighbourhoods as "populaire", often translated as working-class, but also "mixed", alluding to its ethnic and religious diversity (Lelévrier et al, 2015). Frequently describing themselves and others by way of their dominant ethnic or migration backgrounds (for example, "Malian" and "foreigner"), but also racial and religious categories ("black" and "Muslim"), residents construct a definition of mix particular to Parisian working-class neighbourhoods. While time living in the neighbourhood and degree of assimilation are also categories of differentiation, they are not necessarily correlated. One could live a lifetime in the neighbourhood yet not be perceived as "French" and, in fact, living in such a culturally diverse place may be highly stigmatised. Another common-sense category is "bobo", short for bourgeois-bohemian, which is used to describe a privileged lifestyle distinguished by certain dress, food and home décor preferences (Lelévrier et al, 2017). Other groups are differentiated by how they appear to pass their time: "mothers" who organise activities for their children, "youth" who hang out on street corners, and "dealers" and "junkies" who produce a sense of insecurity. Some of these perceptions are further examined below.

Imagining the friendly, intercultural working-class neighbourhood

Residents of these "populaire" Parisian neighbourhoods often claim that a good mix is different from elsewhere in the city, especially in the wealthier districts. They talk about a convivial atmosphere of being "vibrant" and "animated", and of looking after one another (Lelévrier et al, 2015). This conviviality – the French *vivre ensemble* – has to do with solidarity as well as saying hello and being courteous in public. Such 'civility' is interpreted as open-mindedness, and interviewees' sensitivity to impoliteness reveals concerns about prejudice or intolerance toward minority cultures, but also claims of disrespect toward "French" norms.

The neighbourhood's ethnic mix is widely seen as an opportunity to learn about other cultures, to be exposed to numerous languages and to widen one's point of view about others, the opposite of living parallel lives. When discussed in this sense, interviewees were fond of living with cultural diversity. A 38-year-old part-time employee at a non-governmental organisation (NGO) who settled in the area in 2003 claims that it provides safety: "The fact that this neighbourhood has a largely African and Maghrebian community means that the adults are all very attentive to the kids. You really can't imagine much of anything bad happening here to a child."

Defining belonging: valuing and devaluing difference

In everyday public encounters, positive stereotypes and notions of class and interethnic solidarity can unravel, revealing how social groups are stigmatised and othered, valued and devalued. In these instances, race, ethnicity and religion are especially emphasised over categories such as age, gender or class to explain conflicts, but also the desirability of some groups over others. Arielle, who is white French, describes her experience with young men in public spaces: "Well, the Africans they don't harass you. And the Maghrebians they … they're always commenting on you. They look at you, you see, they always comment on you."

She uses geographic identifiers, like "African and Maghrebian" or "North African", to differentiate two groups of men, perceived through visible characteristics related to skin colour and ethnicity. On the other hand, gender, age and class are only implied. The men may be French-born and educated, but she goes on to say, "it looks like you are in Bamako". Arielle distances herself by orientalising them to distant parts of the world. She says she can "pass right through" the African men and feels cool, confident, dominant even; in another area, Goutte d'Or, she feels dominated, passing through another's territory. While gender relations are deeply engrained in the encounters, perceived cultural differences, sense of belonging and control of space become the main points of tension.

In a similar sense, some social groups are perceived as normal and belonging to the space, but also valued above others. Coco (a 37-year-old woman from West Africa, active in organising family activities through the municipality) perceives the presence of white residents in the neighbourhood as vital to an appropriate mix:

'The building, there, there are whites but more blacks than white. It is not normal! When the whites begin to leave, it is not normal! I don't agree; we should mix.'

While "we are all the same", her concerns about some groups disclose a fear of abandonment and social exclusion. She describes the neighbourhood composition according to racial, ethnic and religious differences, but assesses its wellbeing by giving a higher importance to the presence of white residents.

Unlike Coco, Djibril grew up in the neighbourhood, the son of parents who had immigrated to Paris from Mauritania. His perspective differs on who and what is normal or "original" to the place. He discusses the new type of gentrifier moving to the neighbourhood sometimes referred to in French as "bobo". He deconstructs this category that implies a certain class and lifestyle, but no longer implies one skin colour as he once thought; instead there is a mix of ethnic backgrounds:

> 'In my imagination, the bobo was white and of good means. When I look at our resident committee, there is a bit of everything. In other words, it consists today of a certain category of population that cares less about ethnic origins, and more about their way of life. And that is what brings them together. They are sensitive to all that has to do with respect for the housing environment and that's their common cause.'

He assesses the role of this ethnically mixed group in changing the neighbourhood by differentiating it according to their power or *savoir-faire* to affect change in the neighbourhood. These newcomers strive to improve local conditions, he believes, but their arrival has led to "the neighbourhood emptying a little of its original substance, the people born here, who grew up here.... Now that it's a better place to live, [they] can no longer stay because the rents have become too expensive."

Discussion

Analysis of the three cases has shown that identifying groups and making distinctions between groups within the neighbourhood is a complex process of social construction contingent on different factors. In all cases, people are generally less familiar with using the term 'diversity'. In Leipzig, interviewees use expressions such as "other ways of life", "different lifestyles", "colourful" or by employing a rhetoric of mixing and 'othering'. In both Leipzig and Athens, the idea of diversity is hidden or intermingled with other notions, feelings or perceptions. Categorisations applied are ethnicity, age, gender, duration of residence and socioeconomic status. Ethnicity is the dominating category with lines drawn between different groups and related to the time of arrival in the neighbourhood. There is strong evidence that people develop relations of proximity or distance in accordance with the construction of their own identity and through their local engagement. This influence of one's own position is very evident in Paris. Here, differences in the positionality of the speakers, how they perceive themselves in relation to other groups, and their encounters with them shape discourses as empathetic, valuing or othering. While long-term experience with social heterogeneity may lead to a better appreciation of the positive qualities of others, it does not guarantee that stereotypes disappear. Experience seems to be a way of justifying one's beliefs about an essential nature to cultural differences. Difference is not understood as just being different from others, as the term 'diversity' might imply. Some groups are valued more, and this seems linked to the power they are believed to hold in improving neighbourhood conditions, or in worsening them. The examples also show how inhabitants perceive belonging based only partly on incumbency but also on judgements about other residents' contributions to the 'conviviality' of the neighbourhood.

In Leipzig, where experience with cultural difference is a much younger phenomenon, interviewees express a superficial tolerance (see Bannister and Kearns, 2013) together with a clear expression of distinction and distance towards others. Generally, distance is expressed most pronouncedly by using a bundle of categories such as "young migrant men" or "poor uneducated Germans". At the intersection of these categories, differences are felt more strongly and 'othering' is more hostile. Categorical intersections increase stigmatisation; the more categories are interrelated, the more the stereotyping picture of a group hardens. Similarly, in Athens, if bounded by fear, the migrant is perceived as a "black male delinquent *xenos*" responsible for the crisis. But here, unlike Paris or Leipzig, the crisis produced new alliances and expressions of similarity across former differences. Once residents are open to different cultures, lifestyles and ethnicities, the neighbour is just another person suffering the economic recession "like us". This expression of a new all-embracing 'we' turns all other characteristics random. Distinction, on the other hand, draws on specific intersections of gender, race, ethnicity and economic status to construct the others who do not belong here. Such sentiments lead to further isolation promoting a dynamic invisible segregation.

From the analyses, six significant observations emerged across the cases. *First, the construction of the social environment depends on the residents' own positionality.* Here, ethnicity, age, gender, socioeconomic status, but also duration of residence in the neighbourhood are factors defining the position from which an interviewee draws boundaries and identifies groups. While doing so, interviewees also define their own identity and express group belonging. In Leipzig and Athens, ethnicity coincides with duration of residence: the long-time residents are white natives and already a bit older, whereas in Paris, long-term residents might be white as well as people with a migration origin. Certain groups are explicitly 'gendered' (for example, young migrant men), which causes discomfort. However, gender is not applied reflexively. Usually, interviewees treat their own position as given, with little awareness of change and dynamics. However, the Athens case shows how a collective drop in socioeconomic status did change the way residents saw themselves in relation to others. This then resulted in contradicting perspectives on the social environment.

Second, the construction of social groups draws on a variety of rather classic social categories that come with various assessments of these groups. The most prevalent category to demarcate groups in all three cases is ethnicity, in the French case combined with notions of race and religion. Interviewees sometimes use stereotyping categorisations as known from the literature on 'othering' as a hegemonic practice of excluding or marginalising groups. As the case of Athens shows most prominently with the category *xenos*, a 'we' is constructed around native Greek residents in claiming supremacy over migrants irrespective of origin, age, gender or social status. In the case of Paris, a similar disdain was expressed although the 'they' was extended to French-born men who were simply non-white. In Leipzig, precariousness is also a moment leading to othering, for example, against long-term unemployed, deprived Germans. People are othered for being socially marginalised and excluded and perceived as hostile and dangerous.

We observed that defining the desirable composition of the neighbourhood draws a certain and ambivalent picture of social heterogeneity, such as the construction of what comprises a 'normal mix'. For example, according to recent immigrants in Paris from the Ivory Coast, normality means that there are also white people in the area; if white people leave, it is interpreted as a sign of neighbourhood degradation. In Leipzig, a mix of age groups and household types as well as educational backgrounds with some (unspecified) ethnic variation is perceived as 'normal', also prominently expressed in the term 'colourful'. Sometimes 'normal' is used to describe an average socioeconomic status, distancing oneself from higher-status groups and potentially threatening newcomers who signal the emergence of gentrification. Age is a category used in a rather neutral way when it marks duration of residence in the neighbourhood; it also signifies belonging to the area. In Leipzig, we found contradictory moments where both stigmatising and positive assessments were made about the same group, for example, "the Fidjies" for Vietnamese migrants, which resembles Bannister and Kearns' (2013) idea of 'passive tolerance'.

Third, stigmatisation often occurs at the intersection of categories. When it comes to expressions of fear and hatred or stigmatisation, prototypic images of the criminal, as dangerous or disgusting (Anthias, 2016) 'other', are created at repeated intersections of ethnicity, and sometimes race, gender, age and socioeconomic status. It is the young male Arab in Leipzig and Paris who turns parts of the area into places to be avoided, and young black men in Athens who are said to threaten other residents and contribute to the decline of the neighbourhood. Thus, in those stigmatisations, socioeconomic inequalities (poverty, precarity) as well as stigmatised differences (ethnicity, gender, skin colour, age) are intersected, marking the most threatening other as a kind of stereotype. In Leipzig, a clear social distance, sometimes even disgust, for the white German underclass is expressed. In Athens, a ladder of distinction can be observed. Greeks disparage Pakistanis and Roma as two groups leading to degradation of the neighbourhood. As Pakistanis arrived earlier, they distance themselves from the Roma population as a new threat in the neighbourhood. Distance and fear are felt towards new groups, something also observed in Leipzig where the Vietnamese as the migrant group with the longest duration of residence in the neighbourhood and the Russian-Germans who arrived second in the 1990s are more accepted, while immigrants from Arabic-speaking countries are feared and marginalised more. When new groups appear, initially arrived migrants are seen in a more positive light, and the scapegoating is passed on to the next (new) groups. An intersectional lens therefore helps to analyse how residents of socially heterogeneous, underprivileged neighbourhoods perceive and construct the social environment around them, but instead of the classic triangle of race, class and gender, more categories and crossings need to be considered.

Fourth, neighbourhood change influences the construction of groups and the valuation of their presence. Inequalities and vertical differences come to the fore when residents express their fear about a change of status and reputation of the neighbourhood, either in the form of degradation and stigmatisation or gentrification and displacement. This frequently intersects with the duration of residence in the neighbourhood. Across our cases, long-term residents expressed their anxieties about newcomers such as newly arriving students in the case of Leipzig or the influx of 'bobos' in the case of Paris. Although the neighbourhoods are diversifying through such newcomers, the experience is that this process is uneven and not all groups are benefiting equally. In potentially gentrifying neighbourhoods, newcomers evoke ambivalent perceptions. On the one hand, there is hope for improvement of the neighbourhood and its reputation; on the other hand, residents fear increasing costs and losing their position to gentrifiers. As the Athens case shows most prominently, incoming migrants in neighbourhoods with an already low status and reputation fear further deprivation and increasing stigma.

Fifth, national discourses influence the construction and assessment of groups. Interviewees expressed their categorisations and assessments in ways that relate to features of national political and policy discourses. In Paris, the emphasis on the normality of social mixing – that normality meaning more white people – reflects the national social mixing policy discourse. In Leipzig, we interpret the careful use of categories, a hesitant political correctness in talking to us as interviewees, as a reflection of the prevalent conflict between liberal, leftist and cosmopolitan political positions and populist, right-winged groups. In Athens, lacking a multiculturalist policy, where the political mainstream discourse demands assimilation, most of the interviewees' positions reflect this in rejecting the cultural other.

Sixth, encounters with social heterogeneity lead to very different outcomes, ranging from friendship to hostility. The results about the nature of contact with people different from one's own social groups confirm the scepticism of more recent scholarship on living literature on living with diversity. Encounters resulting in positive contact – meaningful contact in Valentine's (2013) terminology – depend on clear positive foci, as highlighted by Nast and Blokland (2014). Our cases confirm that children are a door opener for contact between parents of different backgrounds. Otherwise, depending on one's own positionality, openness to different groups depends much on the background, attitudes and life circumstances of the interviewee. This is wrapped up in the notion of normality in Leipzig or of a good mix in Paris. Even interviewees who claim openness to other groups at some point express excluding boundaries – all those not belonging to the normal or good mix. Encounters even seem to harden such boundaries. They always involve intersections with vertical socioeconomic differences, be it poor migrants or impoverished natives. Passive tolerance (Bannister and Kearns, 2013) – or a superficial civility (Valentine, 2013) – is prominently found in the German case. Yet it comes in different shades, ranging from politically correct notions of barely hidden othering ("I had no problems so far") to acknowledging the legitimacy of the presence of different groups while using stigmatising language ("the

Russians and the Fidjies are quiet"). Different from the other cases, Leipzig has the least experience with immigration, which may be one explanation.

The results, and thus the contrasting of the three cases, open some interesting hints to the role of social dynamics in this context. Greece, as an extreme example of collective loss of socioeconomic status, reveals that as vertical differences diminish, two opposing reactions can be observed: marginalisation and solidarity. From our material we cannot tell what makes the difference here. It is possible, as we have shown above, that since the 'crisis context' in Athens, sharing in mutual support activities has given rise to a sense of solidarity and sameness in 'suffering together'. Also, some interviewees already stigmatised by others tend to marginalise the next groups below them in the social ladder or those arriving later in the neighbourhood.

Conclusion and outlook

Interpreting these findings using the diversity concepts in social science enables us to acknowledge the broadening variation of social identities in urban societies, but it seems less fit to understand people's perceptions of this broadening heterogeneity. Here, the intersectionality approach can help to better understand reservations towards others and experienced inequalities since it focuses on thinking across intersections of people's characteristics and how discrimination occurs at those intersections. We could show how intersecting characteristics are important to understanding both the perspective on others and the positionality of those expressing this perspective. The intersectional lens reveals unequal power relations within our globalising cities (Anthias, 2013). The importance of gender was striking in understanding expressions of otherness and the marginalisation of groups; gender both influences categorisation and explains the position of the speaker, even if speakers may not themselves bring up gender as an issue. They may focus on race, ethnicity or cultural differences as the source of problems, but when forming a clear stereotype of the other, gender comes in, usually stigmatising male youth.

Our analysis enriches the debate on living with social diversity by re-politicising it as it incorporates inequality and asymmetries in power relations. Although the diversity approach is well equipped to bring attention to and explain the variety of differences along distinctive single categorisations, it is not that powerful in replacing concepts such as inequality or intersectionality that are more appropriate to explain how differences become inequalities. Therefore, our recommendation is to analyse urban social heterogeneity through various lenses, and in combining them, make use of their strengths and point out their limits and weaknesses.

Our analyses also reveal open questions and issues for further research. A main issue would be to focus on the relation of people's perceptions to the local or political contexts within which the perceptions are expressed. This encompasses the trajectories of neighbourhoods as well as the political discourse and how it relates to daily life in heterogeneous neighbourhoods. Another important field of research is to better understand the potentials and limits of encounter. Context effects would be a meaningful path for further investigation here. Investigating the role of time and migration dynamics could reveal insights into growing tolerance – passive or dynamic – stemming from public discourse rather than personal encounter. Moreover, we suggest using the intersectionality lens not only for understanding marginalising discursive practices but also to understand empathetic, supportive discourses that also use specific intersections to identify groups in need of support. Through this, research could help to better identify mechanisms of inclusion and exclusion in today's European urban environments. Finally, this chapter has focused less on the role of space in determining people's perceptions of their social environment, but shows that there are again numerous open questions to be addressed.

Notes

[1] As will become clear from our approach, 'ethnic' diversity cannot be considered a clear-cut category since it is not used (consistently) in national statistics across Europe. 'Ethnic' or 'ethnicity' roughly refers to different national backgrounds, cultural belongings and migration histories influencing values and practices. In his article on super-diversity, Vertovec (2007) used the term in different ways: ethnic/ethnicity and country of origin diversity as synonyms (pp 1025, 1039), ethnicity and country of origin as two different categories (pp 1035, 1043) and ethnicity as subset trait of country of origin (p 1049). Yet he referred to the UK context, where this is a census topic and country of origin is actually a census category. In our three national contexts this is not the case and categories are, moreover, not comparable. The migration histories in Paris, Leipzig and Athens have different scopes and dynamics so that the actual meaning of a 'country of origin' for someone's identity, which in itself is a very complex issue (Anthias, 2013), cannot be captured by any clear definition of ethnicity that is useful across different contexts.

[2] The results presented in this chapter are based on an analysis of interview material collected for the European Union's (EU) Seventh Framework Programme project 'DIVERCITIES – Governing urban diversity in today's hyper diversified cities' (see www.urbandivercities.eu).

[3] The samples in each case study can be described as follows. The Leipzig sample is composed according to different periods of in-migration in the case study area

within the last three decades. The composition of the sample of interviewees reflects the variety of inhabitants according to their sociodemographic characteristics, life stage and migration background. The Paris sample reflects the complex history of the research area through a sample of interviewees that vary in socioeconomic, educational and occupational backgrounds, with a mix of national and cultural belongings, migration histories and life stages. Interviewees also ranged from long-time residents to newcomers and returnees. In the case of Athens, sampling procedures were designed carefully to reflect the social and ethnic composition of the research area considering the migration inflows in the past 30 years. Concomitantly the interviewees' profiles introduce a variety of income, educational, socioeconomic, cultural and ethnic profiles that correspond to the existing mix of Athens inner-city neighbourhoods.

[4] Antiparochi refers to the system developed after the 1950s, where housing production was negotiated between landowners and small construction companies. Its implementation led to the demolishing of mainly low-rise housing stock, especially in the central areas of Athens, and its replacement by high-rise and dense blocks of flats.

[5] Names for all interviewees and case studies are pseudonyms.

[6] Fidschi is a commonly used, discriminatory expression for Vietnamese migrants in the former GDR.

[7] A housing project ('Hausprojekt') is a form of collective housing where a group of people develop, live and maintain a house together and share certain facilities.

[8] Golden Dawn is a neo-Nazi party elected into the Greek parliament since 2012.

References

Allemann-Ghionda, C. and Bukow, W.-D. (2011) *Orte der Diversität Formate, Arrangements und Inszenierungen*, Wiesbaden: VS Verlag für Sozialwissenschaften.

Anthias, F. (2013) 'Moving beyond the Janus face of integration and diversity discourses: Towards an intersectional framing', *Sociological Review*, 61(2), 323-43.

Anthias, F. (2016) 'Locating diversity: Making and unmaking boundaries of identity and belonging', Keynote speech at the Conference 'Diversity encounters: Intersectional and post-colonial perspectives', Humboldt University of Berlin, 24-26 May.

Amin, A. (2002) 'Ethnicity and the multicultural city. Living with diversity', *Environment and Planning A*, 34(6), 959-80.

Arampatzi, A. (2016) 'The spatiality of counter-austerity politics in Athens, Greece, emergent "urban solidarity spaces"', *Urban Studies* (http://journals.sagepub.com/doi/abs/10.1177/0042098016629311).

Ashcroft, B., Griffiths, G. and Tiffin, H. (2013) *Postcolonial studies: The key concepts*, London: Routledge.

Bannister, J. and Kearns, A. (2013) 'The function and foundations of urban tolerance: Encountering and engaging with difference in the city', *Urban Studies*, 50(13), 2700-17.

Bell, C., Hartman T. and Newman, B. (2014) 'Decoding prejudice toward Hispanics: Group cues and public reactions to threatening immigrant behaviour', *Political Behaviour*, 36(1), 143-63.

Budnik, M., Grossmann, K., Haase, A., Haid, C., Hedke, C., Kullmann, K. and Wolff, M. (2016) *DIVERCITIES: Living with urban diversity – The case of Leipzig, Germany*, Utrecht: Utrecht University, Faculty of Geosciences.

City of Leipzig (2015) *Statistics quarterly report*, Leipzig: Department for Statistics and Elections.

Faist, T. (2009) 'Diversity – A new mode of incorporation?', *Ethnic and Racial Studies*, 32(1), 171-90.

Faist, T. (2010) 'Cultural diversity and social inequalities', *Social Research*, 77(1), 297-324.

Fincher, R. and Iveson, K. (2008) *Planning and diversity in the city: Redistribution, recognition and encounter*, Basingstoke: Macmillan International Higher Education.

Kreckel, R. (1972) 'Toward a theoretical re-orientation of the sociological analysis of vertical mobility', *Social Science Information*, 11(5), 153-78.

Lelévrier, C., Rivière, C. and Shokry, G. (2015) *Fieldwork inhabitants, Paris (France)*, Paris: Université Paris-Est Créteil.

Lelévrier, C., Rivière, C., Escafre-Dublet, A. and Shokry, G. (2017) *DIVERCITIES: Dealing with urban diversity – The case of Paris*, Paris: University of Paris-Est-Créteil.

Lutz, H. (2014) *Intersectionality's (brilliant) career – How to understand the attraction of the concept*, Working Paper Series 'Gender, Diversity and Migration', Frankfurt: Goethe University.

Massey, D. (2005*) For space*, London: Sage Publications.

McFarlane, C. (2010) 'The comparative city: Knowledge, learning, urbanism', *International Journal of Urban and Regional Research,* 34(4), 725-42.

Michaels, W.B. (2006) *The trouble with diversity. How we learned to love identity and ignore inequality*, New York: Henry Holt.

Nast, J. and Blokland, T. (2014) 'Social mix revisited: Neighbourhood institutions as a setting for boundary work and social capital', *Sociology*, 48(3), 482-99.

Robinson, J. (2011) 'Cities in a world of cities: The comparative gesture', *International Journal of Urban and Regional Research*, 35(1), 1-23.

Tasan-Kok, T. van Kempen, R., Raco M. and Bolt, G. (2014) *Towards hyper-diversified European cities: A critical literature review*, Utrecht: Utrecht University.

Therborn, G. (2013) *The killing fields of inequality*, Cambridge: Polity Press.

Valentine, G. (2013) 'Living with difference: Reflections on geographies of encounter', *Progress in Human Geography*, 32(3), 323-37.

Vertovec, S. (2007) 'Super-diversity and its implications', *Ethnic and Racial Studies*, 30(6), 1024-54.

Vormann, B. (2015) 'Urban diversity: Disentangling the cultural from the economic case', *New Diversities*, 17(2), 119-29.

Ward, K. (2009) 'Commentary: Towards a comparative (re)turn in urban studies? Some reflections', *Urban Geography*, 29, 1-6.

Wrench, J. (2015) 'Diversity management', in S. Vertovec (ed) *Routledge international handbook of diversity studies*, New York: Routledge, 254-62.

11

Conclusion: Super-diversity, conviviality, inequality

Stijn Oosterlynck and Gert Verschraegen

In the Introduction to this book (Chapter 1), we argue that the concept of super-diversity captures a number of ongoing diversity-related societal transformations, but also has its limitations. The chapters in this volume each in their own way improve our understanding of living with super-diversity in deprived and mixed neighbourhoods. They aim to contribute to the literature on super-diverse urban neighbourhoods in two important ways. First, overly generic, pessimistic and one-sided narratives on the failure of multiculturalism are nuanced by focusing on the myriad ways in which citizens actively and creatively regulate, live and deal with super-diversity in the concrete urban places in which their life unfolds. Second, we aim to show how ethno-cultural differences matter for social inequality and vice versa by explicitly focusing on the intricate relationship between ethno-cultural diversity and social inequality. In this concluding chapter we briefly reflect on the main insights that we can draw from the contributions on these two topics, and end with some directions for future research.

Living with super-diversity

The scholarly literature on living with super-diversity offers a welcome antidote to overly pessimistic accounts on the 'failure of multiculturalism' and the return of concerns with 'national civic culture' (Zapata-Barrero, 2017) and even assimilation (Brubaker, 2001) in academic as well as public debates. As explained in the Introduction to this book, much of this countervailing literature can be loosely categorised under the concept of 'conviviality', although there is a range of rather similar terms in circulation such as 'everyday multiculturalism' (Wise, 2009), 'commonplace diversity' (Wessendorf, 2013) and 'urban multiculture' (after Gilroy's distinction between multiculturalism and multiculture; see Gilroy, 2004; Jones et al, 2015). Instead of focusing on conflict and rupture in interethnic relations, conviviality refers to human modes of togetherness in diversity (Nowicka and Vertovec, 2014). As Nowicka and Vertovec argue, conviviality privileges individuality and individual agency over the multiculturalist concern with the collective identification and agency of ethnic groups. Following Gilroy, they question whether belonging to a particular ethnic group necessarily results in 'discontinuities in experience' and grave difficulties in communicating with others. According to Nowicka and Vertovec, then: 'for many authors, it [conviviality] offers a new vocabulary to speak of a collective without referring to fixed categories of ethnicity' (2014, p 347).

Several authors in this volume adopt (although often implicitly) this new vocabulary and refrain from referring to fixed ethnic categories. Jamie Kesten and Tatiana Moreira de Souza (Chapter 3), for example, seek to understand the dynamics of living together in the super-diverse London Borough of Haringey. Their empirical analysis is very much in line with Pemberton and Phillimore's call to shift our analytical focus beyond the role of monolithic ethnic identities in migrant place-making and analyse instead how diversity itself may generate place attachment in neighbourhoods where no single ethnic group dominates (Pemberton and Phillimore, 2016). In Haringey, there are sizable numbers of a wide range of different ethnic and cultural minorities, but no single ethnic group dominates statistically. Almost all respondents view the diversity of their neighbourhood positively, which shows that 'migrant' place-making is not necessarily based on fixed ethnic identities, but may be equally successfully constructed around the ethnic diversity in the neighbourhood. For residents of Haringey, the neighbourhood's diversity offers them opportunities for new experiences, higher levels of tolerance and comfort and access to more diverse places of consumption.

Ayda Eraydin (Chapter 4) makes similar observations in an in-depth case study of how the residents of the diversified Istanbul neighbourhood Beyoğlu perceive and define each other. The majority of the interviewed residents regard living with diverse others as positive because of the possibility it offers to get to know different people and learn about their cultures and the tolerant atmosphere in the district. Residents tend to use socioeconomic and occupational and lifestyle attributes to define other residents in Beyoğlu. Ethnic and cultural categories are not dominant. However, as Pemberton and Phillimore also observed (2016), developing place attachment around the neighbourhood's diversity (rather than one particular ethnic identity) may exclude some groups. In Beyoğlu this is especially the case for some established residents. They fear that their lifestyles may be under threat by the inflow of poor immigrants who are seen to bring in opposing lifestyles linked to the revival of religious and conservative attitudes.

In the Introduction we explain that some authors criticise the super-diversity literature for being conceptually fuzzy and question its analytical added value. In this regard, Maxime Felder's contribution on how inhabitants of four residential buildings in central, densely populated and socially mixed areas in Geneva is insightful (see Chapter 2). Felder does not adopt the new vocabulary on super-diversity and conviviality, but takes his inspiration from the more established micro-sociological vocabulary of Simmel (metropolitan personality), Goffman ('civil inattention') and Lofland (world of strangers). His theoretically well-informed empirical analysis of how urbanites learn about their neighbours while still maintaining their strangeness gives a good insight into how conviviality can be created.

Felder draws an important distinction between not knowing someone personally but being familiar and not knowing of someone's existence. Most of the residents he interviewed had become familiar with each other through fluid encounters and occasional chats, but still have only limited and partial knowledge of the other. Familiarity, however, seems sufficient to live together peacefully. Felder observes that residents tend not to classify each other in groups based on sociodemographic criteria, but describe their neighbours in terms of how they conform to the ideal of the 'good neighbour', which refers to friendliness, helpfulness and respect for others' privacy. Good neighbours hence do not need to be like us as long as they are friendly and do not threaten our interests and privacy. Even then, living among strangers remains challenging because residents have only very incomplete knowledge of their neighbours. Felder describes how residents respond to this condition with a back-and-forth movement between 'normalising' and 'fantasising'. He observes how residents feed their 'existential need for normalcy' by normalising the observed peculiarities and incongruities in the behaviour of their neighbours. At the same time, residents also make use of the incompleteness of information they have about their neighbours to fantasise about the latter's lives, which is almost always more stimulating than the real lives they are observing.

Scholarly research on social mix has convincingly shown that positive perceptions of diversity do not necessarily translate into mixed social networks (Arthurson, 2012). Research on conviviality in super-diverse neighbourhoods seems to lead to a similar conclusion, but also provides further indications about why this is the case or under which conditions mixed social networks might develop. Kesten and de Souza observe among the big majority of residents who value the neighbourhood's diversity a clear contrast between those who engage in meaningful and sustained interactions across difference and those whose social networks are relatively insular. The latter group far outnumbers the former. Conviviality is mainly a feature of urban public space. In the private sphere, residents prefer to spend time and be in places with others who have similar characteristics. Social class differences seem to play an important role here. This finding should serve as an important reminder not to overestimate the potential of conviviality for creating cohesive societies (for similar observations, see Wessendorf, 2013). Despite this, Eraydin, in her case study in an Istanbul neighbourhood, identifies a set of conditions under which conviviality effectively carries over in mixed social networks. She notes that differences in socioeconomic status are clearly reflected in social networking relations. Lower-income groups in particular maintain strong neighbourhood relationships with family members, relatives and people originating from the same hometown, because these are essential for their survival (for example, care support and borrowing money or foodstuffs). These kin relations, however, are not an obstacle to developing relations with residents of different ethnic and cultural backgrounds because of the sheer need for mutual assistance. One might conclude, then, that difficult living conditions make people more tolerant and understanding of others and incite them to develop mixed social networks.

Anika Depraetere, Bart van Bouchaute, Stijn Oosterlynck and Joke Vandenabeele (Chapter 5) also focus on the conditions under which people may forge solidarity relations across ethnic and cultural lines. Unlike the other chapters that analyse how diverse social networks do (or do not) come into existence spontaneously, Depraetere and colleagues take a professional intervention perspective. They analyse the impact of the introduction of a local currency by a social work organisation, supported, among others, by the city council, on social interactions in the neighbourhood. They find that the local currency triggers new joint activities in the neighbourhood and stimulates a diverse group of inhabitants to participate. By doing so, it strengthens interdependency in the neighbourhood and generates solidarity in diversity, albeit mainly between residents in similar economically disadvantaged positions. In their theoretically informed analysis, they strategically adopt the 'stronger' discourse on solidarity rather than conviviality in order to engage with wider and long-lasting sociological debates on the possibility of fostering solidarity in ethno-culturally heterogeneous societies (see also Oosterlynck et al, 2016). This allows them to combine the 'here-and-now' focus of the concept of conviviality with a more explicit concern with identifying the social structures that generate solidarity. They argue against the strong tendency to seek solidarity in the shared history and the presumably homogeneous culture of the nation–state, which is especially notable in the social capital literature (see the introductory chapter in Oosterlynck et al, 2017). Instead, their case study shows how a local currency succeeds in nurturing new solidarities by expanding and creating interdependencies among diverse neighbourhood residents.

In his analysis of national and local models for incorporating international migrants into Italian society, Eduardo Barberis (Chapter 6) also takes an intervention perspective. Whereas the bulk of conviviality research prefers on-the-ground empirical analysis of how people cope with living in and with diversity in everyday life, Barberis connects a political philosophical debate on the respective values of multiculturalism and interculturalism (Modood, 2017; Zapata-Barrero, 2017) with an empirical assessment of concrete intercultural policy-making practices at national and local level. Since interculturalism promotes contact, communication and dialogue between diverse groups and rejects the reduction of identity-formation to fixed ethnic and national categories, it pays more attention to micro-level dynamics of face-to-face contact between diverse citizens in urban public space than multiculturalism. On the basis of a discourse analysis of national and local policies, Barberis concludes that at least in Italy interculturalism can best be understood as a form of assimilationism that works through an implicit subordination of immigrant rights and life chances to the goal of social cohesion. This conclusion is supported by an analysis of two local measures in Milan that target migrants, which suggests that these local measures fail to address systematically migrant needs, and shows how the visibility of diversity is seen as disturbing.

The analyses of Barberis and Depraetere et al are important for highlighting how the micro-level dynamics of living in diversity are thoroughly shaped by national and local policies, the policy paradigms that inform them and all matter of professional interventions. These interventions do not necessarily constrain the active and creative ways in which citizens regulate, live and deal with super-diversity in everyday life, but – as Depraetere and co-authors show – may also have transformative effects in the sense that existing social structures and relationships are questioned and adapted to better accommodate the diverse nature of the citizenry.

Inequality and urban diversity: Connecting research agendas

Van Kempen recently noted that, 'separate research agendas have developed on the themes of (income) inequality and urban diversity. While questions of income inequality are often answered by using data on high spatial levels ... researchers on urban diversity (almost by definition) look at the urban and neighbourhood level' (2015, p 2). As we explain in the Introduction to this book, the separation of the diversity and inequalities social research agendas was already visible in the very first studies on ethnic relations of the urban sociologists of the Chicago School. The observation of separate research agendas led van Kempen to call on inequality researchers to spend more attention on how inequalities play out in daily life in cities and on diversity researchers to explicitly ask questions on how inequalities impact on the social and economic opportunities of citizens in diverse urban neighbourhoods. To connect these two research agendas, van Kempen suggests focusing on the connection between the macro-level socioeconomic developments that produce structural social inequalities and the human agency that people engage in in their daily lives in urban mixed and disadvantaged neighbourhoods. On the one hand, urban citizens and neighbourhoods are unevenly impacted by macro-level socioeconomic developments, while on the other hand, urban citizens do not remain passive in the face of these socioeconomic developments, but actively react and respond to them. Several contributions in this volume advance our understanding of the interaction between social inequalities and diversity, especially with regard to how people react to and cope with the unequal life chances generated by structural social inequalities.

Anouk K. Tersteeg and Ympkje Albeda (Chapter 9) analyse neighbourhood choice and satisfaction in mixed and disadvantaged neighbourhoods in Antwerp and Rotterdam. Following van Kempen's call to pay due attention to human agency, they focus on the motives for choosing to live in particular neighbourhoods. Unlike most research that focuses on the residential choices of white, middle-class residents (see, for example, Atkinson, 2006; Lees, 2008), Tersteeg and Albeda look at the residential choices of a range of other sociodemographic categories as well, implying that agency does not just reside with well-off middle-class families. Contrary to what is suggested by the 'diversity-seeking' hypothesis, they find that the primary motive for choosing to live in a diverse neighbourhood is the availability of affordable housing, despite the often-negative discourses on these neighbourhoods in public debates. For poor residents and migrants, other motivations count as well, namely, the presence of family and friends in the neighbourhood. We may add that this could reflect their weak socioeconomic position in society, which makes them more reliant on social networks for support.

A central focus in several contributions is the issue of social mix (see, notably, Chapters 7, 8 and 9), which is currently perhaps the most commonly analysed interaction between diversity and social inequality (see the Introduction for a brief overview of the literature). Van Kempen aptly summarises the overall conclusion of most recent research on social mix strategies and the impact it has on social inequality: 'mixing does not guarantee contact between different groups, contact does not guarantee positive social outcomes and the chance that inequality will be reduced, either by social contacts or mixed communities is probably close to zero' (2015, p 9). This sceptical perspective on social mix is supported by the empirical analyses in the contributions to this volume. Tersteeg and Albeda (Chapter 9), for example, do not find much evidence for the existence of more diverse social networks in mixed and impoverished neighbourhoods in Antwerp and Rotterdam, although they do observe some quite diverse weak ties with neighbours and acquaintances, which seems to confirm arguments around the existence of conviviality in mixed urban neighbourhoods (see also Nowicka and Vertovec, 2014).

Dimitris Balampanidis and Panagiotis Bourlessas (Chapter 8) come to similar conclusions in their case study on Athens, where they observe both a great deal of social distance, lack of contact and even xenophobic attitudes, but also practices of solidarity, tolerance and friendship in multi-ethnic residential buildings. Testimony to the importance of keeping social inequalities in the analytical focus of empirical studies of how urbanites live with diversity is their remarkable finding of 'vertical social differentiation within buildings'. Although Athens as a city is characterised by comparatively low levels of spatial segregation and high levels of ethnic mix in neighbourhoods as well as within residential buildings, they observe a strong correlation between ethnicity and floor of residence. The conclusion is that living together does not mean that inequality disappears. They characterise multi-ethnic coexistence within apartment building in Athens as 'living together but unequally between conflicts and encounters', once again showing the complex ways in which inequality and diversity interact in urban contexts.

Javier Ruiz-Tagle attacks head on the assumption that 'intergroup physical proximity' in diverse urban neighbourhoods would necessarily enhance social integration and promote upward social mobility

(Chapter 7). This is true regardless of whether we look at integration in mainstream social institutions such as the labour market or public services, at the micro level in daily social interactions or at the level of processes of shared identity-formation and identification. Quite to the contrary, Ruiz-Tagle finds that intergroup relations in the mixed and disadvantaged neighbourhoods in Chicago and Santiago are marked by negative emotions such as fear and distrust, governed by competition, and often lead inhabitants to avoid one another. Ruiz-Tagle's contribution is a powerful reminder not to lose sight of the persistence of social stratification and the forceful ways in which it keeps on shaping urban life in cities and neighbourhoods, notably through housing markets and welfare systems. It teaches us not to focus excessively on the spatial causes of social problems, which is clearly present in the popular research field on neighbourhood effects (Galster, 2012), as well as to put power relations more central in empirical analyses of how citizens live together in super-diverse neighbourhoods.

The aforementioned contributions look at the interaction between social inequalities and diversity through the lens of rather conventional concepts such as spatial segregation, neighbourhood choice, social mix and social networks. However, bringing the two research agendas together not only requires a broader and more inclusive empirical focus, but also calls for conceptual rapprochement. The contribution of Katrin Großmann and co-authors (Chapter 10) precisely responds to this need for conceptual innovation. They adopt an intersectional perspective to analyse which categories neighbourhood inhabitants use to describe social groupings and their relationship to particular places, and to formulate normative assessments about a social grouping in the neighbourhood. Although Großmann et al do not focus on income inequality, their comparative analysis of inhabitants' perceptions of the neighbourhood in mixed neighbourhoods in Leipzig, Paris and Athens establishes a clear linkage with social inequalities by relating perceptions to stereotyping and stigmatisation. These psychological and sociological processes construct social differences between groups and organise them in a hierarchical fashion, which may have knock-on effects on the allocation of valuable resources. Although they observe that stigmatisation often occurs at the intersection of different social group identities, the most prevalent category to demarcate groups in all three cities is ethnicity. As becomes clear from their chapter, the intersectional nature of constructed group identities may offer an explanation for the observation that encounters in diverse neighbourhoods do not weaken stigmatisation and stereotyping, but sometimes even harden such boundaries. The inflow of poor migrants or impoverished natives in neighbourhoods with an already low status and reputation may trigger fears for further deprivation and increasing stigma or quite the opposite, fear of increasing costs and weakened social position in the case of the influx of middle- or upper-class gentrifiers.

To conclude, the contributions in this volume not only advance our understanding of how urbanites actively and creatively live with and in super-diversity and how urban diversity interacts with social inequalities in disadvantaged and super-diverse neighbourhoods. They also point to directions for future research and analysis. Analyses of super-diversity and conviviality should be brought in closer dialogue with more established debates on solidarity and social capital in the context of increasing ethnic and cultural diversity and normative philosophical debates on migrant incorporation. Since the former tends to see diversity – at least in the short to medium term – as a threat to social solidarity and social capital, the super-diversity and conviviality literature offers a refreshing perspective of how diversity plays out in everyday urban life. At the same time, the focus on macro-level societal trends and social structures can enrich the micro-level analysis of conviviality since daily urban life in neighbourhoods does not unfold in a vacuum. For this reason, normative philosophical debates on multiculturalism, interculturalism, (neo-)assimilationism and the like should also be drawn into the conversation. These philosophies inform national and local policy-making, which, in turn – although mostly not directly – shape the context for urban daily life. Connecting super-diversity and conviviality research with these other fields of research is necessary to make a thorough assessment of both the potential and limitations of conviviality in nurturing social cohesion and solidarity. Crucial in this regard as well is following up on van Kempen's call to bring the research agendas on social inequality and urban diversity together to disentangle their respective effects on neighbourhood dynamics.

References

Arthurson, K. (2012) *Social mix and the city. Challenging the mixed communities consensus in housing and urban planning policies*, Clayton, VIC: Csiro Publishing.

Atkinson, R. (2006) 'Padding the bunker: Strategies of middle-class disaffiliation and colonisation in the city', *Urban Studies*, 43(4), 819-32.

Brubaker, R. (2001) 'The return of assimilation? Changing perspectives on immigration and its sequels in France, Germany, and the United States', *Ethnic and Racial Studies*, 24(4), 531-48.

Galster, G.C. (2012) 'The mechanism(s) of neighbourhood effects: Theory, evidence and policy implications', in M. van Ham (ed) *Neighbourhood effects research: New perspectives*, New York: Springer, 23-56.

Gilroy, P. (2004) *After Empire. Melancholia or convivial culture*, London: Routledge.

Jones, H., Neal, S., Mohan, G., Connell, K., Cochrane, A. and Bennett, K. (2015) 'Urban multiculture and everyday encounters in semi-public, franchised cafe spaces', *The Sociological Review*, 63(3), 644-61.

Lees, L. (2008) 'Gentrification and social mixing: Towards an inclusive urban renaissance?', *Urban Studies*, 45(12), 2449-70.

Modood, T. (2017) 'Must Interculturalists misrepresent multiculturalism?', *Comparative Migration Studies*, 5(1), 1-15.

Nowicka, M. and Vertovec, S. (2014) 'Comparing convivialities: Dreams and realities of living-with-difference', *European Journal of Cultural Studies*, 17(4), 341-56.

Oosterlynck, S., Schuermans, N. and Loopmans, M. (2017) *Place, diversity and solidarity*, London: Routledge.

Oosterlynck, S., Loopmans, M., Schuermans, N., van den Abeele, J. and Zemni, S. (2016) 'Putting flesh to the bone: Looking for solidarity in diversity, here and now', *Ethnic and Racial Studies*, 39(5), 764-82.

Pemberton, S. and Phillimore, J. (2016) 'Migrant place-making in super-diverse neighbourhoods: Moving beyond ethno-national approaches', *Urban Studies*, 1-18.

van Kempen, R. (2015) 'Inequality and urban diversity: Different discourses or a crucial connection', Unpublished draft.

Wessendorf, S. (2013) 'Commonplace diversity and the "ethos of mixing": Perceptions of difference in a London neighbourhood', *Identities*, 20(4), 407-22.

Wise, A. (2009) 'Everyday multiculturalism: Transversal crossings and working class cosmopolitans', in S. Velayutham and A. Wise (eds) *Everyday multiculturalism*, New York: Springer, 21-47.

Zapata-Barrero, R. (2017) 'Interculturalism in the post-multicultural debate: A defence', *Comparative Migration Studies*, 5(1), 1-14.

Index

Page references for notes are followed by n